JOB #: 121647

Author Name: Paul

Title of Book: Women in Buddhism

ISBN: 9780520054288

Publisher: U Cal

Trim Size: 5.5x8.25

Bulk: 20mm

Women in Buddhism

Women in Buddhism

Images of the Feminine in Mahāyāna Tradition

BY Diana Y. Paul

WITH CONTRIBUTIONS BY Frances Wilson

FOREWORD BY I. B. Horner

UNIVERSITY OF CALIFORNIA PRESS

BERKELEY LOS ANGELES LONDON

University of California Press
Berkeley and Los Angeles, California

University of California Press, Ltd.
London, England

Library of Congress Cataloging in Publication Data
Main entry under title:

Women in Buddhism.

Bibliography: p.
Includes index.
1. Women in Buddhism. 2. Women in Tripitaka.
I. Paul, Diana Y. II. Wilson, Frances.
BQ4570.W6W65 1985 294.3'378344 84-23960
ISBN 978-0-520-05428-8 (pbk.)

Printed in the United States of America

12 11 10 09
14 13 12 11 10 9 8

The paper used in this publication is both acid-free and totally chlorine-free (TCF). It meets the minimum requirements of ANSI/NISO Z39.48-1992 (R 1997) (*Permanence of Paper*). ♾

Contents

*Translated into English for the first time.

Preface to the Second Edition

Since the first edition of *Women in Buddhism* was published in 1979, there still has been virtually no research by scholars on this very important subject matter within the field of Buddhist Studies. There has been much demand, however, from students and the general audience of readers and scholars interested in Asian culture. For them I have been invited by the University of California Press to present a second edition of my book on feminine imagery in the Mahāyāna Buddhist traditions of ancient India and China. I especially appreciated the opportunity to work with Phyllis Killen and Barbara Zimmerman, editors at the Press, on this edition.

Religion may give women certain freedom of expression, but there is often a considerable price paid for recognition by a given religious institution. Today women desire equal status and full participation in religion. Scholars disagree about women's status, authority, and power in religious organizations. Moreover, they do not interpret images and symbols of religious literature in exactly the same way. They all acknowledge, however, that traditional religious stories, images, and ideals absorbed by members of a culture are potent forces which can give power and dignity to women or, in some instances, deprive women of even the ability to dream of higher aspirations and goals.

All of us are becoming increasingly aware of assumptions made about women and how these assumptions affect women and men. Scholars in Feminist Studies have focused on theories about gender and its relation to power and prestige, resulting in highly innovative and pioneering humanistic and social scientific studies of American and European societies. Scholars in other disciplines as well are beginning to investigate the depth and pervasiveness of sexual and gender stereotypes and images in our society. This is part of the legacy that the women's movement has given us. I believe that all research in human culture must rightfully acknowledge the contribution of the women's movement to a new direction in intellectual inquiry.

In the 1960s, publications on women, religion, and politics concentrated on the history of institutions that promoted sexism and patriarchal symbolism of the sacred. By the late 1970s and early 1980s, scholars, both feminist and nonfeminist, began to look cross-culturally for feminine sacred symbols that could inspire contemporary women in reaffirming their self-esteem and values. These scholars were likely to be literary figures as well as specialists in a particular religious tradition. All of these studies were in agreement that religion formulated an underlying structure of common cultural stereotypes about men and women, which still affects many of our social, political, and economic institutions.

A new dimension for understanding religion's influence on the self-concept of women can be seen through an examination of the religious portraits of women and the feminine in a broad range of religious traditions, both East and West. These traditions have generated a wide variety of attitudes and beliefs toward women. Although I am not trained in any of the feminist methodologies and have not applied any of the methodological approaches derived from some of the splendid work in Feminist Studies, it is my hope that some of my feminist colleagues and readers will take my textual material and apply their powerful critical modes of analysis to Buddhist attitudes toward the body and sexuality, toward motherhood and family, and toward religion as a means of social, political, and economic control. Many of the most persuasive critiques of traditional psychological and economic theories have been brought out by feminist historians and social scientists. A desperate need exists for more research with data in Asian cultures, particularly of classical religious values and institutions. While my personal journey will always be indebted to feminism, the scholarship in this book remains based upon textual and historical methodologies in Buddhist and Asian Studies.

Women in Buddhism is first and foremost a study of ideological concepts and not a social history of women's actual behavior in Indian and Chinese society. I am concerned with gender definition. The process and analysis of gender-role redefinition is occurring at various and uneven rates throughout much of the world today. Buddhists and other religious thinkers were deeply concerned about gender in their time as well (although they did not always distinguish gender from sexuality). The role expectations for men and women in classical times were dictated by religious as well as political elites, but these expectations or ideal roles were not necessarily clearly defined or without competing or alternative role options. There were gender-role expectations or definitions for those women and men who wished to make their way outside the normative family model. Equally important were the features of socialization responsible for bringing about the performance and observance of political and religious gender roles that often excluded women from spheres of influence to which men, especially those from the upper classes, had access. These gender roles were grounded on images and ideals of masculinity and femininity. For those who ventured outside the family, there was at times an equal sharing of roles and responsibilities. For others, there were intractable lines marking gender-role divisions. Adherence to a position that men and women are essentially different beings was the most restrictive view of women in society. Men and women were thought to have separate spheres of activity according to their talents and abilities. Those talents and abilities accorded to gender roles were felt to be natural and legitimate rather than ideological. Instead of a focus on those gender roles and expectations as they were situated in their broader sociopolitical and economic context, images of the feminine and masculine were frequently viewed as permanent and unalterable. I will be treating these images as distinctive features in the overall value system of Mahāyāna Buddhism in ancient India and China and interpreting the internal contradictions and pressures within those systems of belief.

The following study interprets stories from Buddhist scripture that give rise to an understanding about gender roles and ideals in Mahāyāna Buddhist culture. These stories disclose who women were expected to be, what the ranges of feminine character and behavior should be. They provide a contrast to corresponding definitions of masculinity, although the latter are not a central focus in this book. The tales and myths are not only evaluative and informative but also invitational: they invite us to imagine and to wonder. They are intended to be read not as history but as descriptions suggesting values and ideology, disclosing perspectives of the feminine, of sexuality, and of gender roles. These stories raise questions and suggest answers simultaneously. An attempt is made to deal with the question of gender and its relation to states of spiritual being and the potential for religious practice. There is no definitive answer; instead, tentative propositions are presented against the cultural background of gender definitions for men and women and their degree of social acceptability.

I have investigated both the tension between sexual discrimination and religious ideals of equality and the competing and conflicting theological interpretations of the feminine and masculine. Each text that Frances Wilson or I have translated is introduced by a critical analysis and commentary on the positive or negative definition of the feminine. We put forth no conclusive answers to how women acted upon those definitions in ancient times nor to how the lives of actual women were affected by these portraits of their feminine nature, because of the historical and textual difficulties in reconstructing those lives. In this study I emphasize that gender roles and definitions were constantly *changing* and that notions of sexuality and its relevance or irrelevance to religious practice have no definitive answer or consensus throughout Mahāyāna Buddhist literature. To this inquiry concerning myths, images, and symbols of the feminine I now turn. I invite you to join me.

Diana Y. Paul
Palo Alto, California
October 1984

Foreword

The only generalization that can perhaps be made with any validity about the position of woman in Buddhist lands and the role she played and still plays is that neither her position nor her role was ever negligible or trifling. In all cultures and during all times, women have never been considered mere entities or totally ignored. However, they have never been accorded the same kind of universal respect conferred upon men. But the course of history also shows that however much men were regarded as superior, women frequently challenged this conception and sometimes won a more honored standing both in life and in literature. This challenge was also true in Buddhism and its various manifestations in the Eastern countries where it took root, grew, and expanded. Sometimes, encouragement from outside women's own ranks also contributed to their improved status in the household and in the world of public affairs.

The present work breaks new ground in offering a number of Buddhist texts concerned with Mahāyāna Buddhism, a mine of information on women. The author has chosen this material, which has come down to us in Sanskrit and Chinese, with an eye to maintaining a high level of interest and, thus, it should have wide appeal. The source material, nineteen episodes, of which nine are translated here for the first time, forms part of the great corpus of Buddhist literature. The ambivalent attitude toward women that has been apparent in Buddhist lands in all ages and epochs is well portrayed. On the one hand, woman was regarded as a danger, potential and actual, to a man's perilous progress along the way to welfare; and, on the other hand, she was shown, as in the guise of the Nāga princess who was nothing less than a Bodhisattva, on a footing equal to that generally claimed by man as his special spiritual prerogative. This study presents these two aspects without prejudice, fear, or favor.

I. B. Horner
London

Acknowledgments

I wish to express my gratitude and appreciation to Frances Wilson, not only for her contributions but also for her encouragement in this work. In addition, warmest appreciation is due to Nancy Falk, Andrea Halliday, I. B. Horner, Estelle Jelinek, Nancy Lethcoe, Wendy O'Flaherty, and Sandra Sizer, who provided creative and useful comments on portions of early drafts. A grant from the Center for East Asian Studies, Stanford University, and from the University of Wisconsin-Madison made it possible for me to prepare this publication. Without their generous support, this work would have been virtually impossible.

The spirit of this book is most of all dedicated to my husband, Douglas, who kindly reminds me that there is both a serious and humorous side to any religion, including Buddhism. To the many friends and colleagues who helped in some way, thank you for your support.

MAYA'S DREAM. A.D. 2ND–3RD CENTURY. COPPER REPOUSSÉ SCULPTURE.

The mother of the Buddha Śākyamuni dreams of an elephant, symbolizing that she will soon give birth to a wise and religious child. (*Asian Art Museum of San Francisco, The Avery Brundage Collection*)

Introduction

Scholars investigating sexual stereotypes in our society are becoming increasingly aware of assumptions made about women and the effect of these assumptions on women. Traditional religious stories, images, and ideals absorbed by members of a culture are frequently vehicles of misogynist views. This presentation of literature from the more recent Buddhist tradition known as Mahāyāna attempts to provide examples of the variety of images of the feminine which may have been potent forces in formulating the self-concept of women in Buddhist societies.

Are Buddhist portraits of women the same as those in Western society? Do the images of the sacred and the divine, as constructed by male Buddhists, include the feminine? Are notions of sexuality viewed as compatible with notions of the sacred? The following readings are designed to furnish answers to these questions.

Many sympathetic to the teachings of Mahāyāna Buddhism believe it to be an egalitarian religion, more supportive of women than either the earlier form of Buddhism or other religions. Indeed, there are positive images of the feminine in the Mahāyāna tradition, and laywomen and nuns play an active role in Buddhist religious practices. However, texts preserved in the Buddhist canon reveal a wide spectrum of views, most of which reflect male attitudes, the educated religious elite, whose views do not often reflect sexual egalitarianism.

Like Judaism and Christianity, Buddhism is an overwhelmingly male-created institution dominated by a patriarchal power structure. As a consequence of this male dominance, the feminine is frequently associated with the secular, powerless, profane, and imperfect. Male Buddhists, like male religious leaders in other cultures, established normative behavior for women by creating certain ideals of femininity. At the same time, men's opportunities for interaction with women were minimized by the restrictions of devout practice. In early Buddhist monastic communities, interaction with laywomen was necessary for economic support but otherwise was avoided. When we find texts in which the sacred is represented as masculine while the profane or imperfect is represented as feminine, we have a polarization that suggests both internal psychological conflicts and external social barriers between the sexes.

These Buddhists texts, many of which are translated for the first time, should be of considerable interest to students of religion as well as to feminists. At a time when Buddhism is rapidly increasing in importance both as a subject of academic investigation and as a popular religion in the West, Western women are undergoing a fundamental change in their understanding of their roles in society. As this tradition of religious thought moves into a Western society that is self-consciously reexamining sexual roles, it is important to explore the Mahāyāna Buddhist images of the feminine, which offer an opportunity for Western readers to examine the sexual typification in an important religious tradition.

The texts, a small sampling of the vast corpus of Mahāyāna literature, offer a fascinating perspective on sexual role formation. From a feminist perspective, one perceives a destructive, complex set of images preventing women from fulfillment within the Buddhist religion. From a male perspective, one can sense fascination and alienation. These texts reveal as much about men's self-concept in relation to women as they do about the effects of these texts on women's self-image. The imagery of a mysterious and elusive woman shows men's feelings of wonder and curiosity. At times, women must have felt isolated and removed from full participation in Buddhist society because of their diminished status in Buddhist orthodoxy. Some men must have felt curiosity about the marginal feminine world that perhaps, because they could not share, they devalued.

The translated texts in this volume represent an attempt to document a range of problems concerning the depiction of woman and her feminine nature in Mahāyāna Buddhist literature. Affirmative and negative portraits of the feminine are included. Some texts represent a dualistic system of beliefs and values, in which women are excluded from fulfillment of their religious convictions. Other texts reflect a nondualistic system in which women are included as fully human and religious. The arrangement of texts is organized according to a typology, progressing from the most negative images of the feminine to the most positive and affirmative ones.

A major precedent for this study was set in 1930 by the publication of I. B. Horner's *Women Under Primitive Buddhism.* In her volume on women's roles in Theravādin Buddhism, Horner investigates the earliest known Buddhist textual sources from the Pāli Theravādin canon, written approximately during the first century A.D. but dating back several centuries before that time. The roles of Buddhist laywomen and Buddhist nuns or "almswomen" are discussed. The focus of the present work is on traditional attitudes toward women, their soteriological paths (paths to salvation), and the images of the feminine in Mahāyāna Buddhist literature, written from approximately the second century through approximately the sixth century A.D. My investigation of textual materials from the Mahāyāna Buddhist tradition includes many texts which have been generally ignored by other scholars. These samples are characteristic because they discuss recurring themes found in other Mahāyāna Buddhist texts as well. I have considered a number of the texts as paradigmatic and influential in representing the views of female sexuality in Mahāyāna Buddhism. The Tantric Buddhist tradition, which affirms sexuality as sacred and which is rich in sexual imagery, has been treated by others and is not discussed in this book.

The interpretation of textual materials in this volume has presented some problems. Of the nineteen texts, sixteen are sutras, that is, purportedly the sermons and lessons spoken by the historical Buddha to his disciples. Comprising more than twenty-five volumes in the Chinese Buddhist canon, the sutras developed over hundreds of years in different regions and by different authors. The audiences to whom these texts were addressed ranged from the religious orders to the laity and included men and women, both literate and illiterate. Sutras may have been selected by Buddhist teachers in terms of their appeal to the audience being addressed. However, little information is available concerning the type of audience and locale because the sutras are not dated and the authorship is unknown.

Of the other texts, which are not sutras, one text describes the disciplinary rules of the nuns and two are folktales, incorporated into a Mahāyāna Buddhist anthology known as *The Collection of Jewels*. The materials include poignant folktales, rhetorical diatribes, myths, devotional poems, and religious vows. Even some of the sutras mentioned above probably were originally folktales or myths which were later incorporated into the genre of Buddhist literature known as sutras. Because of the overlap in categories or types, texts are often difficult to identify. What may have originally been a folktale or rhetorical diatribe may have been revised according to the standardized format and style of a sutra, with the word "sutra" appended later to the title. In the titles of the texts in this volume, the word "sutra" is included if it appears in the original Sanskrit or Chinese text from which the translation is made.

All these texts reveal various shades of attitudes toward the feminine and of attributes of the feminine imposed on Buddhist women. Some of the selections are humorous and imaginary, others morbid and pessimistic. Some materials were originally in Sanskrit; others in Chinese. To place these diverse texts into their geographical and historical contexts is speculative, not only because of their anonymity but because they developed over a long time, with continuous emendations and accretions to the originals.

A Buddhist text may have had two periods of development. A Sanskrit text, after its original composition, sometimes underwent generations of revision even before further development, revision, and editing, when the text was exported to China. These factors preclude identifying all variables necessary for reconstructing the historical context of each text. Besides, the views put forth in any given text may not have been a dominant view of the general populace and may, in fact, have been either ignored or unknown to many followers and practitioners of Mahāyāna Buddhism. Thus, many of the texts no doubt have incorporated what were originally non-Buddhist ideas and attitudes, but it is almost always impossible to identify the cultural context of such borrowings.

The argument may be put forth that Hindu and Confucian values, as well as indigenous folk beliefs, are the origins of Buddhist nonegalitarianism. However, if Buddhists accepted nonegalitarian beliefs from outside their original teachings and incorporated them as sutras, that is, as part of their scriptural canon, they had to have accepted such beliefs as worthy of the status of scripture. To that extent, they could not have considered such nonegalitarian views as the antithesis of the Buddha's doctrine; therefore, they cannot be said to have consistently or wholeheartedly advocated equality of the sexes.

Textual materials do not necessarily reflect the practical

religion, the religion of people at large. Representing the orthodox view of a religious establishment, Buddhist texts were the approved doctrinal statements of the monastic elite in much the same way that Vatican pronouncements and council papers represent an orthodox view that is not necessarily carried out by practicing Roman Catholics. Questions concerning the significance of Buddhist texts to practicing male and female Buddhists remain to be answered. The illiterate lay Buddhist of both sexes may not have even known about misogynist texts. Furthermore, literate Buddhist women may not have cared to read antifeminist texts even if they knew of their existence. All the information in the textual materials may represent only orthodoxy and not the common tradition of lay Buddhist practitioners. The intent of presenting these materials is to compare and contrast the various orthodox attitudes toward sexual stereotyping within a broad range of Mahāyāna Buddhist doctrine.

Given these limitations and problems with regard to Mahāyāna Buddhist materials, what kinds of information and inferences can be derived concerning femininity and women's status in Buddhist societies? The worth of these texts lies in their revelation of permutations of two central themes found cross-culturally. The first is the notion that the feminine is mysterious, sensual, destructive, elusive, and closer to nature. Association with this nether world may be polluting and deadly for the male and therefore must be suppressed, controlled, and conquered by the male in the name of culture, society, and religion. Female sexuality as a threat to culture and society provides religion with a rationale for relegating women to a marginal existence. Simultaneously, the mystery of the female body and its powers are associated with disruptive cosmological powers. Exceptions to this view, however, are found in some Buddhist literature as well as in other religious literature, particularly with regard to the prostitute. A prostitute's sexuality, although feared, is also desired. She is powerful because she is not subjugated by any single male authority figure. She is appreciated because she gives of herself indiscriminately.

The second theme is the notion that the feminine is wise, maternal, creative, gentle, and compassionate. Association with this affective, emotional, transcendent realm is necessary for the male's fulfillment of his religious goals and for his release from suffering. Sexuality may be either controlled or denied in the feminine as sacred. In the role of nun or virgin, sexuality may be transcended as irrelevant to fulfilling human potential. In the role of mother, sexuality is usually viewed as in a controlled state, a state of equilibrium. Mahāyāna Buddhists usually preferred the notion of transcendence of all sexuality in religious women, rather than in the controlled sexuality of the mother.

Women may derive their power either through their sexuality as evil, threatening, and mysterious or in accordance with their religiosity defined as an asexual spiritual potency and creativity. When women's sexuality is regarded as an anomalous, potentially destructive force, it limits their power in society. However, regarded as creative spiritual persons, women may be given a complementary religious status, equivalent (or nearly equivalent) to men. Women's relationships with other women, as a legitimate source of spiritual inspiration, are omitted from scripture, with the exception of a few verses allegedly composed by nuns. Women as religious figures are almost always counterparts to men and are portrayed in some relationship to them.

The interplay of these two central themes can be seen as the mediation in Buddhism between two world views. The first view is dualistic: Masculine and feminine are seen as discrete categories, like spirit and matter. The second view is integrative: Masculine and feminine are seen as complementary aspects of a unified spirit, in the manner of compassion and wisdom. This is the more prevalent Mahāyāna Buddhist view.

The reiteration of these themes and the resolution of the contradictions between opposing views of the feminine are not told in the same ways from culture to culture or even within a single culture's various subgroups. In Buddhism, a panorama of texts evidencing the two themes creates an intricate web of threads woven into a fabric of male stereotypes of the amorphous female. The manner in which these elements describe the female is provocative and complex.

In organizing this variety of primary sources progressively from the most inferior image of the feminine to its most egalitarian presentation, I have followed the typology based on the early Buddhist myth of the origin of society, the *Agañña-suttanta,* a text in the Pāli canon. In this text, the two central themes of femininity, in particular, and sexuality, in general, are delineated in a generalized way. We see the absence of sexuality and of all opposing elements in the beginning of personal relations in a Golden Age.

According to this myth, there was a Golden Age in which asexual, self-luminated, and noncorporeal beings dwelled blissfully in the heavens, existing without need for food. One day one of them tasted the earth with one finger, and the others followed. As a result, these beings lost their luminous natures, and the sun, moon, and stars appeared. The beings continued to eat and gradually became corporeal and heavier in form. Those who ate little were beautiful whereas those who were gluttonous were ugly. Pride in one's beauty caused the devolution of the cosmos; the physical appearance of the beings became even grosser in form, and divergence in beauty became greater. The sexes then emerged and, with them, passion and sexual intercourse. Sexuality became immoral and violent, a degeneration from the previous state of perfection. Gradually, sexual intercourse became sanctioned under prescribed situations. With continual devolution, property resulted, and crimes were committed until the best one of the human race, a male, was elected king.

This Buddhist myth assumes the potential of a state of perfection which is asexual, noncorporeal, and beyond notions of good and evil. Physical devolution is concomitant with moral degeneration. There were neither sexual nor social distinctions in the perfected state nor any tendency for passions (for food, property, or sexual intercourse). As soon as the celestial beings of the Golden Age lost their divine state (by falling from heaven), their nature was associated with desire and craving. The earth, the object of their craving (or "taste"), was characteristically a feminine symbol in pan-Indian religion.

The relationship between devolution and feminine earth may or may not be causal. Although no cause for the degeneracy of the age is offered, pride and sexuality emerge immediately after the increase in eating, the gross degeneracy of the human form, and the appearance of male and female characteristics. Sexual intercourse, the first act which violates a member of the opposite sex, is an object of revulsion. This account helps clarify our understanding of sexuality in early Buddhism and prefigures a trend found in Mahāyāna texts as well. The Buddhist accounting for the origins of sexuality is thus associated with the fall of humanity. Sexuality as a fallen state is associated with eating and the acquisition of property.

In this myth both men and women are equally responsible for their fallen state. However, in some Buddhist texts women are represented as more responsible for bringing about the fallen state, although the reasoning is not always clear. Devolution is the way of the world and of ordinary human behavior. Evolution, on the other hand, is the way of Buddhist practice. Buddhism works against the grain of devolution by reversing the process of sexuality, acquisition of property, and all other forms of sensuality and desire. The religious objective is to reverse the entire process of attachment to the world of desire in which sexuality is one important factor. The question to be raised is whether women have the capacity to "reverse" or at least control their sexuality and worldly desires.

The selection of Buddhist texts translated here documents major varieties of female stereotypes in the Mahāyāna Buddhist tradition, reflecting both the propounded ideals of Mahāyāna Buddhist teaching and the prejudices of a society that challenges those ideals. Eleven of the selections are translated from the Chinese recensions, some of which are also extant in Sanskrit. When the Chinese recension has been preferred over the Sanskrit, it is due to clarity of style and to a more interesting development of the narrative (as in the case of "Sadāprarudita and the Merchant's Daughter" from *The Sutra of the Perfection of Wisdom in Eight Thousand Verses*). The other eight selections are translated from the Sanskrit recensions. Identification of the texts and their primary recensions are given, and the English translator is indicated at the bottom of the first page of each translated text, as well as notation of first English translations. Not all of the translations correspond to the entire text of the original; some of the material has been extracted because of the length of the original text, its lack of relevance to the issue of feminine stereotypes, or the repetition of details unnecessary to the central themes under discussion.

PART I

Traditional Views of Women

But in the end, when we read what women write about "woman," we are justified in a good measure of distrust that women really want—really *can* want—enlightenment about themselves.

Nietzsche, *Beyond Good and Evil*

CHAPTER 1

"Temptress": Daughter of Evil

Traditional Buddhist attitudes toward woman as inferior reflect a view of woman as temptress or evil incarnate. The lustful woman is seen with unrestrained sensuality, perhaps irrevocably so. She has an animalistic nature associated with innate sexual drives not found in the nature of the male. Buddhist literature implies that woman is biologically determined to be sexually uncontrollable. By despising her own nature, woman can perhaps deny her biological destiny of depravity. This view is clearly illustrated in the translations presented in this chapter.

In the study of woman as an instrument of evil, a distinction must be made between the symbolic representation of woman, generalized as the dark, sensual, emotional nature of the personality or "eternal feminine," and the actual being of woman as an individual. Woman, as the "eternal feminine," the temptress and seductress, is a common element in religious thought. Woman is Eve, precipitator of the fall of man, and Pandora who wreaks havoc on the world. The examples of woman as the embodiment of evil in Buddhist literature reflect: (1) the limitations of the human condition, which is a continual process of suffering and rebirth (saṃsāra*), frequently denoted by the

*In the body of this book, we are using roman type for Sanskrit words because of their frequent occurrence. In the footnotes, however, we are using italic type when Sanskrit words are given in juxtaposition to other foreign words.

feminine; and (2) the projection of masculine resentment, denoted by the projection of the feminine onto women.

In Genesis, Eve is the primeval mother of the human race, yet simultaneously the representative of the serpent who is evil incarnate. The central intention of the myth is to show that both Eve and Satan are antagonistic to Adam, the protagonist.[1] In this Adam-centered myth, original sin is sometimes represented as sexuality, symbolized by woman as the serpent's mediator. Sexuality did not exist until Eve was tempted and then subsequently tempted Adam. Although Adam was already sexually awakened and rejoiced at Eve's creation, the projection of the evils of sexuality upon women is suggestive of masculine resentment and dissatisfaction with the limitations of the human condition.[2] Although the temptation was a responsibility shared by Adam and Eve, symbolically represented in every man and woman, evil was not interpreted as a self-induced seduction and frailty but as "other," that is, as woman. The Buddhist myth in the *Agañña-suttanta,* like the myth of Genesis, also portrays woman as the cause for the fall of the human race.

Greek mythology, specifically the Pandora myth, is similar in intent with that of Eve but is more explicit in its representation of woman as the perpetrator of all existential suffering. The irresistibly beautiful Pandora was fashioned by Zeus in retaliation for Prometheus' unauthorized gift of fire to man. Although Zeus initiated the gift of misfortune, Pandora is the scapegoat and perpetrator of destruction, again demonstrating masculine malcontent projected onto women.[3]

In Indian mythology the representation of woman as evil is continued, but we have a more complex form of the myth of Eve. The dominant and invincible goddess is Devī, who slays the gargantuan buffalo in the *Purāṇas.* As the Hindu goddess Kālī, she is fearsome and loathsome, depicted as an old hag with skull-laden necklaces, gluttonously drinking the blood of her victims;[4] she functions more powerfully than an Eve-like mother of the human race. As Devī, she is the primeval force of the cosmos, the maternal power, which has a dualistic dimension of demonic and creative proportions. As the power of the universe, she may either bestow life or annihilate it. She may also be the life-giving force of fecundity as a positive energy.[5]

Buddhism inherited the Indian mythological structure in which tension existed between the maternal aspect and the destructive aspect explicitly illustrated by Kālī. Whereas Kālī represents both the maternal and destructive forces of the cosmos, the Buddhist representation of woman as evil is one traditional attitude, the woman as mother another. The two representations are not combined in one image as in the case of Kālī.

In sharp contrast to the traditional attitude of positive feelings toward the woman as maternal, to be described in Chapter 2, woman was portrayed as the purely sensual with uncontrollable desires in a number of early sectarian Buddhist texts.[6] Non-Buddhist Indian texts generally believed a woman's sexual drives were stronger than a man's. Women were believed to be recipients of a portion of the Brahmanic god Indra's excess energy or sexuality.[7] Buddhist literature frequently incorporated this belief in some of its misogynist literature. Woman represented limitations of human nature in much the same manner as Eve and Pandora, but woman glowed with a more intense sexual vitality and was the primeval force of fecundity,[8] as she was in the Hindu religion. Unlike the Hindu Mother Goddess, however, the sexual energy was unequivocably repugnant in early Buddhist sects such as the Theravādin sect. What was feminine or sensual was saṃsāra, the world of bondage, suffering, and desire, which led to cycles of rebirths. This world of the feminine had to be vanquished at all costs.[9]

The negative aspect of the woman was not only due to the mythological context Buddhism inherited. It is true that early Buddhist texts such as the *Jātakas* (birth) tales of the Buddha incorporated many strident misogynist remarks from the orthodox tradition of Brahman ascetics.[10] However, the interpretation of woman as temptress and seductress represented a tenacious masculine resentment in monastic Buddhism. The projection of resentment and dissatisfaction onto women is evidenced from the time of the early Saṃgha, the Buddhist community of monks. The pragmatic objective of the monastic order was to maintain the organization while the religious objective was to achieve spiritual growth. Symbolically, woman represented the profane world, saṃsāra. Perhaps more detrimentally, women were potential obstacles in actual life to man's spiritual growth. The male novitiate left his wife and family for the order, and naturally at times he yearned to return to the company and security of his family. In fact, the woman as wife could pose a very real threat to the individual monk's observance of celibacy.[11] Moreover, from the organization's perspective, the wife or lover was a powerful competitor for the member's loyalty and support. While the Saṃgha could offer spiritual solace and salvation through self-discipline, the woman could offer sensual comfort and emotional support, alleviating loneliness and austerities.[12] If fear of a woman's appeal and power were instilled, albeit reactionary, the preservation of both the individual's chastity and the organization's stability were felt to be assured.

The prototype of woman as evil, the equivalent of Satan's whore in Christianity, is found in the Theravādin scriptures known as the Pāli canon.[13] When the Buddha was on the threshold of enlightenment, Māra, the sovereign of the desire realm—and it is desire that binds us to the human condition—desperately attempted to prevent the imminent enlightenment of the Buddha. In order to tempt the Buddha, Māra dispatched his three daughters, personifications of Lust (Rāgā), Aversion (Arati), and Craving (Tṛṣṇā), to appear before the Buddha. The ultimate in feminine seduction was embodied in these three, but the Buddha-to-be was utterly repelled by them. The Buddha's transcendence of the bonds of existence and desire in this tale had become synonymous with the transcendence of the bonds of women, a favorite theme employed by later monastic thinkers.[14]

A derivative of the prototype of Māra's daughters developed early in Buddhist literature in the description of hell. Woman, as cosmic physical energy, was perceived as temptress and seductress and was associated with the death of the spiritual being.[15] Hell is populated, both in Theravādin and Mahāyānist literatures, with elderly, repulsive women who were grotesquely formed. Of the eight hells in Buddhist cosmology, two dealt with sexual indulgences, but none of the hells was populated only by women. To avoid any attraction to women, that is, to the sensual pleasures their wives and others represented, the monks were required to meditate upon the human body as old, diseased, dying, or as a rotting corpse.[16] Such visualizations, when performed on occasions when captivatingly lovely women were present, would ward off the probability of succumbing to a woman's charm.

As a result of the threat that women represented to the stability of the monastic community, disciplinary rules emphasizing the avoidance of women at all costs became the standard for chastity, as is evident in this dialogue between the Buddha and his favorite disciple, Ānanda:

> [Ānanda:] "How are we to conduct ourselves, Lord, with regard to womankind?"
> [The Buddha:] "As not seeing them, Ānanda."
> [Ānanda:] "But if we should see them, what are we to do?"
> [The Buddha:] "Not talking, Ānanda."

[Ānanda:] "But if they should speak to us, Lord, what are we to do?"

[The Buddha:] "Keep wide awake, Ānanda."[17]

The contact with women was further complicated by the fact that monks had to beg for alms from house to house as part of their daily routine. Since a housewife would be the principal almsgiver, the monks were dependent upon them, yet afraid of the order's punitive actions for misconduct.[18] Psychologically, there would be a reinforcement of a low self-image for those monks who hated the women upon whom they were economically dependent. The monks' feelings of being manipulated and dependent would result in self-hatred projected upon women. An antagonistic attitude toward women inevitably resulted, with the evil nature of women dramatically emphasized in some early Theravādin literature, such as the *Jātaka* tales.[19]

Mahāyāna Buddhism was more sympathetic to the existential concerns of the laity, but it likewise did not escape an element of misogyny in a portion of its literature. The preservation of the social order and the monastic community may have also dictated that a woman's position in both society and Buddhism should not be elevated. Texts, like the two translated below, *The Sutra of the Buddha Teaching the Seven Daughters* and "The Tale of King Udayana of Vatsa" from *The Collection of Jewels,* focus on the "hellish" quality of diabolical women who tempted the monks and dragged them to degeneracy.

Meditational formulae for alleviating lustful thoughts were prescribed. The cathartic release of meditative ecstasy *rivaled* that of an orgasm. Consequently, the latter's emotive and physiological outcome was denigrated in comparison. The image of woman had gradually developed as the antithesis of religion and morality.[20]

Both in terms of the feminine as sensual, as vital

energy, and as a threat to the organizational stability of the monastic order, a sympathetic portrayal of a woman's spiritual needs was sometimes lacking.[21] Ignoring the spiritual nature of woman, the monks attributed destruction of the spiritual to woman. The monk's jealousy toward his competitor was evident in texts such as "The Tale of King Udayana of Vatsa," in which women were given tremendous power to manipulate men like animals and children. Sexual intercourse was bestial and associated with evil. The woman was both procreator and lover, and the universe was disposed of and controlled by women. In this tale, the Buddha states:

Those who are not wise,
Act like animals,
Racing toward female forms
Like hogs toward mud

. . . .

Because of their ignorance
They are bewildered by women, who
Like profit seekers in the marketplace
Deceive those who come near.

In short, the misogynist literature of Mahāyāna Buddhism was based, in part, upon the mythological context of India in which woman as the feminine was the embodiment of the physical and ultimate sensual power in the universe. Each woman was a microcosmic power who could render havoc in her negative aspect. In early Buddhism the existentially confining condition known as saṃsāra, identified with the feminine, had to be overcome:

The king [Śuddhodana, the Buddha's father] said: "What is your awareness of a woman?" The prince [the Buddha] said, "It is an awareness of contrariety."[22] The king said, "My son, what is your awareness of contrariety?" The prince said, "It is that of this body

> which comes and goes where it is fixed; where it stands, sits down; where it is active, is quiet; where it is an external thing, it is void, inactive, strong or weak, a delusion and untrustworthy—such do they say is the totality of things.[23]

The residual identification of the feminine with the negative aspect of existence was never entirely removed from some scriptural texts. The pragmatic concerns of the monastic order to preserve and stabilize their organization demanded the exclusion of familial responsibilities, particularly to the wife. As a natural outcome of the fear which the wife represented to one's organizational membership and to one's spiritual progress, certain Mahāyāna Buddhist factions projected their fears upon all women as a means of spiritual survival,[24] as evidenced in the following two texts.

The one-sided portrayal of women in these two translations is by no means the predominant attitude toward women in Buddhist literature in general. The extreme prejudice against women in these texts illustrates the reactionary biases of only one portion of the Buddhist population, a segment of the monastic community. Their rejection of the household life represented, in part, the rejection of women.

In the two texts, woman is the abstract cause for evil and the cosmic principle of degeneracy. The early Buddhist myth summarized in the Introduction above did not attribute the devolution of the universe to woman. In sharp contrast to that myth, the following translations acknowledge woman as the "daughter of evil," the origin and prime mover of sexuality. In Parts II and III, I will investigate more moderate views with regard to ideal paths for women and images of the feminine.

A. Introduction to *The Sutra of the Buddha Teaching the Seven Daughters*

The Sutra of the Buddha Teaching the Seven Daughters is extant only in Chinese, translated by the Buddhist layman Chih Ch'ien, who was from the Central Asian state known as Tocharia.[25] His grandfather, accompanied by several hundred countrymen, settled in China. Chih Ch'ien was born in China and had a Chinese literary education in the classics. He entered the capital of the state of Wu about A.D. 220, before the downfall of the Han dynasty. At court he received the patronage of the ruler Sun Ch'üan and became the court scholar. Chih Ch'ien was the only important translator of Buddhist texts in South China until the late fourth century. Because he was familiar with the literary elegance of the classics, Chih Ch'ien's style of translation is fluid and brief, freely eliminating much of the repetitiveness Indian Buddhists cherished in their texts. Chih Ch'ien is also credited with composing the first Chinese Buddhist hymns to be accompanied by musical instruments.

Between 223 and 253 Chih Ch'ien translated the first edition of the *Vimalakīrtinirdeśa,* the *Dhammapāda,* the oldest translation of *The Larger Sukhāvatīvyūha (Pure Land Sutra),* and *The Sutra of the Perfection of Wisdom in Eight Thousand Verses.* Until Kumārajīva's translation of the *Vimalakīrti* in the fifth century, Chih Ch'ien's recension was immensely popular among the Chinese gentry, with whom he enjoyed amicable relations.

The Sutra of the Buddha Teaching the Seven Daughters is rather peculiar in subject matter with little or no Mahāyāna doctrine. The story opens in Kapilavastu where a very wealthy Brahman, a member of the highest of classes in Indian society, has seven daughters of exceptional talent. Although the seven girls are not explicitly considered Buddhists from the textual material, they practiced almsgiving and were extremely generous to the people of the kingdom, teaching the principle of justice to all that would listen.

A householder hears of their reputation and decides to ask the Buddha if these young girls truly are so lovely in character. The Buddha relates an odd story about King Kiki and his seven daughters. The focus of the story is a graveyard where dwelling upon the decrepitude of the human body is a means to eliminating sensual desires and to understanding the cause of rebirth. Female corpses were often the object of this meditation. While the graveyard was a usual place for meditation by Buddhist monks and nuns to eliminate sensuality, a vivid scene in which the girls surround the corpses and chant verses to save the "spirits" of the corpses suggests non-Buddhist influence, perhaps shamanistic in tendency, since "spirits" or "souls" were denied by all Buddhists. The vows made in front of Indra are enigmatic, contradictory claims. The daughters never explain the meaning of their vows to Indra but rather chide him for not comprehending them since he is lord of the gods. Arhats, the early Buddhist saints, and Pratyeka-buddhas, the solitary enlightened ones, cannot understand the conundrums because they do not know the teaching of nonsubstantiality (Emptiness) which is central to Mahāyāna Buddhism.

King Kiki[26] is mentioned in Pāli literature. He was the king of Vārāṇasī (Benares) during the appearance of the previous Buddha named Kāśyapa. One of Kiki's daughters was Uracchadā, who became an Arhat (saint) when she was sixteen years old. His seven other daughters are also mentioned in the *Jātaka* tales, the *Apadāna,* the stories of previous existences of monks and nuns, and the *Therīgāthā*, the collection of hymns written by nuns.

Samaṇī is the eldest daughter who observed celibacy for twenty thousand years in her past lifetimes and built a monastery for the Buddha.[27] She appears in several *Jātaka* tales[28] and is described as the ideal Buddhist woman. As the nun Khemā in the time of Śākyamuni,[29] she becomes an Arhat.

The second eldest daughter of King Kiki was Samaṇā (or Samaṇaguttā) who, in other rebirths, was the sister of the Bodhisattva[30] Śākyamuni and of various goddesses which are related in the *Jātakas.*[31] In her last rebirth she is considered one of the Buddha Śākyamuni's two chief women disciples. Within two weeks after her ordination as the nun Uppalavaṇṇā, she becomes an Arhat.[32]

The third daughter was Guttā, who became a nun during her life as King Kiki's daughter. She built a cell for the Saṃgha and was celibate for twenty thousand years. During the Buddha Śākyamuni's lifetime, she became the nun Paṭācārā who was a great teacher and the most expert among the nuns in the *Vinaya Piṭaka (The Book of the Discipline),* the disciplinary rules of the Saṃgha. Many women sought her instruction and she became an Arhat.[33]

Bhikkhunīdāsikā (or Bhikkhunīdāyikā) was the fourth daughter, who lived in celibacy for twenty thousand years and built a monastery for the Saṃgha. During the time of Śākyamuni she became one of the most excellent nuns named Bhaddā-Kuṇḍalakesā. At the end of the first sermon which she had heard from Śākyamuni, she was ordained by the Buddha and attained Arhatship.[34]

The fifth daughter of King Kiki was Dhammā, who became a nun and lived a celibate life. During the time of Śākyamuni she became a nun named Kisāgotamī, who had had a very unhappy married life. She begged the Buddha to accept her as a nun, and she soon realized Arhatship through listening to him preach.[35]

The sixth daughter was Sudhammā, who also lived a life of celibacy for twenty thousand years. During the time of Śākyamuni she became the nun Dhammadinnā, who was accomplished in preaching and became an Arhat while living in solitude.[36]

Saṃghadāsī was the youngest of King Kiki's daughters, who performed good works and generously gave alms after her marriage. Unlike King Kiki's other daughters, she did not become a nun, and in a later life as a female lay disciple to Śākyamuni named Visakhā she became one of the most important laywomen disciples earning a reputation for her tremendous generosity. Later she became a Streamwinner on the path to Arhatship while the Buddha preached to her.[37]

In *The Sutra of the Buddha Teaching the Seven Daughters* it is implied that the young girls of Brahman Mahāmāya have not learned the Buddha's teaching or Dharma. They apparently are still very young and have distributed their wealth throughout the kingdom. Considering the fact that all seven of these girls were believed to be virtuous, Śākyamuni's denunciation of their good reputation occurs for no apparent reason. The implicit reason seems to be a denunciation of non-Buddhist practices. However, there are several statements about the hellish quality of women. The reader is led to conclude that a biased and antagonistic author deliberately imposed his views upon the teaching of the Buddha, either in defiance or ignorance of the earlier tradition of the Pāli canon, in which the daughters of King Kiki are eminently virtuous. The text appears to be split, with a diatribe against Mahāmāya's daughters interspersed with a tribute to King Kiki's seven daughters.

Although the seven young daughters of the Brahman Mahāmāya are deprecated by the Buddha, the story of the seven virtuous daughters of King Kiki balances the prejudicial statements attributed to the Buddha in the first half of the text. The emphasis shifts from sexual desires and attachments associated with the feminine to the attachment to the transitoriness and illusion of existence itself. The use of graveyard imagery is especially vivid in communicating the ephemeral quality of human existence. The text, in its concluding passages, states: "The citizens of Kapilavastu, not as male or female, were ecstatic. With harmonious hearts they entered meditation." Both the men and women in the text attain a spiritually advanced stage along the Buddhist path. Consequently, the initial polemic against women is softened by peaceful coexistence between the two at the very end of the text.

The Sutra of the Buddha Teaching the Seven Daughters* *(Fo shuo ch'i nü ching).* T. v. 14, n. 556, pp. 907-09.[38]

THUS I [Ānanda][39] have heard [from the Buddha who preached this sermon to me]:

At one time, I, the Buddha, was residing in Kapilavastu in the Nigrodha[40] grove with one thousand Arhats, five hundred Bodhisattvas and the gods, spirits, and Nāgas.[41] At that time in Kapilavastu there was a Brahman named Mahāmāya,[42] who was both stingy and greedy and did not believe in my Dharma. He was extremely wealthy with many precious jewels, livestock, and homes, and his cleverness was unique. In his kingdom he was a teacher who always had five hundred students. The king's chief minister would receive him respectfully. The Brahman (Mahāmāya) had seven daughters who were exceptionally refined and incomparable in wisdom and speech. From

*This first English translation is by Diana Paul.

their heads to their feet they wore gold, silver, and white precious jewels [pearls?]. At all times they were attended by five hundred women. They delighted in their own worth, high integrity, and refinement. Lazy and self-indulgent people relied upon their wealth, calling out [to them] constantly. Every day they taught the principle of justice to the other citizens of the kingdom. Always they [the daughters] were excellent [in their teaching].

There was a householder named Nigrodha who had heard about the loveliness[43] of these girls. He went to the Brahman's residence and said: "In your honorable house your daughters are said to be refined. Although by this time everyone in the kingdom should have seen them, if anyone rebukes these girls you should give me five hundred gold coins. If they do not rebuke them, I will give you five hundred gold coins."

Then, for ninety days, wherever he called out throughout the kingdom, no one anywhere deprecated these girls. The Brahman accordingly received five hundred gold coins [from the householder]. Nigrodha spoke to the Brahman: "Now the Buddha is in the Jeta garden. He knows all past, present, and future activities. To verify [the girls' virtue] and see if they are not lying, you should go see the Buddha."

The Brahman spoke: "Very well, I will go with five hundred Brahmans as retainers and with five hundred women from our kingdom." They then went to my residence. At that time I was teaching the Dharma to countless thousands of people. Each paid reverence before me and left their seats to one side. The Brahman spoke humbly before me, saying: "Gautama, you have continually roamed throughout various kingdoms and have you not seen such loving and refined women as these?"

I disagreed: "These women are not loving. All of them are wicked without one lovely good quality."[44]

The Brahman asked me: "But these women are not deprecated by anyone in the entire country! Now, Gautama, why do you alone deprecate these girls?"[45]

The Brahman [again] asked me: "For people in the world why is there love?"

I spoke: "If the people in the world did not see shapes with their eyes nor hear evil sounds with their ears, then there would be love.[46] If they did not smell perfume with their noses nor relish taste with their mouths, then there would be love. If they did not crave the delicate and smooth with their bodies nor remember evil with their minds, then there would be love. If they did not steal others' possessions with their hands nor speak evil of others with their mouths, then there would be love. Do not value beautiful speech. If one knows that what is born will end in death, then there will be love. If one believes in generosity and that later one will have blessings, then there will be love. If one believes in the Buddha, the Dharma, and the Saṃgha of monks, then there will be love."

I spoke to the Brahman: "Loveliness of face and form are not lovely. The loveliness of the body is not lovely. The loveliness of clothing is not lovely. False speech and flattering words are not lovely. The refinement of the heart and correct thoughts are lovely. Return to Nigrodha his five hundred gold coins."

I [again] spoke to the Brahman: "In the past there was a Buddha who came from the city called Vārāṇasī. All the future Buddhas were in this [land]. Then the king of the state named Kiki became a [Buddhist] layman who thoroughly understood the sutras. On behalf of the Buddha he built a monastery. The king had [seven] daughters who became laywomen. Their understanding of the sutras and their wisdom were refined and unique. On their bodies they wore gold, silver, and jeweled garments which were extremely lovely. His first daughter was Guttā. His second daughter was Sudhammā. His third daughter was

Bhikkhunī (Dhamma). His fourth daughter was Bhikkhunīdāsikā. His fifth daughter was Samaṇī. His sixth daughter was Samaṇā. His seventh daughter was Saṃghadāsī.

"They were always generous to the utmost degree in accordance with the moral precepts."

The seven daughters together went to their father's palace and humbly spoke: "We sisters desire to have you come with us to a graveyard to take a look."

The king spoke: "But graveyards are extremely frightful. There are only the skeletons and hair of corpses scattered and cast on the ground. The grief-stricken and weeping fill the place. There are savage wild beasts and vultures which eat the blood and flesh of corpses. Why would you sisters go to a graveyard? The garden in my palace has ponds for you to gaze at. In it there are flying birds and mandarin ducks chasing each other and screeching. In it there are many flowers of five different colors, brilliant to the eyes, irises, and exquisite trees with many succulent fruits you can eat to your heart's content. You can easily take a look. Why would you sisters go to a graveyard?"

The seven daughters answered: "Your majesty, how could these fruits supply a serving to everyone? We have seen the people in the world who, when old, approach death. There is no one who is born and will not die. We are not small children who are distracted by food. Your majesty is distressed thinking of us. You should listen to us sisters and come to the outskirts of the city to see the corpses."

The king spoke: "Very well, I will pay attention to what you do."

Then the seven daughters and their five hundred women attendants regally rode out of the palace in carriages. The seven daughters then removed their jewels from their necks and scattered them on the ground.

At that time there were one thousand people in the kingdom who saw them. They ran after them, grabbing the jewels rapturously. When they had reached the graveyard on the outskirts of the city, there was a huge stinking spot which was not clean. They heard only the sounds of weeping. The female attendants and townspeople fidgeted with their clothing on their bodies, their hair standing on end. The seven daughters saw the corpses in front of them. Some had their heads cut off. Others had their arms and legs amputated. Some were missing noses and ears. Some had already died, but others had not. Some were in coffins, others inside mats or tied with ropes. The entire household wept desiring the liberation [of the deceased]. The seven daughters gazed on many corpses to the left and right. On all sides birds and beasts who came to prey upon the corpses fought among themselves to devour them. The blood and pus from the swollen bellies of corpses oozed. Millions of insects crawled out of their stomachs. This stinking spot was difficult to tolerate.

The seven daughters did not cover their noses but surrounded them [that is, the corpses] in a circle and said these words: "The bodies of us sisters will, in a short while, be like these."

The first daughter: "Why doesn't each of us compose a verse to save the spirits[47] of these corpses." The other six daughters: "Fine."

The first daughter: "When these people were born, they loved to splash perfume on their bodies and wear new and lovely clothes. While walking in a crowd every detail [of their appearance] was pleasing to the eye. They made an impression among others and wanted others to look at them. Now the dead on the ground are scorched by the sun and blown by the wind. Those who considered making an impression important [for their self-image] now rest here."

The second daughter: "Small birds hidden inside bottles with covered openings cannot fly out. Now if these bottles were broken, the small birds could fly away."

The third daughter: "If a horse-drawn carriage goes along and stops in the middle of the road leaving the carriage behind, the carriage cannot proceed as before. If the owner sends a driver, they can go to their destination."

The fourth daughter: "If a man steers a ship and all the passengers are ferried across to the shore, then he can anchor the ship. Parting from one's body and leaving it behind is like parting from a ship and leaving it behind."

The fifth daughter: "Within the fortifications of the city many citizens were born. Now, within its great walls, the city is empty and one does not see its citizens—where have they all gone?"

The sixth daughter: "The dead are laid to rest in the ground. Their clothing, which was always lovely from head to foot, is now destroyed. Today they cannot walk or move about. Now where have all the people gone?"

The seventh daughter: "Supposing someone who lives alone leaves his house. Then there is no one to protect that house which is empty. Now that house will daily fall to ruin."

At that time the lord of the gods, Indra, in the Trayastriṃśas heaven, the second [of the six desire realms], had been sitting but became agitated when he heard the seven daughters explaining this sutra. As if he were stretching, he descended from heaven to praise the seven girls [and said]:

"What you have explained is remarkable. I wish to know what kind of vows you have professed so that I can undertake them as you have."

The seven daughters: "This is Śakra! This is Brahmā! We did not see you supernaturally come before us and we want to know why."

Indra: "Daughters, I am Indra, lord of the gods. I have

heard your fine explanation [of this sutra]. Because your words are so lovely, I have come to listen to you."

The seven daughters: "Your excellency wishes to know our vows. Then, most reverend lord of the thirty-three gods in heaven [Trayastriṃśas], the second [of the six desire realms], you will undertake them with us. We sisters will explain our vows."

The first daughter: "I vow to be born among trees without leaves, branches, or roots. This is what I vow."

The second daughter: "I vow to be born on a land without shadows or shade."

The third daughter: "I vow to be born on a high mountain without any sounds or echoes, which is unknown to man."

Śakra: "Stop! I can't make such vows! If you women wish to be born among the four gods, Brahmā, myself, and the others, then I could undertake [such vows]. Now what you have vowed I truly cannot comprehend."

The seven daughters: "Your excellence, the supreme sovereign in heaven, has supernatural powers. Why can't you undertake these vows? Are you like an old bull who can't pull a wagon or pull a plough and is perfectly useless to his owner?"

Śakra: "Because I have heard you explain this sutra, I have come to listen. I should be excused for what I do not know."

The seven daughters were silent and did not answer.

Then the gods spoke from the heavens: "Now the Buddha Kāśyapa is very near these graves. Why don't you go ask the Buddha Kāśyapa?"

The seven daughters heard them and were delighted. With their five hundred women attendants they went to see him. In the graveyard there was much mourning, weeping, and wailing. Five hundred people had been absorbed with such thoughts [of sorrow]. At that time the Buddha Kāśyapa was teaching the Dharma to innumerable thousands of people. Immediately every individual paid reverence before the Buddha Kāśyapa, leaving their seats to the side. Indra, the lord of gods, humbly spoke to the Buddha:

"I have presented myself because I have heard the king's seven daughters explain this sutra and I have come to listen to them. Because of my inquiry about their vows, the seven daughters said: 'I wish to be among trees without leaves, branches, or roots, a place without shadows or shade, a high mountain without any sounds or echoes, which is unknown to man.' I then could not answer and vowed to have the Buddha explain the meaning of the seven daughters' statement."

Buddha Kāśyapa: "Very well, you have asked about what is beyond [most people's comprehension]. Such matters cannot be known by the Arhats and Pratyeka-buddhas. So, of course, that is the reason [why you don't understand]."

Then the Buddha Kāśyapa smiled. A five-colored brilliance shone from his mouth, illuminating all the Buddha lands, then returning to encircle his body and enter his head. The attendants knelt before the Buddha Kāśyapa and spoke: "Buddha, please do not laugh, for we wish to understand the meaning of their vows."

The Buddha Kāśyapa spoke to the protector of all beings:[48] "Do you see these girls? After having seen them, along with these seven daughters, you will awaken to the thought of the Supreme, Perfect Enlightenment and worship five hundred Buddhas. After you have also worshipped ten thousand Buddhas for ten eons, all of you will become Buddhas bearing the same name, Fu-to-lo-pen.[49] The Buddha land will be named Śuddhāvāsa.[50]

"The lifespan of these Buddhas will be thirty thousand eons. During this time the food and clothing of the people [in this Buddha land] will be like those who are in the heaven of the thirty-three gods, the second [of the six desire realms]. After the final Nirvana of these Buddhas, the path will be retained and will flourish for eight thousand years. When these Buddhas teach the Dharma, seventy-five million people will realize the paths of the Bodhisattva or Arhat."

When the Buddha Kāśyapa gave this prediction to the seven daughters, they leaped with joy to the sky, about twenty feet off the ground. When they descended from above, they had changed into boys and realized the irreversibility[51] [from the path of a Bodhisattva]. The five hundred women attendants and fifteen hundred gods and men saw the seven daughters change into boys and leaped with joy. All of them awakened to the thought of the Supreme, Perfect Enlightenment. One thousand people separated from impurity and attained the Dharma vision.

I spoke to the Brahman: "The seven daughters of this king delighted in their own worth, high integrity, and refinement. They were not dependent upon their bodies to be lovely. Why? Since the body cannot live for long, think of it as transitory. Because everyone in the world is only engrossed with their doubts, they fall into the twelve-linked chain of causation which gives rise to the cycle of existence. All people are born from attachment [to existence].[52] From birth there is old age. From old age there is sickness, and from sickness there is death. From death there is weeping until one is grief-stricken. All people are born from attachment [to existence]. One should see one's own body as well as that of others [in this way]. Rising from your seat, one should reflect on the vile excretions of the body in the stinking spot which is unclean, of heat and cold where tears fall [namely, the grave]. What kind of body, when destroyed, changes into meat for insects to eat? The bones and joints disintegrate to dust. So remember 'the death of my body is like this.' One should not depend upon the body for loveliness. One should think of it as transitory. If a person practices good and does not praise himself with flattering words, after death he will be born in heaven. If he commits evil, he will enter hell.

[The Buddha continued:] "Why do so many women fall into hell? Because many of them are engrossed in jealousies." When I had explained this, the Brahman women leaped with joy. Their jewels fell off their bodies and were strewn on me. By my supernatural powers, the jewels which were scattered became a jeweled umbrella appearing in the sky. From it a voice rang out: "Excellent, it is just as the Buddha has said."

Then I, the Buddha, by my supernatural powers, moved from my seat, pressing the ground with my toe. The three thousand great world systems all quaked. Brilliant light radiated everywhere. One-hundred-year-old withered trees bore fruits and flowers. All the empty aqueducts were spontaneously filled with water. Musical instruments such as lutes, without being played by another, automatically played. The women's jeweled bracelets jangled by themselves. The blind could see and the deaf could hear. Mutes could speak and the hunchbacked were straightened. The lame were healed and those with deformed extremities were healed. The insane were cured. The poisoned were not affected by the poison. The imprisoned were freed. Hundreds of birds and beasts were harmonious in their cries. Then, the citizens of Kapilavastu, not as male or female, were ecstatic. With harmonious hearts they entered meditation.

When I had created these magical changes, the king of Kapilavastu gave away his jewels and leaped with joy. The hundred ministers and the Brahman women, their retainers, and five hundred Brahman men all awakened to the thought of the Supreme, Perfect Enlightenment. Five hundred monks realized the path of the Arhat. Five hundred people in the kingdom entered the path of the Streamwinner. After I had explained this sutra, the Bodhisattvas, monks, laymen, and laywomen, the king, ministers, and citizens, the gods, spirits, and Nāgas all were ecstatic and prostrated themselves on the ground. Having paid reverence to me, they then left [for home].

B. Introduction to "The Tale of King Udayana of Vatsa" from *The Collection of Jewels*

The Collection of Jewels (Mahāratnakūṭa) is an anthology which now includes forty-nine tales, also called assemblies, fourteen of which were independent texts at one time. *The Collection of Jewels* referred originally to the Kāśyapa assembly, which is one of the oldest discourses on Emptiness now accepted as Mahāyānist and incorporated as the forty-third assembly. This anthology of forty-nine tales, translated into Chinese by Bodhiruci of the T'ang dynasty between 706 and 713, approximately 600 years after the composition of the Kāśyapa assembly, is now collectively designated *The Collection of Jewels.* The original compilation of forty-nine texts may have taken place in either China or Central Asia.[53] Due to the diversity of texts incorporated in *The Collection of Jewels,* there was no single place of composition.

The twenty-ninth tale or assembly is "The Tale of King Udayana of Vatsa."[54] King Udayana[55] of Kauśāmbi had two wives. His chief queen, Śyāmāvatī, was a devout Buddhist. His second queen, Anupamā Māgandika,[56] wanted to slander the chief queen because she was jealous. Due to Anupaınā Māgandika's lying and flattery, King Udayana tried to kill Śyāmāvatī by shooting three arrows at her. Śyāmāvatī then entered concentration (samādhi) and forgave the king. Instead of injuring her, the three arrows remained suspended over the king's head. Astonished and perplexed, the king repented and went to see the Buddha to find out why women are evil. The Buddha explained that one must know man's evil ways before one can know woman's, but from the discourse which follows, women are viewed as a problem of insurmountable proportions.

Ironically, although Śyāmāvatī in the following tale was the most innocent and holy character in the story, the Buddha is made to present a scathing indictment of all women by the author of this text. The king is a "straw man" for the monks who projected their own insecurities and weaknesses onto women, as will be evident in the following story. Relationships with women are generalized first as being evil and the source of suffering. One should enter into worthwhile relationships, which exclude those with women. Second, relationships with women draw energy away from valuable relationships with monks and Brahmans. Those who deal with women have misplaced values since they view their relationships with women as valuable rather than as corrupting the valuable. Third, relationships with women are all-consuming and preclude involvement in other relationships. Fourth, attraction toward women is extremely powerful and implies a natural force which draws men and women together only to end in destruction. The author vacillates between woman's deception as the cause for the strong attraction and helplessness of the male, on the one hand, and a man's desire for self-inflicted pain, on the other.

Women are given tremendous power in "The Tale of King Udayana of Vatsa." They manipulate and confuse men with their powers of deception. Yet men's self-inflicted pain is somewhat contradictory in view of their victimization by women. The monk's jealousy becomes evident, especially in the passages in which women are depicted as powerful competitors for attracting potential followers to the Buddha's teaching. In "The Tale of King Udayana of Vatsa" we find a vituperative polemic against women which demonstrates a polarization of women on one side and the Buddha's Dharma on the other. For the monk, his situation demanded the exclusion of women in order to practice the rules of celibacy. His lifestyle has been projected on society at large in the following tale in which women and the desire to associate with them should be totally rejected. The severity of this "monkish" attitude and the one-sided nature of the rhetoric is especially noticeable when the author extols the benefits of filial piety but glosses over the duties to mother, sister, and wife in contrast to the compulsion to denigrate sexuality at all costs.

"The Tale of King Udayana of Vatsa"* ("Udayanavatsarājaparivartaḥ") from *The Collection of Jewels (Mahāratnakūṭa)*, assembly 29. T. v. 11, n. 310, pp. 543–47.

THUS I [Ānanda] have heard [from the Buddha who preached this sermon to me]:

At one time I, the Buddha, was residing at Ghosilārāma[57] in Kauśāmbī with 1,250 monks. King Udayana's chief queen, Śyāmāvatī,[58] continually gave alms and paid reverence to me, the Tathāgata,[59] and to the holy Saṃgha with fervent faith, continually praising my merits. The king's second queen, Anupamā Māgandika, was jealous and loved flattery. At the palace she would recklessly deprecate me and my disciples and called the chief queen wicked. When the king heard her, he was furious at Śyāmāvatī and immediately shot an arrow at her. Śyāmāvatī, forgiving the

*This first English translation is by Diana Paul.

king, entered a state of meditation. The arrow, which had been shot, settled in mid-air above the king's head. This arrow blazed brilliantly like a conflagration, instilling great fear. Likewise the [second and] third arrow hovered around his head. Seeing this feat, King Udayana's hair stood on end. Bewildered and flustered, he repented, speaking to the queen:

"You are a goddess, a Nāga princess, or a spirit (Yakṣiṇī). A satyr. A semihuman being (Kiṃnarī). An ogress (Piśācī) or a demoness (Rākṣasī).[60]

The queen answered: "I am not a goddess nor a demoness or any of the others. Your majesty, you should know me. I have heard the true Dharma from the Buddha. I have accepted the five moral precepts,[61] becoming a lay practitioner. I forgave your majesty and entered a state of meditation. Although you, my king, are not favorably disposed toward me, I have compassionately vowed not to harm you."

Then she recommended to the king: "Your majesty, you should seek refuge in the lord, Arhat, Completely Enlightened One, paying reverence to him and attaining peace."[62]

King Udayana reflected: "The true Dharma which she heard from the Buddha made her a lay practitioner. Moreover, she has such supernatural powers! The Tathāgata, Arhat, Competely Enlightened One is even greater [in supernatural power]."

With that thought, the king went to my residence and prostrated himself at my feet. Circumambulating three times, the king then humbly spoke to me: "Conditioned by desire, I was deceived by the lies of that woman [Anupamā Māgandika] and harbored malicious thoughts toward you and the holy Saṃgha." Having made that statement, he again humbly spoke to me: "I only wish that you, the Tathāgata, and the holy Saṃgha would give me happiness, listen to my confession, and cause my offenses to cease."

Then I spoke to the king, saying: "What you have said about me and my holy Saṃgha is like an ignorant fool who has many faults. He recklessly hates the fields of merit. Now if you depend upon the moral precepts of the holy Dharma, repenting for your offenses without accumulating any others,[63] then you will have no future births and you will never transgress again. I will now accept you and cause you to grow in the holy Dharma in the future."

King Udayana again humbly spoke to me: "Lord, because of woman's deception, I am perplexed and ignorant. For this reason I have intense hate. Lord, because you bring peace and benefits to living beings, I want you to explain, out of compassion, the flattery and deceit of women. Do not let me have close relationships with women. Then, after a long time, I will be able to avoid all suffering."

I spoke: "Put aside these actions. Why don't you ask about what is important and not about extraneous matters?"

The king spoke to me: "I will ask without digressing. Women make me commit acts which will send me to hell. From now on I wish to completely understand the faults of women, their obsequiousness, and their lying and treachery. I would like you to explicate these three requests which I have just stated."

I answered: "Your majesty should first know a man's faults. Then he'll have insight into those of a woman."[64]

King Udayana replied: "All right, lord, I wish to listen."

I explained: "Because all men engage in four kinds of wrong and excessive actions, they are perplexed by women. What are the four? First, they are addicted to desire, insatiably looking at women for their own self-indulgence.[65] They do not experience a close relationship with either monks or Brahmans. They are not close to all those who practice good actions in accordance with the moral precepts of purity. Such men as these turn away from faith, morality, learning, and [the perfections of] generosity and wisdom. Since they have no faith, morality, learning, nor [the perfections of] generosity and wisdom, they are not good men and act like hungry demons. They are without wisdom, addicted to desire, and dissipated. They are attached to desire, harnessed to desire, and living for the sake of desire. They have close relationships with fools, avoiding those who are wise. Having evil friends as their companions, they engage in whatever is not right. Greedily addicted to women who are living in an impure state,[66] they submit to them like male slaves who are shackled, degenerating without shame or embarrassment. They associate and cavort with them like the eternal flow of pus, slime, and mucus from boils festering in a grave.

[I continued:] "They disregard their obligation to their parents. They ignore the monks and Brahmans. They do not have reverence and respect for them. They habitually abuse the rights of animals. They do not have sincere faith in me, the Dharma, nor the Saṃgha. They are continually turned away from Nirvana. These men enter the hells from that of Saṃghāta to Avīci. They also degenerate to rebirth as antigods [Aśuras] and animals without deliverance. Although they hear my teaching, they frequently have thoughts of the dancing and laughter of evil women and do not avoid them. One should know that such are the habits of fools who do not seek the actions of the good man. Your majesty, you should know that when men have close relationships with women,[67] they have close relationships with evil ways. This is the first fault of men."

[Then I recited these verses:]

"All desires are suffering,
The vilest of evils,
The impurity of pus,
Extremely despicable.

Where many wrongs
Are compounded
Why should the wise
Delight in them?

Like the overflow from a toilet
Or the corpse of a dog
Or that of a fox
In the Śītavana cemetery
Pollution flows everywhere.
The evils of desire
Are contemptible like these.

Fools
Lust for women
Like dogs in heat.
They do not know abstinence.

They are also like flies
Who see vomited food.
Like a herd of hogs,
They greedily seek manure.

Women can ruin
The precepts of purity.
They can also ignore
Honor and virtue.

Causing one to go to hell
They prevent rebirth in heaven.
Why should the wise
Delight in them?

The person who
Desires the poisons of material comforts
Has torments both physical and mental
And cannot assuage them.

Because these desires
Become the basis for suffering
They are poisons to the body.

Fools cannot know
Nor realize
The illusory qualities of phenomena.
They carelessly seek
Only self-inflicted pain.

Fools, in addition,
Out of desire,
Continually seek suffering
And fall into hell.

Some engage in food and drink
Dancing and singing with prostitutes
And having affairs with other women.
Even though they have wives
They accumulate much
Suffering without any benefits.

Fools perform these futile acts
Increasing their vices.
They avoid good habits
And in futility
They do not care for their lives.

Because of these depravities,
Their evil ways become a deep pit.
Once more they're sent to a hell
Of blazing flames and iron pellets,
Spears, bayonets and mountains of swords
And the pain of poisoned arrows.

Women can compound one's suffering.
By their perfume
One falls in love.[68]

The fool,
Confused, yearns for her.
Being close and admiring
Insignificant things,
He turns away from wisdom.

Falling into the three blunders[69]
Because of his foolishness,
He becomes deluded
Like the exhausted seagull
Who is confused by the other shore.

The fool
Has molten iron[70] poured
On his neck
Like a yoke on a cow.

His desires are like liquor
Intoxicating to men.
Why do fools not
Recognize the basis for pain?[71]

They easily forget their parents' kindness.
Because of their desires
They commit vices
Continually in this way.

They praise and follow
Their lewd inclinations
Without shame.

Because of their foolishness
They are confused.
Having committed these vices
They precipitate the three blunders.

Heavily addicted to desires
The intoxicated
Also abandon
The kindness of their parents.

If those who are greedy
Associate with desires,
They will turn away
From the field of virtue.

For innumerable periods of time
Their misconceived afflictions

Cause their perpetual grief.
From these, they are reborn.

In addition, some seek
A position of wealth in the world.
By unrighteous acts
They propel themselves
Into revolving and rebirth.

Because of these (acts)
They will be summoned now
To suffer beatings,
Dying and falling into
The Avīci hell.

Now look at these sufferings.
In the future they will cluster on you.
Good friends will depart.
The celestial palaces will be forever lost.
Why should the wise
Delight in them?

Thrown into a hell of Iron
Racing over sword mountains
Sleeping on blazing ovens
They cannot be close to a woman's form.

If you continually lust
For objects of desire
You will lose many
Beneficial pleasures.

Women can be
The cause of great suffering.
If desire[72] is destroyed
There will be everlasting happiness.

Evils are compounded
And good friends depart
When one is addicted
To women who are the basis.[73]

If one listens
To what I have said
They can be reborn, separated
From women.

Then theirs will be
The majestically pure heaven
And they will attain
Supreme Enlightenment."

[I continued:] "Your majesty, because your parents wished for happiness and prosperity for their children, they would perform whatever practices were difficult, have patience in facing all difficulties, and withstand all kinds of evil. Because they also wanted their children's physical abilities and appearance to be outstanding, they would let them see extraordinary things like the roseapple tree, caring for their children tirelessly in order that they might have profound happiness without distress. Obtaining whatever their children wanted, together they provided whatever material possessions their children needed and would live with the families of those they would marry. Having married, however, their children become addicted to other women.[74] Because of their addiction, they are confused.

"Seeing their parents gradually age, they turned against them and insulted them. They would use their [parents'] wealth without shame and drive their parents from their home. Because of desire there is such perversion.

"Your majesty, you should know that these are the causes for rejecting one's obligation to one's parents.[75] To value and flatter other women, providing them with various things without satisfaction, is the foundation of hell. This is a man's second fault."

[Then I recited these verses:]

"You should know
The one who respects and reveres

His mother and father
Will always have
The world protectors Indra and Brahmā
To protect him.
They can give his family
Peace and happiness.

Because of business,
Some men travel overseas.
Their trips will be safe ones
And they will acquire wealth.

I refer to these
Invaluable treasures
Which can bring benefits
As an excellent field.

Similarly, at present,
If wealth and benefits
Are all offered in reverence
To one's parents,
In the future
You will not have
The body of a beast of burden
Who carries heavy loads.

Neither will you be subjected
To cremation near the river
Nor suffering by
Mountains of swords, spears, and bayonets,
Nor molten metal.

In the future
You will be born among men.
You will have wealth,
Abundance and prosperity.[76]
Your wife, children, and relatives
All will have harmony.

Some will be reborn
In heaven
Among palaces and gardens

And the sounds of music.
Joyful and at ease
They will have the most profound happiness.

Who are the wise?
Those who hear the Dharma,
And to their parents
Never waver in giving reverence."

[I then explained:] "Your majesty, due to erroneous views, men who do not know that their bodies are soon extinguished, commit evil, and make fools of themselves. These ignorant men vainly pass their time. Like lifeless engravings, they have a human image but are not aware of it. Habitually desirous, they commit actions which lead to the evil destinies. This is a man's third fault."

Then I spoke [again] in verses:

"Men, because of desire,
Become confused.
For this reason, they commit
Numerous vices.

Perverted views preclude
And obscure their minds.
Carrying on in this way,
They will be reborn
In the evil destinies of hell.

Those who commit offenses
Will again separate
From all blessings.

They do not respect
Monks and others.
Because of these perverse views,
They will seek refuge
In evil doers on mountains and near rivers.

Because of their lust
Some will slaughter

All the birds and beasts,
Sacrificing to gods and spirits.

Perverted views are the cause.
Without the Dharma, they seek happiness.
For this reason, they forever are deprived
Of peace.

Those who are in such a state
Perform evil actions.
They do not experience true faith
And are viciously cruel without remorse.

Men such as these
Are forever separated from the holy
And inevitably will fall
Into the Mahāraurava hell.

Some, because of their desires,
Use force on others,
They will fall into the Tāpana
And Pratāpana hells.

Because of their perverted views,
They cannot associate
With the Buddha, Dharma, and Saṃgha.
Respect and reverence
For the true teaching of the Dharma jewel
Is not learned.

Separated from the holy,
They fall into evil ways.
Therefore, the wise
Are able to be human.

Do not engage in
Perverted, false views.
Practice generosity
And morality.

Then one will attain
Rebirth in heaven

And realize
The path of Enlightenment."

[I continued:] "Your majesty, there are some men who, with regard to their lives, are overachievers, accumulating material luxuries. Because they become involved with women, like young slaves, they pay respect to them. For these reasons, they are miserly with their wealth and do not give to the monks or Brahmans.

"Now, everyone is able to endure the penalties, license, and extremes of the king's law. Some are beaten and scolded by women. Some are afraid, submissively paying respect to them. Reflecting on their sorrow, they say to themselves: 'How can I be joyous today?' I should say that these men are slaves to desire. In the impure and inferior, they conceive of the pure and are impassioned. When they have close relationships with women, they are engulfed in evil ways. This is a man's fourth fault."

Then I [again] spoke in verses:

"Men who are intoxicated by desire
Truly are without peace.
Because they associate with evil
They are not called good men.

If a man is self-indulgent
And is without morality,
Acting as he pleases
He will lose merit.

Those who are not wise,
Act like animals,
Racing toward female forms
Like hogs toward mud.

Fools cannot see
The vice in desires
And ignorantly focus on them
Like blind men.

Bound to [female][77] forms
They become ever more desirous
Like a fox
Who is never away from a grave.

To sound, taste, touch, and smell
They are addicted,
Revolving in the cycle of life and death
Like monkeys tied to a post.

Because of their ignorance
They are bewildered by women who,
Like profit seekers[78] in the market place,
Deceive those who come near.

Foolish men close to desire
Enter a realm of demons.
Like maggots
They are addicted to filth.

As rain and hail
Destroy farms,
So a potter close to a fire
Is often burned.

Those who still have not seen the truth
Lose the pure Dharma because of desire.
As the wind blows the smallest kernels
The meaning is similar.

If a good man
Were seized by a killer
The injury incurred would be better
Than that from closeness to women.

If one delights in a woman's form
His lust will be reborn.
Born as an ordinary man,
He will be increasingly lustful.

When, in the heat of summer,
One roams into a desert

Ravaged with thirst, gulping salty water
Becoming even more parched.

Those who still have not seen the truth
Fool themselves.
Associating with women,
Their desires become hardened.

If one touched a poisonous insect
He would be harmed by the poison.
Similarly, the ordinary man,
Committed to desire, is also injured.

Like a multicolored bottle
Containing a potent poison,
The interior is feared
Though the external appearance is serene.

Ornaments on women
Show off their beauty.
But within them there is great evil
As in the body there is air.

With a piece of bright silk
One conceals a sharp knife.
The ornaments on a woman
Have a similar end.

Just as a fire in a deep pit
Can cause fire damage without smoking.
A woman also can be
Cruel without pity.

As the filth and decay
Of a dead dog or dead snake
Are burned away,
So all men should burn filth
And detest evil.

The dead snake and dog
Are detestable,

But women are even more
Detestable than they are.

In the age of destruction
A great holocaust will arise.
All forests and plants
Will be consumed by fire.
Where elephants reside,
All waters will run dry.

Mt. Sumeru, the other jeweled mountains,
And the entire world will be destroyed by fire.
During this age of destruction
Brilliant flames will be on land and sea.

There will be no living beings
Who can be protected.
Because of women's desires
The ignorant will be consumed in fire.

In the age of fire
All will be consumed.
The impure will forever be immersed
In a body of spit, mucus, and blood.

Why should such fools
Be addicted to these,
To a skeletal post
Covered by skin and flesh.
Their stench is offensive
Like rotten food.

Within the gates of the public granaries
There is a surplus of grain.
In the body filthy secretions
Are replete.

The filth of the stomach, kidneys, liver, and bladder,
The bowels and lungs
With the marrow, brain, pus, and blood
Have eighty thousand germs.
Within the body, they are always eating.

The blind fools,
Hiding through self-doubts,
Do not know
The pollutions from various foods
Cause the nine holes [in the body] to ooze.

Such corporeal evils
Are impure from the onset.
Fools are bound to the appearance
Of women.

Because of these lewd attachments
They do not truly know
Lust adheres to the heart
As flies around vomit.

Likewise, the environment
Of the fool who yearns for a woman,
Falling upon her body
He only contaminates himself.

How does the fool
Cavort in such pleasures?
Like a bird seeking food
He does not avoid the net.
Lusting for women,
One also suffers.

Like a fish in water
Who flips into the net,
If one is held by another
How can one not be harmed?

Women are like fishermen.
Their flattery is a net.
Men are like fish
Caught by the net.

The sharp knife of the killer
Is to be feared.
The woman's knife is to be feared
Even more so.

As a moth in a fire
Is singed,
Insects set afire
Have no refuge.

Confused by women
One is burnt by passion.
Because of them
One falls into evil ways.
There is no refuge.

The fool, committing adultery,
Lusts over another's wife
Imagining there is joy.
But, like the domestic chicken
Or the wild pheasant,
While wandering, he is killed.

Self-inflicted pain
Is without respite.
Avoiding my teaching,
One associates with women.

Because of their actions
They fall into evil ways,
Like the female monkey
Who leaps precariously in the trees.

Isn't self-destruction
Due to delusion?
Those addicted
To women
Are spun by delusion
And subjected to life and death's pains.

In dealing with the world's criminals
One uses sharp tools to cause pain.
Those addicted to desire
Will be suspended in forests of swords.

Into scalding water
Heated by a blazing fire

He will be thrown with the wheat
Floating, bubbling, and sinking.

So, the licentious man
Does not know the right path.
At death he falls into evil
And boils in scalding water.

In scalding water
For sixty-four eons
Men's evils
Reside with them.

From one boiling cauldron to another
Each period is ten years.
The fire blazing everywhere
Covers all areas.

For one hundred years,
For two, three, or four hundred,
They suffer by boiling
Because of their deeds.

Hell wardens with sharp sickles
Repeatedly raise them, causing
The skin to tear off and fall
And the bones to turn white like shell.

Hell wardens such as these
Will place them in iron vats,
With clubs to pound them.
There is no escape.

Then their bones and marrow
Will be shattered to dust.
The howling wind of their deeds
Will return them to existence after death.

If one assaults another's
Wife, concubine, or a virgin,
One will make iron-thorned trees
And axes and clubs one's misfortune.

There are three iron forks
And four or five mountain paths.
For assaulting another's wife
One will receive these punishments.

There are iron-beaked birds
Which peck deeply into the marrow and brain.
Foxes and other such beasts
Will fight for this food.

The licentious man
Will fall into the grave of hell.
Chased by bayonets,
He will climb sword mountains.

The licentious man
Falls into the flames of hell.
Injured by fire,
He then falls into ice.

The licentious man
Again falls into a raging fire;
Shrieking and screaming,
Pulled both ways by a black rope.

The licentious man
Will float down a burning river;
Passing through intense heat
Never reaching the bottom to die.

Hell has thorned bushes
With five-pronged thorns.
Forced by dogs
These men are chased into them.

Those who lust for women
Will fall into a fearsome place;
Swallowing iron knives
Drinking molten iron.

There are two molten-iron mountains
Which will be joined together.

In the past those who were desirous
Suffered in between the two.

When one experiences this pain
There is no salvation.
Retribution for one's crimes
Are all due to one's actions.

In the past, lust and joy were the same.
Today what remains of them?
We experience retribution
And there will be no escape.

In former generations,
Because of one's own deeds
Toward one's parents,
There can be no escape.

In former generations
Because of one's own deeds
Toward men and women,
There can be no escape.

In former generations
Because of one's own deeds
Toward one's brothers,
There can be no escape.

In former generations
Because of one's own deeds
Toward one's sisters,
There can be no escape.

In former generations
Because of one's own deeds
Toward one's friends,
There can be no escape.

Fools who are desirous
Lust after women.
Incessantly in hell
They experience pain.

Explain the impurity
And evil in women.
Actions by fools
Are avoided by the wise.

Relationships with women
Are extremely base.
Evil among evil—
What satisfaction is in lust?

The addictions of the common
Are in the manure heap.
Because of their actions
They will suffer without end.

For women, fools will endure
Various torments.
Beaten and bound
They have no hate toward them.

For women, fools will undergo
Various tortures.
Enduring that pain
They have no hate toward them.[79]

Some are placed on sharp instruments.
Some are killed by drowning.
Some are thrown into huge pits.
They receive the poison of suffering.

Although one sees that pain
Lies in sensual desires,
He flatters women
And does not hate them.

Some have a little wisdom
And know the souı ce of their pain
But continue to associate with it
Like the confused who see fire.

Although they hear my teaching
And arouse faith in me,

They still breed with women
Like cattle or sheep.[80]

Some hear my lessons
Then feel remorse.
Instantly, greed reemerges
Like a lingering poison.

Just as a pig which is frightened
Momentarily stops,
If he sees manure,
Lust reemerges.

An ignorant man who hears the Dharma
Momentarily feels astonished.
But when he sees a sensuous form,
Lust reemerges.

Men such as these,
From their own heads
Throw away golden garlands
For crowns of molten iron.

Fools, because of their desires,
Throw away my teaching.
Greedily seeking inferior things
They commit evil deeds.

Intoxicated with desire
They fall into Yāma's[81] world.
Forever swallowing molten swords
They drink liquid metals.

Intoxicated with desire
They reject good and commit evil.
Abandoning the pure
They long remain in hell.

If the wise
Listen to my Dharma
They will reject all desire
And quickly depart from it."

Then, after I had recited these verses, King Udayana humbly spoke to me: "What I have heard today is extraordinary! You, who are the Tathāgata, Arhat, Completely Enlightened One, have explained the vices of desire very well. Now I seek refuge in the jewels of the Buddha, Dharma, and Saṃgha. For as long as I live, I will seek refuge in the Buddha, Dharma, and Saṃgha as a layman. I only wish for you to accept me."

After I had taught this sutra, Udayana and the assembly of gods, men, spirits, and the like heard my teaching and were exalted, practicing what I had taught.

Notes

1. Paul Ricoeur, *The Symbolism of Evil* (Boston: Beacon Press, 1967), p. 235.
2. Ibid., p. 255.
3. J. Edgar Bruns, *God as Woman, Woman as God* (New York: Paulist Press, 1973), p. 21.
4. For an excellent survey of the development of the goddess Kālī and her religious literature, see David R. Kinsley, *The Sword and the Flute: Kālī and Kṛṣṇa, Dark Visions of the Terrible and the Sublime in Hindu Mythology* (Berkeley and Los Angeles: University of California Press, 1975), pp. 81–159.
5. The one exception in Vedic myth, representing early Dravidian matrilinear culture is the Mother Goddess Earth (Prthivī) who is a positive deification of maternity and whose parallels were found throughout the ancient Near East. Cf. Heinrich Zimmer, *Myths and Symbols in Indian Art and Civilization* (Princeton: Princeton University Press, 1946), Bollingen Series VI; reprinted 1962, pp. 90–92.
6. See, for example, *The Book of the Gradual Sayings (Anguttara Nikāya),* tr. E. M. Hare (London: Luzac, 1952), i.1, I, 1–2: "Monks, I know of no other single form, sound, scent, savour, and touch by which a woman's heart is so enslaved as it is by the form, sound, scent, savour and touch of a man. Monks, a woman's heart is obsessed by these things." The passage immediately prior to this citation discusses the equivalent obsession men have for women.
7. Wendy Doniger O'Flaherty, *Asceticism and Eroticism in the Mythology of Śiva* (New York: Oxford University Press, 1973), p. 283.
8. For example, *The Book of the Gradual Sayings (Anguttara Nikāya),* i.11, I, 72: "Monks, womenfolk end their life unsated and unreplete with two things. What two? Sexual intercourse and childbirth. These are the two things."
9. For example, *Kuṇālajātaka,* tr. W. B. Bollée (London: Luzac, 1970), p. 160, verses 24–25: "No man who is not possessed should trust women, for they are base, fickle, ungrateful, and deceitful. They are ungrateful and do not act as they ought to; they do not care for their parents or brother. They are mean and immoral and do only their own will."

10. Ibid., p. 121. However, early Buddhist texts were usually not as antagonistic toward women as the Hindu texts were.
11. See, for example, "The Story of Abhiya," *Mahāvastu*, tr. J. J. Jones (London: Luzac, 1949), I, 29–39, in which one monk falsely accuses another of adultery with a merchant's wife. Numerous accounts of wicked women are given in the *Jātakas*, for example, Kuṇālajātaka, which was written "to admonish monks whose ardour had flagged, because they had fallen into the power of women" (p. 177).
12. *The Book of the Gradual Sayings (Angutarra Nikāya)*, xxiii.6, III, 190: "Monks, there are these five disadvantages to a monk who visits families and lives in their company too much. What five? He often sees womenfolk; from seeing them, companionship comes; from companionship, intimacy; from intimacy, amorousness; when the heart is inflamed, this may be expected: Either joyless he will live the godly life, or he will commit some foul offence or he will give up the training and return to the lower life. Verily, monks, these are the five disadvantages. . . ."
13. Edward J. Thomas, *The Life of Buddha as Legend and History* (London: Routledge & Kegan Paul, 1927); 3rd rev. ed., 1949; reprinted, 1969, pp. 72–73. Also, see *Mahāvastu*, III, 261–87. In other accounts of the temptation by Māra, men are included in the armies of evil forces; cf. *Mahāvastu*, II, 224–30.
14. *The Book of the Gradual Sayings (Anguttara Nikāya)*, vi.5, III, 56: "Monks, a woman, even when going along, will stop to ensnare the heart of a man; whether standing, sitting or lying down, laughing, talking or singing, weeping, stricken, or dying, a woman will stop to ensnare the heart of a man. Monks, if ever one would rightly say: 'It is wholly a snare of Māra, verily, speaking rightly, one may say of womanhood: It is wholly a snare of Māra.' "
15. *The Book of the Gradual Sayings (Anguttara Nikāya)*, xiii.128, I, 260: "Here in this world, Lord, I am wont to see with the deva sight [divine sight], purified and surpassing that of men, I am wont to see womenfolk, when body breaks up after death, being reborn in the Waste, the Way of Woe, in the Downfall, in Purgatory. Pray, Lord, possessed of what qualities are womenfolk so reborn? Possessed of three qualities, Anuruddha [the name of a disciple], women are so reborn. What three? Herein, Anuruddha, in the morning a woman stays at home with heart haunted by the taint of

stinginess. At noontide a woman stays at home with heart haunted by jealousy. At eventide she stays at home with heart haunted by sensuality and lust. These are the three qualities, Anuruddha, possessed of which womenfolk . . . are reborn in Purgatory."

16. See Stephan Beyer, *The Buddhist Experience: Sources and Interpretations* (Belmont, Ca.: Dickenson, 1974), pp. 92–93, for the meditation on the repulsiveness of the body.
17. "Mahāparinibbāna-suttanta" in *Dialogues of the Buddha,* trs. T. W. Rhys Davids and C. A. F. Rhys Davids (London: Luzac, 1966), II, 154.
18. For the rules of excommunication pertaining to conduct with women, see *Vinaya Texts,* tr. T. W. Rhys Davids and Hermann Oldenberg (Delhi: Motilal Banarsidass, 1968), pp. 7–8, 16–17; first published by Oxford University Press, 1881.
19. See, for example, "Ingratitude Punished" ("Cullapadumajātaka"), pp. 158–64, "The Tell-Tale Parrot" ("Rādhajātaka"), pp. 167–68, and "Queen Sussondi" ("Sussondijātaka"), pp. 250–53, in *Jātaka Tales,* trs. H. T. Francis and E. J. Thomas (London: Cambridge University Press, 1916); see these tales also in *The Jātaka or Stories of the Buddha's Former Births,* ed. E. B. Cowell (London: Cambridge University Press, 1897), 6 vols.; II: no. 193, 81; I: no. 145, 309; III: no. 360, 123; respectively.
20. For an analysis of woman as the natural power of reproduction, excluded from the monastically defined religion, see Nancy Falk, "An Image of Woman in Old Buddhist Literature—the Daughters of Māra," in *Women and Religion,* eds. Judith Plaskow and Joan Arnold Romero (Missoula, Montana: Scholars' Press for the American Academy of Religion, 1974), pp. 105–12.
21. See Chapter 2 for a portrait ot the long-suffering mother depicted outside the spiritual realm.
22. Pāli: *viparītasañjñā.* An alternative translation is, "a name which signifies contradiction."
23. *Mahāvastu,* II, 143.
24. See Carl Gustav Jung, *Psychology and Religion* (New Haven: Yale University Press, 1938); 16th printing, 1966, pp. 42, 50–53, for the substitution of *anima,* the psychical representation of the feminine in a man's unconscious, by "creed," erroneously called religion. The exclusion of the feminine as earth or the body, connoting evil as well as nature, is discussed in Jung, pp. 76–77.

25. Chih Ch'ien was a member of the Tocharians (Chinese: *Ta-yüeh-chih)*, a Central Asian tribe of Indo-Scythian origin, allegedly the first to send Buddhist scriptures to China after the emperor Ming (A.D. 58–75) had a dream about the state of Yüeh-chih (Erich Zürcher, *The Buddhist Conquest of China* [(Leiden: Brill, 1959)], p. 22). Buddhism must have been imported from Central Asia, through the northwest near Tun-huang, where in fact, the Yüeh-chih had migrated (E. G. Pulleyblank, "Chinese and Indo-Europeans," *Journal of the Royal Asiatic Society*, April 1966, parts 1 and 2, p. 21).
26. Pāli: *Kiki;* in Sanskrit he is called Kṛkī. Cf. G. P. Malalasekera, *Dictionary of Pāli Proper Names* (London: Luzac, 1960), I, 596 (hereinafter cited as *DPPN*).
27. Ibid., I, 727–28.
28. "Uragajātaka," "Rohantamigajātaka," "Haṃsajātaka," "Mahāhaṃsajātaka," and "Mahājanakajātaka." These tales are translated in *The Jātaka*, ed. E. B. Cowell; II: no. 154, 9–11, IV: no. 501, 257–63; IV: no. 502, 264–67; V: no. 534, 186–202; VI: no. 539, 10–37; respectively.
29. Śākyamuni is the historical Buddha (563–483 B.C.).
30. Śākyamuni was called a Bodhisattva in previous lifetimes, before his Buddahood was achieved.
31. "Kharādiyajātaka," "Sārambhajātaka," "Dhonasākhajātaka," and "Sirikālakaṇṇijātaka," in *The Jātaka*, ed. E. B. Cowell; I: no. 15, 46–47; I: no. 88, 217–18; III: no. 353, 105–07; III: no. 382, 165–68; respectively.
32. *DPPN*, I, 418–21.
33. *DPPN*, II, 112–14.
34. *DPPN*, II, 355–57. Sometimes Bhikkunīdāsikā is identified with Mahāpajāpatī, the stepmother and aunt of Śākyamuni; cf. II, 524.
35. *DPPN*, I, 609–10.
36. *DPPN*, I, 1142–43. Sometimes Sudhammā is identified with Mahāmāyā, the mother of the Buddha, instead of Dhammadinnā; cf. I, 596.
37. *DPPN*, II, 900–04.
38. The abbreviated reference (T. v., n.) indicates the volume and numbered text from the *Taishō* edition of the Chinese collection of Buddhist canonical scripture, compiled by Takakusu Junjiro and Watanabe Kaigyoku and entitled *Taishō shinshū daizōkyō*. This edition, which has become the major standard reference for the Chinese Buddhist canon, was first compiled in Tokyo between 1924 and 1929 and reprinted in

1970. It consists of eighty-five volumes, of which fifty-five volumes contain the sutras as well as the commentarial literature and thirty volumes contain miscellaneous Buddhist documents by Chinese, Korean, and Japanese authors.

39. Ānanda, the Buddha's favorite disciple, was believed to have recited all sermons or sutras from memory after the Buddha's final Nirvana. The assembly of monks that convened at this first council held in Rajagṛha listened as Ānanda recited each lesson, allegedly beginning with the words, "Thus I have heard" and then proceeding with the exact words of the Buddha Śākyamuni: "At one time, I, the Buddha, was residing. . . ." These opening words became a convention and style that were not altered in any subsequent sutra compositions.

40. The Nigrodha park in Kapilavastu was the site where the order of nuns was established. An exact equivalent corresponding to the Chinese transliteration could not be found by the author (Chinese: *Fen-ju-ta*). A shrine near Vaiśālī named Saptāmra (Pāli: *Sattamba* or *Sattambaka*) is given as the site for the attainment of the path by the seven daughters of King Kiki, according to the *Mahāvastu,* I. 248, footnote 4.

41. Serpentlike dieties in Indian mythology.

42. Chinese: *Mo-ho-mi;* the tentative Sanskrit reconstruction is *Mahāmāya.*

43. The "loveliness" of the women has a double meaning in Chinese. The character *hao* consists of two elements representing a woman and her child, signifying maternal love, goodness, and excellence. Carried to an extreme, the love becomes an addiction, which is one of the major themes of this sutra.

44. This statement is an anomaly in view of the entirely positive attitude the Buddha shows toward the daughters of Kiki throughout the rest of the story. Because of the intense identification and compassion for all living beings in Mahāyāna Buddhism, this speech is incongruous.

45. The Brahman's question remains unanswered. The text is either corrupt, or these passages are interpolations which were added later to the core text.

46. See footnote 43 for the various meanings of *hao,* translated in the text as "love." In this passage, the implicit meaning is "goodness,' or "excellence" in contrast to the women as objects of love in an addictive manner. There is a play on

words, suggesting that the negation of one kind of love will lead to the other.

47. It is not clear from the context what kind of spirits are indicated. The spirit may be the hungry ghosts (preta) in Buddhist mythology who prey on decaying corpses or some kind of spirit borrowed from Chinese mythology, perhaps from folk Taoism.
48. The tentative Sanskrit reconstruction is *Sattvapāla;* Chinese: *Sa-po-lo*. *Po-lo* is a transliteration of *pāla* in the name Mahāpāla. Cf. Akanuma Chizen, *Indo bukkyō koyū meishi jiten* (Kyoto: Hōzōkan, 1967), p. 385 b. *Sa* is a transliteration of *sarva* in Sarvadana, Sarvadatta, and Sarvamitra (Akanuma Chizen, p. 603); however, from the context, *sa* probably stands for *sattva*. Indra is the protector who is being addressed, and a common epithet for Indra is Sattvapāla.
49. The tentative Sanskrit reconstruction is *Vadanasatyaṇḍatara*.
50. Chinese: *shou-t'o-po*. The Śuddhāvāsa or Pure Abode is the heaven of the five highest classes of gods in the form realm. These gods announce the birth of a Bodhisattva. Cf. Franklin Edgerton, *Buddhist Hybrid Sanskrit Grammar and Dictionary* (Delhi: Motilal Banarsidass, 1970), pp. 530–31. This transliteration is found in Akanuma Chizen, p. 644 b.
51. The "irreversibility" stage usually refers to an eighth-stage Bodhisattva who has only two more stages before Buddhahood. However, there is no textual evidence in this sutra to define what was meant by irreversibility at the time of composition. Stated otherwise, the developed and definitive system of Bodhisattva stages may not have been established by the time this sutra was written. Consequently, irreversibility remains an unclear attribute of a Bodhisattva according to evidence available from this textual recension.
52. The tenth link in the chain of causation is existence (bhava), an attachment which yields suffering. The eighth and ninth links are desire (tṛṣṇa) and possessiveness (upādāna). The last two links, deriving from existence are birth (jāṭi) and old age and death (jarā-maraṇa). Cf. Richard H. Robinson, *The Buddhist Religion* (Belmont, Ca.: Dickenson, 1970), pp. 20–22, for the twelvefold cycle of causation. The cycle of rebirths is broken when there is no desire or attachment to existence. From the monk's point of view, the sexual act was a desire for self-preservation, a yearning for immortality. The entire familial structure would be in jeopardy in cases in which monks carried the cessation of desire to an extreme.

53. Kajiyama Yuichi, "Bhāvaviveka, Sthiramati, and Dharmapāla" in *Beiträge zur Geistesgeschichte Indiens: Festschrift für Erich Frauwallner,* XII–XIII (1968–1969), 196.
54. Vatsa was the name of an Indian kingdom whose capital was Kauśāmbī, near present-day Kamasin of the Banda area.
55. When the Buddha went to the heaven of the thirty-three gods to teach his mother, King Udayana became sick from the Buddha's absence. Only after one of his ministers constructed a statue of the Buddha out of sandalwood did Udayana recover. This is said to be the first statue of the Buddha, which was later transported to China. Cf. Nakamura Hajime, *Shin Bukkyō jiten (The New Buddhist Dictionary)* (Tokyo: Seishin shobō, 1972), p. 48.
56. Pāli: *Anupamā Māgandiyā.* She was the daughter of Māgandiya (Māgandika), a wanderer who lived at Kalmāṣadamja, according to the *Divyāvadāna,* an early sectarian Buddhist text (Edgerton, pp. 28, 428; Ono Masao, *Busshō kaisetsu daijiten* [Tokyo: Daitō shuppansha, 1966], VII, 324 b).
57. Pāli: *Ghoṣitārāma.* Ghoṣila was one of Udayana's ministers, according to the *Divyāvadāna,* who gave the Buddha a residence in Kauśāmbī named after himself (cf. Edgerton, p. 220).
58. Pāli: *Sāmāvatī.* Śyāmāvatī, according to the *Divyāvadāna,* was a consort of King Udayana (Edgerton, p. 534).
59. An epithet for a Buddha.
60. The king's fear of his wife's power is obvious, attributing her powers to those of a ghost, goddess, or demon.
61. No killing, stealing, lying, intoxicating liquor, or sexual misconduct. These are the five observances which are made by all devout Buddhist laymen and laywomen.
62. Note that Śyāmāvatī is a teacher of Buddhism.
63. The offense of accumulating more offenses (samuccaya-khandaka) is found in the *Kandaka,* section 13, of the *Vinaya Piṭaka.* (Cf. *Busshō kaisetsu daijiten,* ed. Ono Masao, V, 4030 b–4031 b; Ui Hakujiu, *Bukkyō jiten* [(Tokyo: Daitō shuppansha, 1971], p. 920 a.)
64. Buddhism criticized those human actions which were initiated from wrong mental states or intentions. Individual responsibility precluded the use of scapegoats for one's own wrongdoing.
65. If men did not have sexual desires, they would not look at women as objects of desire.

66. The ambiguity is intentional. All women are in an "impure state," yet a subset of women such as Śyāmāvatī apparently are not in an impure state.
67. All women and relationships with them are associated with evil and prevent any association with good, i.e., with monks and Brahmans. The two are viewed as competing forces.
68. Falling in love compounds pain. Here, there is avoidance of the problem, namely, women, rather than confrontation of the problem. The avoidance becomes a form of lust and a form of attachment. Consequently, responsibility for one's own actions in these verses seems to be preempted. Instead, women become responsible for men's sexual depravity, apparently regardless of the men's motives. In Hindu orthodoxy, women were considered incapable of being responsible for their own actions. In Buddhism both men and women were to regard evil as ignorance, a mental attitude. Evil was not an external object or force as it is in this text. The concept of evil expressed in these verses consequently is not Buddhistic.
69. Hate, greed, and delusion.
70. This refers to the intense heat of the Tāpana hell.
71. Pain is identified with desire (i.e., a woman).
72. The text confuses woman as incarnate desire with man's desire. Implicit in this verse is the destruction of woman as the cause of desire as well as of man's desire for her. If woman is the instantiation of evil, one must simply remove this obstacle and the desire will cease, according to this text, but such a statement is counter to the Buddhist theme of eliminating a wrong mental outlook toward other persons and things.
73. Women are viewed as the basis for pain.
74. The author of this sutra seems to imply that marriage is an addiction to a woman to the exclusion of one's parents. The meaning of this passage is not clear.
75. Filial piety is the foundation for good, yet the desire for women destroys this foundation. Respect for women, based upon filial piety, is also stressed in the subsequent verses. Consequently, generalizations which are made about women in this text, although ambiguous in nature, apparently are directed to the subset of women who are not treated as wives, sisters, or mothers. See *Samyutta Nikāya,* IV, 110–11 (also found in *Mahāvastu,* III, 254, footnote 4) for the cultivation of the "mother mind, sister mind, and daughter mind."

76. Here, marriage is desirable, being a sign of prosperity. Compare footnote 74, above. There is an ambivalent attitude toward marriage in this text as viewed from the monk's perspective. Marriage, secondary in religious importance to celibacy, appears to be allocated to a segment of the population whose ability to become enlightened is negligible. However, marriage is primary in terms of the quality of life in a secular world. According to the *Agañña-suttanta* sexual intercourse was originally a violation of another human being's virtue. The association between procreation and evil is also found in Hindu cosmogonies. See Wendy Doniger O'Flaherty, *The Origins of Evil in Hindu Mythology* (Berkeley and Los Angeles: University of California Press, 1976), pp. 27–29.
77. Female forms as representative of the limited conditions of human existence (saṃsāra) are implied, based upon the statement made in the two previous verses.
78. Women are deception, hiding and glorifying what is ultimately worthless through "false advertising." Cf. Kanwar Lal, *The Cult of Desire* (New York: University Books, 1967), pp. 5–6.
79. Women inflict pain and should, therefore, be hated. All objects of passion increase one's pain.
80. The sexual act is considered an animal act according to this verse. Desires are animalistic, and women apparently are compared with animals and were actually sometimes believed to be lesser-evolved beings than male humans. "Breeding" with women, then, is like breeding with a very powerful animal.
81. The guardian of the underworld.

CHAPTER 2

The Mother

The religious needs of women are often defined in terms of their "emotional" nature and their dependency on others. In recognizing women as religious beings within certain strict boundaries, the majority of patriarchal religions interpret motherhood as sacred. Ideally, motherhood is nurturing, creative, and continually linked to the child. In the maternal role woman can receive legitimized power within the religious structure. Hinduism sanctified motherhood by allocating religious symbolism to women who were procreators of sons. Buddhism, on the other hand, tended to view motherhood as secular rather than sacred and as outside the religious realm. Mothers represented to Buddhists sufferers and perpetual givers of life in pain, almost as if it were a natural law for women to suffer.

In Mahāyāna Buddhist literature, the religious images of the feminine go beyond the maternal. As embodied in religious imagery, the feminine at times represents the perfection of wisdom, the blissful, the compassionate, the instructor and friend revealing the world of truth. The feminine ideal was independent of maternity and thus not associated with the world of nature, of attachment to existence, and of pain. When women are denied full participation as religious beings in Mahāyāna Buddhist texts, it is most often due to the fact that women's prevailing involvement with reproduction and motherhood as dictated by society does not allow them the freedom to renounce familial responsibilities in the name of religion. Motherhood is secular, and most women are required to be mothers for society's purposes. Portraits of influential female religious characters in Mahāyāna texts, thus, are inevitably of nuns, married laywomen without children, prostitutes, or young unmarried women, all of whom are freed from the responsibilities and burdens of motherhood while simultaneously defying society's norms.

There is a correlation between the broadening of the range of roles for women and the elevation of women's status and more active participation in the Buddhist religion. Texts which describe women as religious beings seldom, if ever, mention motherhood. In sharp contrast, Hindu texts accord women religious status almost exclusively through their functions as mothers. But for the Mahāyāna Buddhist, motherhood represents pain, suffering, bondage, and dependency. The religious aim of Mahāyāna is to be liberated from these situations. Theoretically, the notion of motherhood seems to have been a denial of woman's religious nature in Mahāyāna Buddhism because of the association of motherhood with suffering. Hinduism and Confucianism, in sharp contrast, attributed a sacred value to motherhood because of its image of suffering; woman as sufferer was holy.

Within the law books of Manu, the orthodox regulatory code for the devout "twice-born's" life,[1] the woman was epitomized as an ideal wife if she obediently and daily served her husband and bore many sons to light the ancestral fires. If she performed these duties willingly and continually, she would eventually become a powerful matriarch after her sons' marriages and be accorded the respect she had rightfully earned as the paragon of motherhood. In early Buddhism there are accounts of women who were ridiculed and humiliated by society in general until they bore a son.[2]

Filial piety was regarded as the foundation of virtue,[3] a duty stressed from pre-Buddhist times. A Buddhist tale, similar to that of King Lear, is told of the plight of old age for those with heartless children:

> Those in whose birth I took delight
> for whose existence I had longed,
> They now together with their wives,
> Reject me as one would a hog.
>
> Just as a worn-out horse is forced
> Away from food and driven from his shelter,
> So do these children drive away their father
> To beg for alms at other people's doors.[4]

The mother's love is often portrayed as an intense, self-sacrificing love much stronger than the father's. The mother was the shining exemplar of familial love, evidenced by many beautiful tributes to her in early Buddhist literature.[5] Former disappointment with regard to the birth of daughters diminished, as in the case of the Buddha's dialogue with King Prasenajit at the time of the birth of the king's daughter:

> When the Exalted One [the Buddha] was once at Savatthi, and the king, the Kosalan Pasenadi [Prasenajit], had come to visit him, one of the king's men arrived and, approaching the king, announced to his private ear that Queen Mallikā had given birth to a daughter. And the king was not pleased.
>
> Thereupon the Exalted One, discerning the matter, uttered on that occasion these verses:
>
> A woman child, O lord of men, may prove
> Even a better offspring than a male.
> For she may grow up wise and virtuous,
> Her husband's mother rev'rencing, true wife.
> The boy that she may bear may do great deeds,
> And rule great realms, yea, such a son
> Of noble wife becomes his country's guide.[6]

The Buddha extols the joy for a daughter who is wise and

virtuous but especially for the likelihood of being a mother of sons.

Acknowledgment of both parents' permission as a prerequisite for an aspiring young man or woman's entering the religious order was established prior to the ordination ceremony in order to assure that family ties were not weakened nor that duties to one's parents were neglected. In China, too, the Confucian ethical code of filial piety was scrupulously recognized by early Buddhist missionaries from Central Asia in order to avoid the claim that Buddhist religious orders weakened and dishonored family relations.

The ideal mother, as characterized by the Buddha Śākyamuni's mother, indicates the attitude to motherhood in the early sects of Buddhism. As told in the *Mahāvastu*,[7] the circumstances of the Buddha's birth and extolling of his mother's virtues contribute to the already powerful image of the mother in Indian literature. Buddhas and Bodhisattvas were always said to be born parthenogenetically, that is, without the sexual intercourse of the parents. Although it is never explicitly stated that the mother must be a virgin, she was always the paragon of virtue and chastity. A woman who was to give birth to a Buddha had to be exceptional in every way.[8]

The Buddha Śākyamuni's mother was destined to the fate of all the mothers of Buddhas, namely, to die seven days after giving birth in order to preclude any sexual intercourse after such a marvelous event as giving birth to a Buddha.[9] The implicit assumption is that the ideal mother is disassociated from sexual intercourse and takes vows to abstain from the sexual act, with the prior notification of such an intent in the presence of her husband. Māyā, Buddha Śākyamuni's mother, professes the following vows in front of her husband Śuddhodana:

> Henceforth, I will refrain from doing harm to living things and will live a chaste life. I will abstain from theft, intoxication, and frivolous speech. I will, my lord, refrain from harsh speech, from slander, and from falsehood. This is my resolve. I will not nurse envy of the pleasures of others, nor do them harm, but I will be full of amity toward all, and I will give up false views. I will, O king, live in the practice of the eleven moralities. All night long this resolve has been stirring in me. Do not then, O king, desire me with thoughts of sensual delight. See to it that you be guiltless of offence against me, for I would observe chastity.[10]

Māyā's husband complies with her wishes and promises that he and his kingdom will obey her.[11] Here, we see not only the adulations of the mother's virtue and holiness but also her authority, even over her husband. Her beauty is dazzling as well, having "eyes like lotus leaves." She is the most perfect among women to whom even the gods pay homage. She is set apart from all other mothers in one major experience: the Buddha's mother never experiences the pains of childbirth, that is, the pains of motherhood.[12]

The Buddha is superhuman, even in his mother's womb, by the fact that he discourses on various teachings while waiting for the auspicious time for his appearance. Concomitantly, the mother of the Buddha receives some of her power and respect because of her son, reflecting the prevailing societal attitudes toward the mother of sons in India at that time. As a powerful figure, she becomes the object of reverence and veneration partially because of her own moral integrity but also because of the nature of her son.[13]

From the above portrayal of Māyā, the Buddha's mother, and from other examples of self-sacrificing mothers in early Buddhist literature, one may conclude that a woman in the role of mother had an eminent position among women, which could give her considerable power. In general, the image of the mother is more complex in Mahāyāna Buddhism than in other religions since suffering is not generally associated with a stage of religious growth. By implication, the mother as sufferer is in a stage which stunts religious growth, as do all stages which involve suffering. Furthermore, unlike the Hindu concept of women as both fulfilled and restrained sexually through motherhood, the early Buddhist preference for the ascetic life over married life tended to suggest, rather ambiguously, that motherhood was also somewhat fallen. *The Sutra of the Child and His Five Mothers* suggests that women are bound and severely limited by maternity, tied to a social relationship with children, which is a perpetually suffering state:

> "Now, because I am liberated, I remembered my five mothers [from former lifetimes] who were unable to be free because they grieved over me. I vow that they all will finally end [their grief]."

This type of attitude toward motherhood seems to have been omitted in most literature. Generally, maternity is ignored in Mahāyāna texts. The eventual acceptance of fulfillment of a woman's nature through motherhood and the assumption of religious sanctions may have occurred as an accommodation to Hindu social values in India and to Confucian values in China. Otherwise, motherhood is usually not mentioned in Buddhist scripture as a religious role.

In the portrait of the mother presented below, *The Sutra of the Child and His Five Mothers,* the self-sacrificing, impassioned love of the mother is poignantly described. The boy in the story has the power to recall his past lives and his recollections, which all center exclusively on his mother. The little boy who relates the circumstances of his former lives is first introduced as a very serious and hardworking young student who had extraordinary powers yet never seemed to smile. The memory of his mothers and their devotion stimulates his smile and he proceeds to describe his mothers.

The reader is urged to notice the contrast between the role of the mother in general and that of the Buddha's mother. While Māyā never experienced the pains of childbirth, the mother in this sutra on the five mothers *continually* experiences pain and suffering. Implicit in the text is the premise that a mother's role is to suffer and that the death of a child is her death also. She is defined in terms of her children. Sacrificing for them drains her of life. The mother cannot be free from suffering or from the attachments to existence because of her attachment to her children. Ironically, it is precisely because of the mother's selfless attachment to her children that she is able to have such an important and respectable position in society. To be a good mother implies a strong feeling of attachment. Her grief and attachment cannot end unless she ceases to be a mother. The text appears to recognize the irony of the mother's role and to play on the nature of the contradiction.

The contradictory nature of the mother's role vis-à-vis her relationship with her children, from the Buddhist standpoint, suggests the irony of the Bodhisattva's role[14] with regard to his or her relationship with all living beings. In similar ways the Bodhisattva strongly and intensely identifies with all living beings as a mother identifies with her child. Yet the Bodhisattva, unlike the mother, remains free and detached from living beings through the wisdom of Emptiness. The mother does not view the world as Empty. She is in a never-ending cycle of attachment. The conflict between the mother's role and the spiritually free and detached individual is resolved by the Bodhisattva (as will be shown in Chapters 5 and 6). While the mother in this story is in an impossible situation in which her suffering implies attachment, the ideal life is one without suffering, that is, without attachment, as in the case of Māyā, the Buddha's mother, and of the Bodhisattva who incorporates the ideal mother's character, the character of Māyā.

Introduction to *The Sutra of the Child and His Five Mothers*

This short text is a dialogue between a small boy who wishes to become a monk and his teacher, an Arhat, who lives on top of a mountain. This sutra was translated into Chinese by the Buddhist layman Chih Ch'ien.[15] No other translations, in Chinese, Sanskrit, or Tibetan have been preserved.

Like the small boy in the following story, Chih Ch'ien also lived on top of a mountain with his teacher, although he had no desire to become a monk. In this story the doctrine presented is very basic to all Buddhist schools of both the Theravādin and Mahāyāna traditions. The major thesis presented is nonattachment, the cessation of all desires. Then one can be free, free from suffering, free from evil, free from the cycle of birth and death (saṃsāra), which the Buddhists considered the existential human condition.

Because of the fundamental character of the little boy's teaching, the tendency is to classify this text as either Theravādin in orientation or belonging to one of the early Buddhist sects. Moreover, the boy's teacher is an Arhat,[16] the religious ideal of early sectarian Buddhism, and not that of the Bodhisattva, the spiritual hero and heroine of Mahāyāna Buddhism. However, in later Buddhist texts,

Arhats and Bodhisattvas intermingle amicably and often share the center of the drama. The description of the Arhat in the following tale could just as easily describe any gentle sage and mountain dweller in India or China, having the superpowers, humor, and ability to fly that often characterize their nature.

The Sutra of the Child and His Five Mothers has been selected not because of its doctrinal tenets, which are scarce, but because of the attitude toward death, the psychological character of grief, and, especially, the poignant portrayal of the mother's intense sorrow at the loss of her child.

The Sutra of the Child and His Five Mothers (Wu mu tzu ching)*. T. v. 14, n. 555, p. 907.

THERE ONCE was an Arhat who practiced the path of holiness on top of a mountain. A small boy from Śrāvastī, who had just turned seven years old, left his home to become a monk and follow the teacher who was residing on top of a mountain. From his teacher he diligently learned about the Dharma, without ever slackening. When he was eight years old, he attained the four superknowledges.[17] First, he could discern the most miniscule thing with his eyes. Second, he could hear the faintest sound with his ears. Third, he could fly and undergo transformations. Fourth, he knew about his previous lives. At the place where he was born, he sat down to meditate. Soon he saw the events of his former lives; he saw the five mothers who had given birth to him. He smiled to himself and his teacher asked him:

*This first English translation is by Diana Paul.

"Why are you smiling? While you have been on this mountain with me you have not sung or danced. What is the purpose of your smiling?"

The novice monk [replied]: "I am not smiling. You are looking at me [inquisitively]. I have five mothers who, day and night, lament and grieve for me, constantly saying to themselves: 'Son, I will never forget you.' I am reflecting on the grief of those five families. What could possibly be the purpose of my smiling? I am not smiling, teacher.

"When my first mother gave birth to me, there were neighbors giving birth at the same time as my mother. After my death, when those who had the same birthday started to walk, my mother would look at them and say, 'Wherever my son is, he is also starting to walk.' Then she would be grief-stricken, thinking of me.

"Then my second mother gave birth to me. I did not live long and again died. My mother saw others nursing their children and would painfully think of me. Grieved, she would weep for me. Then my third mother gave birth to me. In a short while I again died. When my mother looked at her food, she would cry. Thinking of me she would say: 'Wherever my son is, he is having food with me, for he would not abandon me after death.' Grieving, she would think of me.

"Then my fourth mother gave birth to me. In a short while, I again died. When those who were the same age as I would have been became engaged, my mother would think of me and say: 'Son, you did not die, but today you are also choosing a wife.' Then she would cry, grief-stricken over me.

"Now I see my fifth mother giving birth to me. When I left home to study the path, my mother wept and said: 'I have lost my son and do not know where he is. Existing in hunger and cold, we will not see each other again.' Sighing sorrowfully, she thinks of me.

"All of my five mothers said they lost their son. Together

they weep. I think that the human spirit, as the son of those five mothers, made them weep, thinking of me. Because of this, I smiled. In the world people do not know that there are other rebirths. Instead, they say there is death. Those who are good will reap benefits, and those who are bad reap retribution. In the world people selfishly rejoice and get angered without fearing evil. Later, their anguish will be inexpressible. In the evil destinies their regret will be unequaled.

"Because I have renounced the world, I have left my parents to seek the path. I have observed the fears of the beasts and hungry ghosts in hell who are exhausted [from suffering] repeatedly. I have the care of my teacher and have accepted the discipline in the Buddhist sutras.

"Now, because I am liberated, I remember my five mothers [from former lifetimes] who were unable to be free because they grieved over me. I vow that they all will finally end [their grief]. People in the world grieve for each other in their minds. When there is no rest [from grief and other attachments], the body is only reborn [brought to earth]. The spirit leaves the sky and follows its given course [of rebirth]. If one cannot extricate himself from [good] habits, then he can be free. Only if one daily accumulates evil, doubting what he has done, then he will not presently associate with the cycle of existence in the same way [as those with good habits]. Only those who do not accumulate [such evil] will enter Nirvana. The bliss of Nirvana is what my teacher has explained."

Having paid reverence before his teacher, he then flew away.

Notes

1. The "twice-born" were the three upper classes (varṇa) of Indian society, namely, the priest (brahman), warrior (ksatriya), and merchant (vaiśya). These three classes were said to be "twice-born" because of their spiritual or second birth at the time of initiation when they received the sacred thread according to the Vedas.
2. See, for example, the story of Kisā-Gotamī, who finally bore a son who died while very young. After his death, she became a nun. Cf. I. B. Horner, *Women Under Primitive Buddhism* (London: George Routledge, 1930), pp. 4–5.
3. See, for example, Chapter 1, *The Sutra of the Buddha Teaching the Seven Daughters.* Support of the parents was a child's obligation: "In five ways should a child minister to his parents as the Eastern quarter. Once supported by them, I will now be their support; I will perform duties incumbent on them; I will keep up the lineage and tradition (kula vaṃsa) of my family; I will make myself worthy of my heritage" [from "Sigālovādasutta," verse 28, in *Dialogues of the Buddha,* trs. T. W. Rhys Davids and C. A. F. Rhys Davids (London: Luzac, 1966), III, 189; cited in Horner, p. 7].
4. *The Book of the Kindred Sayings (Saṃyutta Nikāya),* tr. C. A. F. Rhys Davids (London: Luzac, 1950), I, 175–77; cited in H. Saddhatissa, *Buddhist Ethics: Essence of Buddhism* (New York: George Braziller, 1970), pp. 132–33.
5. For examples of a mother's intense love in early Buddhist literature, see Horner, pp. 11–14.
6. *The Book of Kindred Sayings (Saṃyutta Nikāya),* I, 110–11.
7. The *Mahāvastu* is a historical and legendary collection of tales about the Buddha Śākyamuni. This compilation of facts and tales was undertaken by the Mahāsāṃghika, one of the early forerunners of Mahāyāna, over a long period of time. Many legends from the Pāli canon and the *Jātaka* tales were incorporated. See J. J. Jones, tr., *Mahāvastu* (London: Luzac, 1949), I, ix–xx.
8. *Ibid.,* I, 161: "Rich merit beyond compare has in the course of a long time been acquired by this woman, who will bear him whose worth is illimitable, and who is strong with the merit attained during a long time. . . ." This quote describes

Sudīpā, the mother of the Buddha Dīpaṇkara, who immediately preceded Śākyamuni as a Buddha. There were seven Buddhas who appeared before Śākyamuni, but Śākyamuni is the most significant because he is the historical Buddha of this world system.

9. *Ibid.*, I, 157–58: "Now what is the reason that a mother of an All-Knowing One should die so soon after giving birth to the Best of Men? While he is still dwelling in Tuṣita, the Bodhisattva exercises great mindfulness in his search for a mother whose karma is good. For he must descend into the womb of a woman who has only seven nights and ten months of her life remaining. And why so? Because, says he [the Buddha Dīpaṇkara], it is not seemly that she who bears a peerless one like me should afterwards indulge in love? . . . The Exalted One, indeed, at all times, proclaims the depravity of sensual desires. Shall, then, the mother of the saviour of the world indulge in love?"
10. *Ibid.*, I, 115.
11. *Ibid.*: "I shall comply with all your wishes. Be at ease. You have taken up a noble life, and I and my whole realm will obey you."
12. *Ibid.*, I, 114: "Again, my pious friend, when the Bodhisattva has entered his mother's womb, the host of devas [gods] joyfully approach, bowing and with their hands joined before them, and enquire the happy moment and day of his birth. The Bodhisattvas greet the enquiring devas by raising their right hand, but they do not hurt their mothers. Nor, indeed, do Bodhisattvas, when they are in their mothers' bodies, hurt them either when they sit or when they lie on their side or when they stand up in any position whatsoever. Again, they do not hurt their mothers when they sit cross-legged. Further, my pious friend, when they are yet in their mothers' bodies, by the power of the root of goodness that is in them they relate the story of their existence."
13. *Ibid.*, I, 167: "No weapon can pierce her body, nor can poison, fire, or sword prevail against her because of the power of the Bodhisattva. . . . Again, Mahā-Maudgalyāyana, when the Bodhisattva has entered his mother's womb, because of his power all her escorts deem her worthy of perfect obedience and loyalty, and those who see her go up to her and offer their services."
14. See Chapter 5 for an explanation of the Bodhisattva path.

15. See Chapter 1, *The Sutra of the Buddha Teaching the Seven Daughters,* for a brief account of Chih Ch'ien's life.
16. The distinction between an Arhat and a Bodhisattva is discussed in Chapter 5.
17. Usually listed as five or six, the four superknowledges are ordinarily the following: (1) supervision, (2) superhearing, (3) knowledge of others' thoughts, and (4) knowledge of one's own previous lives and those of others. The fifth and sixth superknowledges are the knowledge to accomplish miracle works and the knowledge to destroy passionate impulses. Cf. Har Dayal, *The Bodhisattva Doctrine in Buddhist Sanskrit Literature* (London: Routledge & Kegan Paul, 1932), pp. 107–34. In *The Sutra of the Child and His Five Mothers* the third superknowledge seems to be substituted by the fifth.

BUDDHA, YAŚODHĀRA, AND RĀHULA. A.D. 3RD CENTURY. GANDHĀRA SCHIST SCULPTURE.

The Buddha Śākyamuni, after attaining enlightenment, returns to his wife Yaśodhāra and son Rāhula to instruct them in the truths he discovered during meditation. (*Asian Art Museum of San Francisco, The Avery Brundage Collection*)

PART II

Paths for Women Leading to Salvation

PRAJÑĀPĀRAMITĀ. A.D. 9TH–10TH CENTURY. PĀLA DYNASTY SCULPTURE.

The Perfection of Wisdom, the highest of Mahāyāna Buddhist virtues, is often personified and worshiped as a feminine Bodhisattva, the good friend and even "mother" of the Buddhas. (*Asian Art Museum of San Francisco, The Avery Brundage Collection*)

CHAPTER 3

The Nun

In contrast to Chapters 1 and 2, in which we interpreted theoretically the traditional attitudes toward women, we will analyze here in Part II the more practical aspects, the soteriological paths, that is, those paths leading to salvation, that were open to women. The first, the religious ideal available exclusively to women, is the path of the nun.*

All soteriological paths, for both men and women, reflect an asexual ideal, in which sexuality has been eliminated or "reversed." The transformation from a fallen state of sexuality to a religious asexual state suggests complete control of one's sexuality. This is the desired result of the soteriological paths in Mahāyāna Buddhism. Men are viewed as the ones most likely to control their sexuality, whereas women, being more closely associated with reproduction and unpleasant bodily functions, are viewed as having more difficulty in controlling their sexual drives. Paths to salvation for women suggest the possibility that women, as well as men, may have the capacity to develop fully and to grow religiously as sexually transformed beings.

However, for women, the only religious path open to them, that of the nun, remains the least desirable one. Since early Buddhism preferred the celibate life as more conducive to Buddhist practice than married life, the nun should have been respected equally with the monk, as a

*This chapter was written by Frances Wilson.

person fulfilling her religious life in ways similar to that of a monk. But, the nuns' community did not survive as a vital force in either early Buddhism or in Mahāyāna Buddhism. Other cultural and societal constraints and assumptions about woman's nature and social position impinged upon the survival of the nuns' community. The path of the nun, although theoretically viable as a religious practice in Buddhism, from the outset was destined for virtual extinction.

The reason for the undesirability of the path of the nun's life is recounted in the textual account of the origins of the nuns' order translated below, which explicitly claims that religion and society will break down if women leave their familial responsibilities, suggesting that a woman's nature as well as her social role necessitated exclusion from religion as well as from any other roles outside the home. In the account, the Buddha states:

> "To go forth from home under the rule of the Dharma as announced by me is not suitable for women. There should be no ordination or nunhood. And why? If women go forth from the household life, then the rule of the Dharma will not be maintained over a long period. It is just as if, O Ānanda, there were a family with many women and few men. It is subject to easy attack and spoilation. It is subject to easy attack, specifically, of thieves and robber bands. Just thus, O Ānanda, if women go forth under the rule of the Dharma, this rule of the Dharma will not be long enduring."

This argument seems to be a non sequitur. Women should stay at home if the Buddhist Dharma is to survive. By implication, men should have a responsibility to stay home to protect women who are vulnerable, but the parallel claim that men outside the home threaten society by causing the family to be susceptible to "attack and spoilation" is never made. A man was ultimately to renounce the family for religion. Family and religion are mutually exclusive for a man, but a woman was placed in an ambiguous position—to remain in the home, which had minimal religious value, but to be, at the same time, a devout Buddhist.

Mahāyāna Buddhists tended to accept familial roles and other lay-oriented roles as conducive to religious practice in more concrete and more varied patterns in their scripture than did pre-Mahāyāna Buddhists. As a consequence of the attention accorded to lay Buddhists, it has sometimes been suggested that the status of the nun would decline as laywomen's status was elevated. However, the concomitant pattern among men, namely, the decline in status of the monk as the layman develops understanding, was not as frequent a theme in Mahāyāna literature as the devaluation or omission of the nun's role. The implication is that the nun, as well as the prostitute with whom she is sometimes associated, are in incongruous roles, in roles disassociated from family life.

For the discussion of Buddhist nuns in the Indian Mahāyāna tradition, two selections from Sanskrit have been translated. The textual sources of Indian Buddhism indicate that in India the nun's role remained undeveloped—at least as a vehicle for literary expression or as an area in Buddhist culture that needed written commentary and redefinition after the early period. Nuns appear rarely in Mahāyāna sutras, more rarely than women lay disciples. This accords with the importance given the laity in Mahāyāna popular literature.

The Mahāyāna of classical India accepted the *Vinaya Piṭaka* (discipline and training rules) set down by the early schools of Buddhism. Both Mahāyāna monks and nuns used the *vinaya* texts of the early schools, having developed no new rules of monastic discipline. Tibetan Mahāyāna Buddhism, for example, uses the *Vinaya* of an early school, Mūlasarvāstivādin, which, unlike the Theravādin early school but like the Mahāyāna schools, used Sanskrit as a canonical language. The perimeter of diffusion of the Mūlasarvāstivādins was much greater than that of the Theravādins whose doctrine was established and maintained early in the countries bordering the Bay of Bengal. The Mūlasarvāstivādins reached east to Sumatra and west to Persia and Gandhara.

The first text translated below describes the subordination of the nuns' community to that of the monks, indicating the lack of autonomy among the women's community and their subsequent deprivation of the power to define their religious obligations along norms that they themselves established. Unlike the Christian organizational structure of nuns which was separate from that of monks, the Buddhist nuns in ancient Indian society were accountable to the monks, and their organizational structure was subordinate to that of the monks. They were directly governed by the monks at joint meetings of both orders. In China this was not the case. The organizational structures were separate at all times, and this no doubt accounts in part for nuns often having formidable powers, not only in religious matters but in the political arena as well.

A. Introduction to "Nuns: The Stating of the Matter" from *The Book of the Discipline*

This first selection, a Sanskrit fragment from *The Book of the Discipline (Vinaya Piṭaka)* appears in an article by C. M. Ridding and Louis de la Vallée Poussin,[1] who consider it to be from the Mūlasarvāstivādin canon; however they admit that it does not entirely agree with the

Tibetan version, "Bhikṣuṇīvibhaṅga." The fragment opens with the traditional history which is associated with women's admission to the Buddhist order of nuns and gives reasons for the existence of the eight chief or important rules (gurudharma). The tradition and the rules for the most part are the same as those in the Pāli Theravādin canon. Horner devotes a chapter to these rules in her *Women Under Primitive Buddhism.*[2] The traditions associated with the eight chief rules are the result of a careful attempt to recount a true history of women's admission to the Buddhist order, but the account is probably a monastic invention. There is some evidence that the myth-making process had intruded. The history of the establishment of the order of nuns in Buddhism is similar to that in Jainism. The Buddha's aunt, who is also his foster mother, Mahāprajāpatī, requests the Buddha to establish an order of Buddhist nuns. In the Jain accounts, it is Mahāvīra's aunt (or cousin).[3]

The translation illustrates a common Indian concern about the care and handling of women as family components. In the opening chapters of the non-Buddhist *Bhagavad Gītā,* Arjuna of the Bhāratas, states to Kṛṣṇa: "We should not slay our own kinfolk. . . . Upon the destruction of the family, the immemorial holy laws of the family perish, . . . the women are corrupted. . . . And [thereby] the eternal family laws [are also corrupted]; . . . then, for men, dwelling in hell certainly ensues."[4]

The Buddha, in refusing the admission of women to the order, states a parallel concern[5] for the disintegration of the family if men are absent from the home. The introduction of nuns as part of the monastic community will make it an analogue of the family—a family for whom, by implication, the monks should provide that function of protection which makes a family a viable unit. The Buddhist texts do not view the monks as protectors, however;

therefore, the community of nuns would not be a viable unit.

The *Therīgāthā,* a collection of hymns believed to have been written by nuns, recounts many stories of both monks and nuns who joined the order after a death in the family. With women there is always the problem, or the accusation, that they enter the monastic life only after the family or the worldly life is no longer, or never could have been, possible, and, further, that the monastic life opens no new life but is only a holding area for life's remainder.

Whatever the reason, the nun's life is not well marked in the Mahāyāna sutra tradition or in the philosophical writing of that tradition. Participation in an intellectual life by the Mahāyāna Buddhist nun is not recorded. The nun seems not to have been a significant part of the student body of the great Buddhist universities which were the central gem in the crown of the monk's order, an order which was extensive, prosperous, and productive of extraordinary thought and art.[6]

After the eight chief rules are given in the fragment of the *Vinaya* presented below, the manuscript recounts the procedure of admission. Repetitive phrases have been omitted. Some interesting items of the ordination of nuns are included, but they are not very revealing in their brevity. For example, an initiate is not supposed to be, among other things, grief-stricken (śokahata). Yet grief at the death of relatives is often associated with joining the order. Society forced women to sever their family ties before joining the order, yet they were not supposed to be grief-stricken to enter the order.

"Nuns: The Stating of the Matter"* ("Bhikṣuṇīkarmavācanā") from *The Book of the Discipline (Vinaya Piṭaka).* Sanskrit text in Ridding and De la Vallée Poussin.

*This English translation is by Frances Wilson.

[Folios 1 and 2 are missing. Folio 3 begins with Mahāprajāpatī's request to the Buddha that women be allowed to join the order.[7]]

Mahāprajāpatī Gautamī said this to me, the Holy One: "If it is possible for your reverence, allow women to obtain the benefits of the mendicant life. Allow them to go forth from a household life under the rule of the Dharma proclaimed by yourself, take ordination, and become a nun. Allow them to observe the chaste and holy life in the presence of your reverence."

When I, the lord, was thus addressed, I said to Mahāprajāpatī Gautamī: "Just you alone, O Gautamī, with shaven head, with robes of a nun, for as long as you may live, will be fulfilled, purified, and cleansed. This chaste and holy life will be for your benefaction and welfare over a long period."

When answered in this way, twice and thrice Mahāprajāpatī Gautamī asked me, the lord: "If it is possible for your reverence, allow women to obtain the benefits of the mendicant life. Allow them to go forth from a household life, take ordination, and become nuns. Allow them to observe the chaste and holy life in the presence of your reverence."

When I was thus addressed, twice and thrice I said to Mahāprajāpatī Gautamī: "Just you alone, O Gautamī, with shaven head, with robes of a nun, for as long as you may live, will be fulfilled, purified, and cleansed. This chaste and holy life will be for your benefaction and welfare over a long period."

Mahāprajāpatī answered thus by me, the Blessed One, three times, bowed her head to my feet and went forth from my presence. Then, Mahāprajāpatī stood to one side in the space outside the gate and began to weep with tears streaming down her face. Ānanda saw Mahāprajāpatī

Gautamī standing outside the gate weeping with tears streaming down her face. And when he saw her, he said to her: "Why are you standing to one side outside the gate, weeping with tears streaming down?"

She said the following: "His reverence, O Ānanda, will not allow women to go forth from home, take ordination, and become nuns under the rule preached by himself."

Ānanda said: "You, O Gautamī, remain here a short while. I shall ask permission for ordination of nuns." The venerable Ānanda went to me, the lord; after approaching, he bowed his head to my feet and stood at one side. While standing there, the venerable Ānanda said to me: "If it is possible for you, the lord, allow women to obtain the benefits of the mendicant life. Allow them to go forth under the rule of the Dharma, take ordination, and become nuns."

I said: "To go forth from home under the rule of the Dharma as announced by me is not suitable for women. There should be no ordination or nunhood. And why? If women go forth from the household life, then the rule of the Dharma will not be maintained over a long period. It is just as if, O Ānanda, there were a family with many women and few men. It is subject to easy attack and spoilation. It is subject to easy attack, specifically of thieves and robber bands. Just thus, O Ānanda, if women go forth under the rule of the Dharma, this rule of the Dharma will not be long enduring. It is as if, O Ānanda, in a big field belonging to a householder, a quantity of thunderbolts with great flashes of lightning fell to the extent that the field was destroyed, ruined, and brought to nought. Just thus, O Ānanda, the rule of the Dharma—if women go forth from a homelife—will not continue for long. Suppose, Ānanda, there were a sugar cane field belonging to a householder. Upon it fell a blight by the name of Crimson disease until the sugar cane was destroyed, ruined, and brought to nought. Just in this way, when women go forth, the rule of the Dharma is not long maintained.

But yet, Ānanda, I shall expound the eight important rules for overcoming the obstructions so that instruction [morality, intellect, and wisdom] can be maintained throughout life. It is as if, Ānanda, a farmer-householder were to build a causeway at the mouth of a river or a canal during the autumn season so that a dam to the water could be effected.

[Folio 4b line 2, begins the enumeration of the eight important or chief rules for overcoming the obstructions.[8]]

"Just thus, Ānanda, I shall teach the important rules to overcome the obstructions. Within these rules the instruction [morality, intellect, and wisdom] can be maintained by women throughout their life. What are the eight rules?

1) In the presence of monks, O Ānanda, women are expected to request ordination to go forth as nuns. I announce this as the first important rule for women to overcome the obstructions so that instruction can be maintained throughout life.

2) In the presence of monks, O Ānanda, a nun must seek the teachings and instructions every half month. I announce this as the second important rule. . . .

3) No nun may spend a rainy season, O Ānanda, in a place where no monks are resident. This, O Ānanda, is the third important rule. . . .

4) After the rainy season a nun must have both orders [monks and nuns] perform the 'end of the rainy season' ceremony for her with reference to the seeing, hearing, or suspicion [of faults committed by her]. This is the fourth important rule. . . .

5) It is forbidden that a nun, Ānanda, accuse or warn a monk about transgression in morality, heretical views, conduct, or livelihood. It is not forbidden for a monk to accuse or warn a nun about morality, heretical views, conduct, or livelihood. This is the fifth important rule I announce. . . .

6) A nun, Ānanda, should not scold or be angry with

or admonish a monk. I announce this as the sixth important rule for women. . . .

7) When a nun violates important rules, O Ānanda, penance must be performed every half month. This I declare as the seventh important rule. . . .

8) A nun of one hundred years of age shall perform the correct duties to a monk. She shall, with her hands folded in prayerful attitude, rise to greet him and then bow down to him. This will be done with appropriate words of salutation. I declare this as the eighth important rule. . . .

"If, O Ānanda, Mahāprajāpatī Gautamī will observe these important rules as a religious duty, then she shall go forth from a home life, take ordination, and become a nun."

The venerable Ānanda, delighting in and rejoicing in my words, bowed his head to my feet and set forth from my presence. The venerable Ānanda went up to Gautamī, and after reaching her, he said this to Mahāprajāpatī Gautamī: "O Gautamī, under the training of the Dharma as promulgated by the lord himself, women will be permitted to go forth from home, take ordination, and become nuns, but, Gautamī, the Holy One has established eight important rules for overcoming obstacles. Within these rules women can undertake lifelong instruction [morality, wisdom, and intellect]. We will teach them so that you will know them."

[Gautamī said:] "Speak, O reverend Ānanda, so that I might hear."

[Ānanda said:] "The Lord said thus, O Gautami."

[Here the text includes a repetition of the above vows.]

[Folio 8 is missing. Folios 9 a to 10 a, line 2, are summarized as follows: Upon their acceptance of the eight important rules, five hundred Śākyan women with Gautamī at their head, set forth from home, took ordination, and became nuns. In due course, other household women approached and were given the triple refuge[9] after they had been examined and it had been ascertained that there were no obstructive conditions. Also these women were given the five chief rules of conduct.[10]]

[Folio 10 a, line 3, begins with the ceremony of setting forth (pravrajyā).]

A nun who is to speak in the community is summoned. She is asked whether there are any obstructive conditions [with reference to the initiate[11]]. If she [the summoned nun], unasked, speaks, then she is guilty of a transgression. She, or each nun of the community in turn, sits squatting on her heels, folds her hands in prayerful gesture, faces the community and speaks: "Listen, O reverend women of the community. This householder-woman, _____ by name, intends to set forth from the household life. Her clothes are white, and her locks are unshorn. She desires to set forth under the rule of the *Vinaya* proclaimed by the Buddha. She, _____ by name, after her hair is shorn and after being clothed in yellow garments, will, with faith, set forth from home. With what instructions will she set forth?"

All the nuns say: "If she is qualified, let her set forth. If she is sent, that is good. If not, she is guilty of a transgression."

After that, an instructress (upādhyāyikā) is requested, and requested a second time. After paying homage, squatting in front of her, and folding her hands in prayerful gesture, [the initiate] says: "Pay heed, O teacher [ācāryikā], I, _____ by name, request a teacher, an instructress [ācāryikā, upādhyāyikā]. Be my teacher, my instructress. With a teacher, an instructress, I shall set forth." Thus, this is said twice and thrice.

Then, the instructress requests the initiate nun to have her hair cut. The instructress asks: "O sister, will you have your hair cut?" If she says no, she must be told: "Just because of this, go!" [The Lord Buddha speaks:] "I, monks, declare the rule applying to the customary action that the nun's hair be shorn. If the weather is cold, the initiate should be bathed with warm water; if the weather is hot, the initiate, whose locks are to be shorn, will be bathed in cold water. If this rule is not followed as stated, there will be guilt of transgression."

Then, at the right time . . . the instructress should give the yellow garments. The initiate, after bowing to the feet of the instructress, should accept these garments and put them on. At this time the initiate should be examined. There must be no absence of proper female characteristics, nor should there be any additional presence of male characteristics. When new initiates are naked and examined, they become embarrassed.

The Lord Buddha declares: "The initiates should not be examined after they are naked. Furthermore, the nuns who are dressing the initiates should examine them without the initiates being aware of this examination." Then, if by this procedure, the initiate is found fit, the instructress should give her the yellow garments and perform for her the rite of "Going Forth from Home." This rite is preceded by the triple refuge.

The initiate, after bowing to the feet of the instructress, is to fold her hands in prayerful fashion and say: "Pay heed, O instructress, I go the the Buddha for refuge. He is the foremost of bipeds. I go to the Dharma for refuge. It is the best of renunciations. I go to the community for refuge. It is the best of assemblies. I go forth to a homeless life, following the Lord Śākyamuni, the lion of Śākyas, the greatest king of the Śākyas, the Tathāgata, the Arhat, the Perfectly Enlightened One who has gone forth. I abandon the superficial characteristics of a householder. I take the superficial appearances of going forth, and I shall always behave in conformity with these superficial characteristics [liṅga]. Because of my intention, I shall take the name given me by the instructress, _____ by name." [This is repeated twice and thrice.]

[Folios 12 through 14 are missing; folio 15a begins as follows:]

The newly initiated nun says to her instructress: "Pay heed, O instructress, I, who am named _____, take formal possession of my nun's garments: the outer cloak [cīvara] and the apron [saṃghāti]. The cloak, which has been completely finished, is correctly made and suitable for use." [This is repeated twice and thrice.] In the same way, the upper, outer robe [uttarāsaṅga], the lower, inner robe [antarvāsas],[12] . . . and the bodice [saṃkakṣikā][13] are to be taken as formal possessions. After that the begging bowl is to be exhibited before the community of nuns: "Pay heed, . . . the begging bowl of this reverend woman is not excessively small, large, or pale." The nuns reply that it is suitable: "It is a good begging bowl." After that, the bowl, as a formal possession, should be taken by the left hand. After it is in the left hand, it should be covered by the right hand, and the newly initiated nun should say: "Pay heed, O instructress [upādhyāyikā] I, who am named _____, take formal possession of this bowl for sage food [ṛṣi], for alms food [food thrown into a begging bowl]. It is fit and suitable for taking food." [This is repeated twice and thrice.]

After that, the novice [the newly initiated nun] is made to leave the range of hearing of the assembly of nuns while remaining in the range of their sight. She bows, folds her hands in prayerful gesture, and then is made to face the assembly. At that time, the presiding nun says: "Whoever she is, let her name herself." Then the presiding officer, as before, summons her to come forward: 'You, _____ by name, are capable to advise the novice, _____ by name, in private session along with her instructress. If you are able, pronounce with her: 'I am able.' " Then the presiding nun makes a motion [without supplementary questions (jñapti)]. "Hear, O reverend community, this preceptress is summoned for a private session with the novice accompanied by her instructress. If, when the community determines the right time, this reverend woman consents, then the Saṃgha approves the preceptress."

The instructress makes a motion: "This nun, _____ by name, the preceptress, will advise the initiate in private session." Then, the initiate proceeds aside, and the preceptress has her squat on her heels and make a prayerful gesture with her hands. The preceptress says: "Hear, _____ by name, this is the right time for you. I shall ask that you truly and fearlessly declare the true as true and the false as false. You are a woman who has dwelled as a householder [or you are a maiden of twelve years or you are a maiden of twenty years]. Your five garments and bowl are complete. Your mother and father are alive—or your husband. You must be permitted by your mother and father or your husband. You cannot be a slave. Say whether this is true or not. You must not be an indentured servant, nor one who has been sold as a slave, nor one who has been taken as a slave, nor one who is worthy of reproach, nor one who is mentally deranged, nor one who is magically created,[14] nor a king's envoy, nor one who has caused a king to be guilty of transgression. You cannot be of furious temperament, nor grief-stricken, nor pregnant, nor a householder, nor without female characteristics, nor with both female and male characteristics, nor with mixed female and male characteristics, nor currently menstruous,[15] nor nonmenstruous, nor of doubtful sexual characteristics, nor a corrupter of monks, nor a slayer of mother, father or Arhat, nor producing blood[16] or wicked thoughts in the presence of a Tathāgata, nor a heretic, nor a thief, nor a flag destroyer, nor a thieflike inhabitant, nor one who has been made to live apart from monks and nuns, nor one who has been expelled from a monastic order. Have you previously 'set forth?' If you reply that you have previously 'set forth,' then I say: 'go from here.'

If you say no, then I say: 'set forth.' You are advised to set forth and lead a life of complete chastity [brahmacārya]."

[The novice says:] "It is led."

"You must request a nun from the community for two years instruction in the six dharmas and the six ancillary dharmas."

[The novice says:] "It is requested."

"You will be instructed for two years in this instruction. You must not give anyone anything however small or large. Are you, _____ by name? Is your instructress, _____ by name?"

[The novice says:] "For this purpose I, _____ by name, take as my instructress, _____ by name."

[The preceptress says:] "Hear, _____ by name, there are many women afflicted in body, afflicted with boils, . . . sores, . . . fever, . . . consumption, . . . white leprosy, . . . broken bones. You should not have any such affliction. If you are sound in health, let it be said in this private session to [me] the preceptress. If I ask you about this in the community, then stand and speak. You must not approach, unless summoned."

Then, while the initiate and the preceptress stand on the end of the path, the preceptress says: "Hear, O reverend community, I have instructed, _____ by name, about the obstructive conditions. She declares herself free from the obstructive conditions. Shall she approach?" All the nuns say: "Let her approach." If they speak, it is good. If not, they will be guilty of a transgression.

Then the presiding nun has the initiate sit and request that she accept observance of chastity [brahmacārya]: "Hear, O reverend community, I, _____ by name, have undergone preliminary examination by the preceptress for ordination by the instructress, _____ by name. I request to observe chastity, etc. For this purpose . . . may the reverend community give me the opportunity to observe chastity." [The community in sympathy repeats this twice and thrice also.]

Then the presiding nun makes a motion that this be done: "Hear, O reverend community, this novice has been examined [by the preceptress] for ordination by the instructress. She requests from the community the opportunity to observe chastity [as instructed] by the instructress, _____ by name. If the community assents . . . let us ask her in this community about 'the obstructive conditions.' " This is a motion without supplementary questions.

[Here the presiding nun asks in open assembly those questions presented the initiate in private session. These answers of the novice may be assented to in silence or may be questioned by the community. The novice is thus stating a matter which allows supplementary questions (karmavācanā) as opposed to the stating of the matter (jñapti), which allows no supplementary questions. (See the above motions made by the presiding nun.) After the presiding nun has questioned the novice in open assembly of the nuns' community, the novice is introduced in open session of both communities (monks and nuns), and she is questioned a third time. After the manuscript presents a partial repetition of the questions and notes about measuring the shade and the five (rather than the customary six Indian) seasons of the monk's year, the procedure of initiation continues.]

[Folio 22 b, line 1:]

[Preceptress:] "Hear, O _____ by name. These are the three supports declared by the lord who knows and sees, the Tathāgata, the Arhat, the Perfectly Enlightened One. A nun should depend on these three supports when she goes forth from home under the rule of the Dharma, takes initiation, and becomes a nun. What are the three?

(1) A cloak from a dust heap is suitable and easy to obtain. A nun, who goes forth, . . . takes ordination, and becomes a nun, should depend on such a cloak. Are you

able, for as long as you live, to wear a ragged cloak from a dust heap?"

The novice replies: "I am able. . . .

(2) Hear, O _____ by name, alms food is the best food, the most suitable and easy to obtain. A nun, who goes forth . . . should depend on alms food. Can you undertake this toward achieving Perfect Enlightenment?" [The novice says:] "I am able to undertake this toward achieving Perfect Enlightenment. . . .

(3) . . . A medical decoction of herbs[17] is the most suitable of medicine. Are you able to use, for as long as you live, only this medicine? Can you undertake this toward achieving Perfect Enlightenment?" [The novice says:] "I am able to undertake this toward achieving Perfect Enlightenment."

[Folio 23 b, line 3, begins the eight (patanīya) offenses:]

[Preceptress:] "Hear, _____ by name, the Tathāgata has proclaimed eight offenses for the commission of which a nun would become not a nun, nor an ascetic [śramaṇī], nor a daughter of the Śākyas, and would lose her nunhood. . . . There are eight such irremediable offenses [parājita]. What are the eight? Hear, O _____ by name. (1) Lust is condemned by the lord. . . . The lord declares that sexual union is not chaste conduct. For the commission of this, a nun will become not a nun. . . . (2) . . . the lord condemns taking what is not given. . . . (3) The lord condemns the taking of life, even of small animals like red ants—not to speak of men. . . . (4) . . . the lord condemns lying and speaking falsely. If a nun should say: 'I speak with gods, Nāgas, and others, and they speak with me. . . .' And although unattained a nun should say: 'I have attained the first and the third levels of meditation. I have achieved Once-Returnership. . . .' For the commission of this a nun will become not a nun. (5) . . . If, further, a lustful nun in company with a lustful man, raises her downcast eyes and assents to touching of the knee, . . . she becomes not a nun. . . . (6) . . . If a lustful nun laughs and is playful in the company of a lustful man, . . . arranges a rendezvous, assents to . . .[18] when he comes, and becomes dependent on him, she becomes not a nun. . . . (7) If a nun has previously committed a serious offense and has been expelled from the community, she, when dead or deranged, or fled to another country and rightly declared to have committed a serious offense, will become not a nun. (8) . . . If a nun undergoes the ceremony of suspension from the order for refusal to recognize or correct offenses [for example, allowing her hair to grow] and she does not desist from her offense—although twice and thrice enjoined, . . . she will become not a nun. . . ."

[In folio 29 b, line 3, to folio 30 b, line 3, the eight important rules given at the beginning of the manuscript are declared to the novice. She says, "I concur." After this, the four conditions which are helpful to mendicants are presented.]

[Preceptress:] "What are the four? When spoken to angrily, not to reply angrily. When angered, not to cause anger in return. When hit, not to hit back. When reviled, not to revile in return." [At this point, folio 31 a, line 5, the manuscript becomes fragmentary and breaks off.]

B. Introduction to "The Nun by the Name Lion-Yawn" from *The Harmony of the Young Sapling Sutra*

The following is an extensive description of an outstanding nun of the Mahāyāna tradition. She was a religious teacher, a good friend, and, by implication of her accomplishments, a Bodhisattva. A chapter is devoted to her in *The Harmony of the Young Sapling Sutra (Gaṇḍavyūha-sūtram),* the concluding section of the *Avataṃsaka-sūtra* in the Chinese and Japanese *Tripiṭakas.* The format of the *Gaṇḍavyūha* has been noted to be like the later picaresque Sanskrit novels. However, the wandering hero is not a rogue but a pilgrim, and the *Gaṇḍavyūha* has been aptly compared with John Bunyan's *Pilgrim's Progress.* At Dhanyākara, a metropolis in South India, Sudhana, the merchant's son, hears the preaching of the Bodhisattva Mañjuśrī, who recognizes Sudhana's vocation for a Bodhisattva life. Unlike the one guide in *Pilgrim's Progress,* fifty-three good friends (kalyāṇamitra) direct Sudhana through the realm to the teacher of the Bodhisattva career. Each lives in a separate city in South India, and Sudhana travels from city to city upon the direction of the last good friend from whom he is taking leave. The good friends have a name plus a designation as teacher, child, goddess, woman lay disciple, perfumer, nun, monk, sailor, Bodhisattva, etc.

It is difficult to recover a "this-worldly" portrait of Lion-yawn (Siṃhavijṛmbhitā) from this sutra. It presents this world (lokadhātu) in terms of the ideal or religious world (dharmadhātu). The *Gaṇḍavyūha,* like the *Vimalakīrtinirdeśa* described in Chapter 6, is a text which expresses the belief that the two worlds are identical. Yet, the *Vimalakīrtinirdeśa* is more helpful for the cultural historian and the women studies scholar, for it presents this world (lokadhātu) in worldly terms and simply asserts that this world and the ideal world (dharmadhātu) are identical.[19] The *Gaṇḍavyūha,* on the other hand, describes this world through the eyes of those who perceive it as the dharmadhātu. The physical environs are composed of natural forms created out of precious gems. Unaltered natural forms, like water, are endowed with purity, sweetness, fertility, and five other good qualities. The people in the *Gaṇḍavyūha* who perceive "this world" as the dharmadhātu are very often Bodhisattvas endowed with powers of instantaneous space travel, instantaneous distribution of goods, and personal communications of an ineffably easy and correct accomplishment. In the *Gaṇḍavyūha* the teaching nun, Lion-yawn, is described in these terms.

In the *Gaṇḍavyūha* there are fifty-three good friends. Most of them live in cities and parks at some distance from each other. There seems to be a natural (lokadhātu) association between the good friends. Each knows of the next and directs Sudhana, the pilgrim-hero, onward. The Lord Śiva (Mahādeva),[20] resident in Kṛṣṇa's capital city Dvāravatī on the Girnar peninsula, directs Sudhana, the pilgrim, to a feminine deity. She, in turn, directs the pilgrim to other feminine deities. After a series of nine encounters with various feminine deities, the last, called night goddess, who is a resident in Śākyamuni's birthplace, directs Sudhana to nearby Kapilavastu where Śākyamuni's wife-to-be (Gopā) is resident. She in turn directs the pilgrim to a terrace of enlightenment where Śākyamuni's mother (Māyā) is living.

In this lokadhātu context, Lion-yawn, the nun, directs the pilgrim to go to the good friend, Vasumitrā, a prostitute in the eyes of those who do not perceive the dharmadhātu. What is the social connection here? It seems that the nun and the prostitute share a lack of a positive characteristic. They are not family women. The sphere of woman is the family, except for the prostitute and the nun.[21]

If more of the *Gaṇḍavyūha* is recovered (we have chapters reporting on only fifty-three of the 108 encounters by Sudhana), we might read about another nun who would direct Sudhana to a monk or someone else with whom she is conventionally associated in the lokadhātu, but in the *Gaṇḍavyūha,* a Mahāyāna sutra where emphasis is on the laity and the dharmadhātu of their lokadhātu, it is not surprising to find the nonfamily women associated with each other.

Furthermore, Lion-yawn, the nun, is included in the *Gaṇḍavyūha.* It is not necessary to postulate that the author of the sutra had in mind a nun alive in his lifetime approximately 600 years after the birth of Buddha. The nun could have been modeled after a figure historical to the Buddha's time, just as with Śākyamuni's mother and wife (who are two of the good friends). The nun could have been taken, if not from the Theravādin tradition of the Therīs (nun Arhats), from a similar source. Horner reports that there were many noted preachers, religious teachers, and brilliant speakers among the Therīs.[22]

It is not possible to determine adequately the nun's role in the Buddhist cultural context of the *Gaṇḍavyūha.* Although the *Gaṇḍavyūha* is not autobiographical, there are even problems with autobiographical songs of the Therīs (nun Arhats). Some have evidence that the songs were written about the Therīs rather than by them. Nonetheless, many of the songs (gāthās) of the Therīs seem to require that one acknowledge their autobiographical actuality. After these songs of personal testimony by "female religious aspirants," there are no further songs of personal testimony by Indian women until the hymns of personal devotion to Viṣṇu and Śiva were composed in the many languages of India, approximately 1,500 to 2,000 years later.

"The Nun by the Name Lion-Yawn"* ("Siṃhavijṛmbhitā") from *The Harmony of the Young Sapling Sutra (Gaṇḍavyūha-sūtram)*. Sanskrit text in Vaidya.

[P. 148, line 1, to p. 153, line 11:]

Sudhana, the merchant's son, in due course went to the Kaliṅga grove in the country of Śronāparānta. After arriving, he went seeking out the nun named Lion-yawn, questioning each person he met. Several hundred boys and several hundred girls came from the four roads of the central intersection and followed him. And several hundred men and several hundred women explained to him: "This nun, good son, lives right here in a great park named Sun-bright [Sūryaprabhā], donated by Victory-bright [Jayaprabhā]. She proclaims the Dharma for the sake of countless beings."

Then, Sudhana, the merchant's son, went to the great park Sun-bright. Wandering through it and surveying the environs, he saw, in that great park, trees by the name of Moon-rise . . . shining with lights, brightening the area for a mile in all directions. He saw leaf trees . . . appearing like rain clouds the color of lapis lazuli. He saw flower trees, "Treasury of Blossoms" by name, variously shaped like the lovely high Himalayan range, raining an inexhaustible flood of variously colored flowers, and like the celestial Pārijāta trees adorning the "cities of the thirty-three gods." He saw fruit trees, . . . jewel trees, . . . trees hung with jeweled clothes, . . . music trees, . . . perfume trees, . . . fountains, . . . lakes, . . . pools, . . . and lotus ponds, . . . surrounded by jeweled benches anointed with sandal paste. . . . He saw the great park Sun-bright possessed of limitless illumination by the force of the wonder working and magic power of the nun, Lion-yawn.

*This first English translation is by Frances Wilson.

Sudhana, the merchant's son, saw these harmonies of the great park, which were exhalted by the inconceivable and limitless virtues, which were the maturation of Bodhisattva deeds, which were free from the own-being of illusory dharmas, which were not accessible to disciples, Pratyeka-buddhas, heretics, the frequenters of the path of Māra [the Evil One], nor the foolish, common people. He looked all about the grounds. On all the great lion-thrones under the various trees was seated the nun Lion-yawn surrounded by her great retinues. She was like a tranquil lake, like a wish gem yielding all desires, like a lotus untouched by the water of worldly phenomena, like a lion who no longer has the bristling mane of fear [because of the purity of her self-confidence], like a great monarch mountain because of the purity of her character [stone],[23] like an enchanting monarch perfume exhilarating the minds of the world, like cool sandalwood quieting the fever of defilements, . . . like a great Brahman unpossessed by greed, hatred, or delusion, like a jewel of tranquil water refreshing the hearts of beings afflicted by defilements, like a beneficent domain promoting the roots of welfare. On all these groups of seats he saw a great assembly seated.

In one circle of seats he saw the nun Lion-yawn proclaiming the Dharma introduction [dharmamukha] by the name of "Presence of Inexhaustible Salvation" [Akṣayavimokṣasaṃbheda] to the foremost sons of Śiva, the gods of the Pure Abode. Elsewhere in another circle of seats. . . [the nun teaches differing Dharma introductions to the differing members of a conventional list of beings including gods, spirits, great serpents, etc., and also to the disciples and Pratyeka-buddhas. She teaches the "introduction to the meditational trance-cognitional light" [samādhijñānālokamukha] to beings who have resolute faith in the Mahāyāna; and to the ten stages of Bodhisattvas and to the assembly of Indra, the thunderbolt bearer [Vajrapāṇi] she teaches the meditative trance introductions.] Thus, as many are the paths of beings and existences in all the varieties of births and spheres, whoever are the beings on those many paths, who are maturing, who are being trained and disciplined, who are fit vessels: For them in this garden Sudhana saw the nun Lion-yawn teaching the Dharma to each who had come and been seated. She taught each according to disposition, resolute intention, and faith so that all became destined to Supreme, Perfect Enlightenment.

Why? Because, of course, the nun Lion-yawn has made ten countless of one hundred thousand ingresses into the entrances of Perfection of Wisdom. And whoever are the Bodhisattvas or other beings entering the great park Sunbright in order to see the nun Lion-yawn or to hear the Dharma, they are brought to the acquisition of the roots of welfare so that they no longer turn back on the path to enlightenment.

Now, you see, Sudhana, the merchant's son, after seeing the endowments of the nun Lion-yawn [namely, the park, living quarters, seats, couches, assemblies, masteries, magical powers, and miracles], after hearing the inconceivable way of the Dharma, while his mind was overflowing with the great Dharma cloud, . . . thought: "I shall make several one hundred thousand circumambulations around the nun Lion-yawn."

Then Lion-yawn radiantly illumined the whole of the great park and the harmonious assembly circles. While circumambulating several hundred thousand times, Sudhana became aware of the illumination. As he continued doing the circumambulations, he saw on all sides [in every assembled group] in front of him the nun Lion-yawn. He prayerfully folded his hands in salutation, stood before her, and said: "I have produced a resolution to Supreme, Perfect Enlightenment. And I do not know how a Bodhisattva trains in the Bodhisattva life, how he practices and acquires it. I have heard, reverend lady, that you give the instructions and teachings of a Bodhisattva. Therefore, tell me, reverend lady, how does a Bodhisattva train in the Bodhisattva life, how does he practice and acquire it?"

She said: "I, good son, have attained the Bodhisattva salvation, 'Abolished vain illusions.' "

He said: "What is the scope of this insightful knowledge?"

She said: "This introduction to insightful knowledge produces the kingly meditative trance named 'Endowment of all dharmas of toiling which are the cessation of toiling.' By the attainment of this meditative trance, I, by mind-made bodies, go forth in all ten directions to do acts of worship [pūjā] with diverse acts of worship equal in number to the countless Buddha fields of each Bodhisattva of those Bodhisattvas who dwell in the Tuṣita heaven and who are bound-by-one-more-birth-only Bodhisattvas. In this way I go to do acts of worship to the Bodhisattvas of the Tuṣita heaven, so I go to the Bodhisattvas in the Kukṣi heaven . . . and to all the Tathāgatas. Those beings who comprehend this performance of service and acts of worship to the Buddhas are all destined to the Supreme, Perfect Enlightenment. I give them instructions in the Perfection of Wisdom. I see all beings with the wisdom eye, and I do not produce the notion of beings, I do not consider them so. I hear the . . . prayers [mantra] of all beings, and I do not consider them so, because I am not attached to the range of any vocalization. I see the Tathāgatas, and I do not consider them so, because I recognize the Dhama body. I uphold the wheel of the Dharma of all the Tathāgatas, and I do not consider it so because I am awakened to the self-existence of the Dharma. I pervade the whole Dharma realm at every instant of thought, and I do not consider this so, because I am awakened to the essential nature of Māyā (illusion). I know the Bodhisattva salvation 'Abolished vain illusions.' How can I know of the conduct of Bodhisattvas who understand the Dharma realm which is without end or center? How can I tell their virtues? They do not reside in the vain illusions of all phenomena, and during one single cross-legged meditation, they pervade the Dharma realm. They demonstrate all the Buddha fields hidden within their own bodies and go to all the Tathāgatas in one instant. In their bodies all the Buddha miracles occur. In one hair pore they lift out many counted and countless Buddha fields. . . .

"Go, good son, right here in South India is a city by the name of Jewel harmonies [Ratnavyūha] in Durga country. There lives a Bhāgavatī by the name of Vasumitrā.[24] Go to her and ask: 'How does a Bodhisattva train in the course of conduct of a Bodhisattva; how does he practice and acquire it?' "

Sudhana, the merchant's son, bowed his head to the feet of the nun Lion-yawn, did several hundred thousand circumambulations, looked back again and again, and set forth from the presence of the nun Lion-yawn.

Notes

1. C. M. Ridding and Louis de la Vallée Poussin, "Fragment of the Sanskrit *Vinaya:* 'Bhikṣuṇīkarmavācanā,' " *Bulletin of the School of Oriental and African Studies* (London), I, part 3, 123–143; India Office, Stein Tibetan Manuscripts, no. 30.
2. I. B. Horner, *Women Under Primitive Buddhism* (London: George Routledge, 1930), especially pp. 119–20.
3. Ibid., p. 102.
4. Franklin Edgerton, tr., *The Bhagavad Gītā* (Cambridge: Harvard University Press, 1952), pp. 11, 13; partial translation of verses i. 37–44.
5. Ridding and De la Vallée Poussin, folio 4 a, lines 3–4, of the "Bhikṣuṇīkarmavācanā."
6. Of course, important nuns are mentioned. King Harṣavardhana became converted or concerned with Buddhism when his sister, Rājyaśrī, became a nun of the Sāṃmatīya school, which, like the Theravādin and the Mūlasarvāstivāda, was called by the Mahāyāna (Greater Vehicle) a school of the Lesser Vehicle (Hīnayāna). It would seem that Rājyaśrī's widowhood was not a time of passive retreat into the order of nuns but a time for active proselytizing of her brother's interest. Rājyaśrī is an example of a nun who was a very strong member of the family through performing her role as a nun. R. C. Majumdar, ed., *The Classical Age* (Bombay: Bharatiya Vidya Bhavan, 1954), p. 395.
7. The actual process of "stating the matter" (karmavācanā), with subsequent interrogation of the novice by the community, begins on folio 17 b.
8. Here is a comparison of the chief rules for nuns as given in the "Bhikṣuṇīkarmavācanā" and in the "Culla Vagga" of the *Vinaya Piṭaka* according to Horner, pp. 118–61.

"Bhikṣuṇīkarmavācanā" (Sanskrit)	"Culla Vagga X" (Pāli)
Chief rule no. 1	Chief rule no. 6
2	3
3	2
4	4
5	8
6	7
7	5
8	1

9. The triple refuge (the Buddha, the Dharma, and the Saṃgha). The procedure is stated below in the translation.
10. The five chief rules of conduct are refraining from killing living things, taking what is not given, sexual misconduct, lying, and intoxicants. These are the śikṣāpada listed here. They are the same as the five pañcaśīla for lay disciples. The other rules for novices are not listed.
11. The terms "initiate" and "novice" are supplied by the translator as an aid in understanding the translation. Very often the subject of the sentence is not stated or the "initiate" is referred to as "nun" (bhikṣuṇī). Only once is the initiate so designated (śrāmanerikā). This designation occurs in folio 11 b just prior to the omission of three folios and is therefore untranslated.
12. Sanskrit: *kusūlaka;* etymologically, this term means "relating to a granary or storehouse." This would suggest that it could refer to a "storage" bag the nun might carry.
13. Translation of bodice (Sanskrit: *saṃkakṣikā)* from Horner, p. 224.
14. Franklin Edgerton, *Buddhist Hybrid Sanskrit Grammar and Dictionary* (Delhi: Motilal Banarsidass, 1970), suggests another possible translation of this term (Sanskrit: *nirmittikā):* "lacking the [female] characteristics," p. 302 b.
15. Sanskrit: *prasrutalohinī;* etymologically, this term means "possessing [menstrual] blood as a discharging fluid."
16. Sanskrit: *rudhiropādikā;* etymologically, this term means "producing blood [or saffron]."
17. Edgerton, *Buddhist Hybrid Sanskrit,* notes that some Pāli commentators interpret "pūtimukta" as "urine" (Sanskrit: *pūtimutra).* Edgerton also notes that "herbal decoction" is attested to by Tibetan, Chinese, and Japanese readings (p. 350 b).
18. This phrase has not been preserved in the manuscript fragment.
19. Edward Conze, *Buddhism: Its Essence and Development* (New York: Harper Torchbook, 1959), p. 157.
20. The dharmadhātu and the celestial geographies and heavens of divine beings are not synonymous. There is a lokadhātu and a dharmadhātu or heaven, earth, and hell. This information is entered here only because it is the first mention of a god. The information will become necessary to keep separated the division of the six possible spheres.

21. The association of the prostitute with the ascetic is a common motif for representing the metaphysical union between the sensual and the spiritual worlds in Hindu literature; cf. Wendy Doniger O'Flaherty, *Asceticism and Eroticism in the Mythology of Śiva* (New York: Oxford University Press, 1973), pp. 43–52.
22. Horner, pp. 201–04.
23. There is a pun: "śīla" means "character"; "śila" means "stone."
24. See Chapter 4 for the story of Vasumitrā.

CHAPTER 4

"Good Daughter" and "Good Friend": Teachers of the Dharma

The woman's path to salvation as a teacher and disseminator of Buddhist doctrine, as spiritual friend or "good daughter," is described in the development of the highest path, that of the Bodhisattva (Chapters 4, 5, and 6). The Bodhisattva is the hallmark of Mahāyāna Buddhism, exemplifying the state of spiritual perfection in which the social and sexual distinctions between living beings have been removed through the universal practice of compassion for all beings.

The essential nature of a Bodhisattva is to assume the suffering of others in order to eliminate the hardships of others. Every living being, male or female, is considered a potential Bodhisattva, capable of eliminating all egoistic desires and passions. This path represents the highest religious development for a Mahāyāna Buddhist practitioner. Accessible to both men and women, the Bodhisattva path provides the means whereby all humans can reverse the degenerative state of ordinary human existence and realize their spiritual potential.

The "son of good family" or "good son" (kulaputra) refers to a man who has entered the Mahāyāna path recently or is already on his way to Bodhisattvahood. Various well-known Bodhisattvas are called "good sons," "sons of the Buddha," and "members of the Buddha's family." His female counterpart, the "daughter of good family" (kuladuhitā) or "good daughter" is a more ambiguous term.

Whereas the good son is often addressed by the Buddha, the good daughter is seldom solely addressed but usually only in association with the good son. A possible explanation which would account for this coupling of good daughters with good sons is that the good daughters may not have been viewed as equals to the good sons but were dependent upon and subordinate to the good sons. There are few examples of good daughters used as epithets for Bodhisattvas, but there are many in the case of good sons.

According to the selections translated below from the *Lotus Sutra,* the good daughter is capable of performing the following, although always in association with good sons: (1) awakening to the thought of enlightenment, (2) receiving a prediction to Supreme, Perfect Enlightenment, (3) worshipping multitudes of Buddhas, (4) professing vows in front of a Buddha, and (5) teaching and respecting the Dharma. All of these actions increase one's merits and imply the Bodhisattva practice (to be discussed in Chapter 5).

The good daughter who is virtuous teaches others about the Dharma and may qualify as a "good friend" (kalyāṇamitra),[1] although the good daughter does not necessarily have to be a good friend. To be a good daughter presupposes one has had a good friend who shows the Buddhist path by example and who instructs in the teaching of the Dharma:

> Those sons and daughters of good family who come to hear this Perfection of Wisdom must have fulfilled their duties under the Jinas[2] of the past, must have planted wholesome roots under [those] Tathāgatas, and must have been taken hold of by good spiritual friends.[3]

The beginner who first sets out on the long journey to Bodhisattvahood, namely, the good son and good daughter, will often feel discouraged, disheartened, and afraid of the experiences which lie ahead. Mahāyāna Buddhism realizes that the beginner in the first stages of training needs support and reinforcement in times of uncertainty. In a general sense, all living beings who are the concern of the good daughter or good son are the spiritual friends. But, more specifically, the teacher who advises how to practice and instructs in the teaching of the Dharma is the true friend who eliminates the fears and depression which the beginner experiences:

> While he is still in the initial stages of his training, on the level of a beginner, the Bodhisattva needs some social support, some "sustenance" [parigraha]. In order to stand the Void,[4] he must be firmly anchored in society. Those who are engaged in completely isolating themselves from everything, and in purifying themselves of it, are in need of association with spiritual friends to keep up their morale.[5]

The good friend's principal function is to instruct in the teaching of the Dharma and to be supportive. Women, as good daughters, were capable of being instructors, that is, good friends, and of being instructed. They were to encourage and support, teaching the Perfection of Wisdom, the highest of Mahāyāna virtues, and assuaging one's fears and uncertainty.[6] In the role of good daughter, a woman must "tend, love, and honor the good spiritual friends"[7] if she is to become or remain a Bodhisattva. This holds true for the good son too.

Good friends include Bodhisattvas, disciples, and those who instruct in the six perfections. The virtues and essence of the Dharma are good friends. The Perfection of Wisdom and the qualities and wisdom of the Buddhas are good friends.[8] As objects of meditation and practice, any quality or person who represents attributes of the Dharma, in principle, could instruct and inspire the beginning student of Mahāyāna Buddhism.

The *Avataṃsaka (Garland Sutra)* beautifully expresses the importance of a good friend by similes: (1) Like a compassionate mother, the good friend gives you birth into the Buddha's family; (2) like a compassionate father, the good friend gives benefits through his unending actions; (3) like a guardian, the good friend helps you in avoiding all evil; (4) like a great teacher, the good friend instructs you in the Bodhisattva practice; (5) like a guide, the good friend brings you to the other shore; (6) like a doctor, the good friend cures your pains from all distress; (7) like the Himalayan mountains, the good friend nurtures you as the mountain nurtures the plants located on them; (8) like a general, the good friend protects you from all fears; (9) like a boat, the good friend carries you across the sea of life and death; and (10) like a boatsman, the good friend helps you reach the jeweled stream of omniscience.

We are concerned here with the path of the good daughter, who is the beginner in training, and with the path of the good friend, who is her spiritual mentor. In the excerpts from the *Lotus Sutra,* translated below, the description of a good daughter as teacher and potential Bodhisattva is indicated. The good daughter's path as a teacher merges with the good friend's path. The selection "Sadāprarudita and the Merchant's Daughter" from *The Sutra of the Perfection of Wisdom in Eight Thousand Verses* also suggests that the two paths of good daughter and good friend need not be mutually exclusive. The merchant's daughter is not labeled as either a good daughter or a good friend. However, the merchant's daughter assumes the path of good friend by giving support, both economically and psychologically, to Sadāprarudita ("Forever Weeping"), a fledgling and very depressed Bodhisattva. Ironically, Sadāprarudita is looking for the *Perfection of Wisdom* sutra to be his teacher (or good friend) but the merchant's daughter, to a lesser degree, is Sadāprarudita's first teacher. Although she is of lower spiritual development than Sadāprarudita, she still is capable of being his teacher. She takes pity on him in his time of crisis, and it is through her support that he is able to find the subsequent teacher, namely, the *Perfection of Wisdom* sutra. Although the merchant's daughter appears to be unaware of the teaching of the Dharma, she is already practicing the Perfection of Giving in some measure by her generous support and assistance to the Bodhisattva Sadāprarudita. In this capacity, one may conceive of the merchant's daughter as a good friend who keeps up the Bodhisattva's morale and presents a way to assist him in his struggle to train in the practice of Mahāyāna. She instructs by her example.

After fulfilling the function of benefactress or good friend, the merchant's daughter and her retinue of female attendants follow the Bodhisattva, becoming part of his entourage or extended family. They worship the Buddhas, learn about the teaching of the Perfection of Wisdom, and revere and honor that sutra as their teacher in the same way that Sadāprarudita reveres and honors it. The roles shift here. The merchant's daughter and her attendants ask for support from Sadāprarudita and pay homage to him for accepting them as disciples.

This episode illustrates that the male Bodhisattva, the good son, has authority over the good daughter and must help her earn merit whereas formerly she had been the one who helped him to earn merit. The women receive their prediction to Supreme, Perfect Enlightenment after Sadāprarudita receives his, concluding the fulfillment of all the requirements by these women for being good daughters, as described in the *Lotus Sutra*.[9]

A. Introduction to Selections from the *Lotus Sutra*

The *Lotus Sutra (Saddharmapuṇḍarīka-sūtram)* is one of the oldest and most popular Mahāyānist texts to have been widely promulgated in India, China, and Japan. This text still appeals to huge audiences and inspires artists throughout Asia. Many of the episodes are dramatic and self-contained short stories, all proclaiming universal salvation or Ekayāna. The reading, writing, or reciting of the sutra becomes a potent instrument for spiritual awakening.

"Puṇḍarīka" denotes the white lotus, a symbol for quintessential beauty. Women who were exquisitely beautiful were often called "lotus-eyed" in Sanskrit literature. As a Buddhist symbol, the delicate, fragrant, and pure lotus which emerges from the mire and from polluted lakes and ponds is a metaphor for the individual who presently exists within the pollution of ordinary existence but will emerge as pure and immaculate as a white lotus if he or she listens to the true Dharma (saddharma) of the Buddha.

The *Lotus Sutra* of the true Dharma was regarded by many Buddhists as the final manifestation of the Buddha's teaching for all living beings, regardless of their differences in capabilities. The essential beauty of popular Mahāyāna Buddhism is gloriously celebrated by this text. There are several stages in the compilation of the text, which now totals twenty-eight chapters of both prose and verse sections, the latter in hybrid Sanskrit. Based upon the date of the earliest Chinese translation by Dharmarakṣa in 276, the *Lotus Sutra* is tentatively dated between A.D. 100 and 200. Chapters 21 to 26 of the sutra are generally believed to be recent additions although even the oldest Chinese recensions now extant include all of these chapters. Kumārajīva's translation of the *Lotus Sutra* in 406 was the most popular version among the Chinese. It is somewhat more conservative in its descriptions of women as compared with Dharmarakṣa's recension.

Both the *Lotus Sutra* and *The Sutra of the Perfection of Wisdom in Eight Thousand Verses* were accepted by all schools of Mahāyāna Buddhism, regardless of sect. The objectives and intent of these two texts are different, however. The objective of the latter was to serve as a manual for the Bodhisattva in training. It emphasized the doctrine of Emptiness[10] and indicated a revolution in metaphysical thought among early Mahāyāna Buddhists of the time. In sharp contrast, the *Lotus Sutra* appealed to the popular, less philosophical Buddhist audience in praising the awesome qualities of the Buddhas (and only secondarily the Bodhisattvas) as objects of cult worship and devotion. The text proclaims universal salvation to all, with pantheons of Bodhisattvas and Buddhas witnessing the sermons and performing miracles. The popular side of the Bodhisattva doctrine is emphasized and dramatized by means of parables, which may have been enacted in ways similar to the morality plays in medieval Europe. The tales and parables are a mixture of humorous and devotional episodes having the fantastic imagery found in many children's tales, but appealing to young and old alike as a form of entertainment.

The philosophical foundation for universal salvation is found in early, pre-Mahāyāna Buddhist teachings in the *Dialogues of the Buddha (Digha Nikāya):* "One path leads to Nirvana, namely, Arhatship." In teaching universal salvation, the *Lotus Sutra* is a critique of the three paths of the Arhat, Pratyeka-buddha and Bodhisattva. All three paths are only an expedient. The Bodhisattva path, as interpreted in universal salvation, included the paths of the Arhat and Pratyeka-buddha. In reality there are no divisions into paths, for, although it may seem as if there are many teachings, there is only one true teaching or true Dharma and only one salvation.

Even though the theory of universal salvation may have been used polemically, that is, in order to accept the wide variety of Buddhists as part of a unified constituency, universal salvation is identified with the nondiscriminative wisdom which is the focus of *The Sutra of the Perfection of Wisdom in Eight Thousand Verses.* If one truly practices the Perfection of Wisdom, one would not distinguish the Arhat from the Pratyeka-buddha or from the Bodhisattva or from even the Buddha himself, for such an action would be discriminatory and, therefore, would not be an act of Perfect Wisdom.[11]

The direct teaching (nītartha) is that of universal salvation as proclaimed in the *Lotus Sūtra,* in which only one path is advocated. The indirect or intentional teaching (neyārtha), which is the teaching of the three paths of the Arhat, Pratyeka-buddha, and Bodhisattva, is presented in order to give encouragement to believers. The three paths are expedients for teaching purposes.

According to the Buddhist eschatology of time, a period of decline in Buddhism would occur, resulting in decadence and corruption. This period of decline was attributed to the establishment of the order of nuns.[12] Irreligious individuals would malevolently teach a counterfeit Dharma in that period of decline. The time of the *Lotus Sutra* is the intermediate period in the schema between the glorification of the Dharma and the decline. Although the impending age will be one of degeneracy, the *Lotus Sutra* is being taught during an auspicious time for proclaiming universal salvation.

In advocating universal salvation, the *Lotus Sutra* is more liberal in its view of women[13] and is more positive in its treatment of the paths of salvation open to women. The paths of the good friend and the Bodhisattva are described as accessible to Buddhist women, in sharp contradiction to the traditional attitudes toward women as obstacles to the spiritual welfare of men.

The passages which follow indicate the woman's potential as good daughter and good friend who may actively participate in disseminating the teaching of universal salvation, the white lotus of Mahāyāna Buddhism.

Selections from the *Lotus Sutra** *(Saddharmapuṇḍarīka-sūtram)*. Sanskrit text in Wogihara and Tsuchida.

[From Chapter 10: "The Lecturer on the Dharma," p. 196, lines 11–19:]

[The Buddha speaks to the Bodhisattva named Physician King:]

"Physician king,[14] after the final extinction of the Tathāgata, I shall predict Supreme, Perfect Enlightenment to those good sons or good daughters who, listening to the teaching of the Dharma, even to only one verse, delight at a single thought of awakening [to enlightenment]. Physician king, these good sons or good daughters will be the worshippers of the hundred thousand multitudes of Buddhas. These good sons or good daughters will profess vows to the hundred thousand multitudes of Buddhas. . . ."

[Continued from Chapter 10, p. 197, lines 6–13:]

"Physician king, if either a man or woman should ask: 'In the future, what kind of living beings will be Tathāgatas, Arhats, Completely Enlightened Ones?'—then that man or woman should observe the good son or good daughter. The one who upholds, listens, or teaches even one four-lined verse because of the teaching of the Dharma or has respect for the teaching of the Dharma is

*This English translation is by Diana Paul.

a good son or daughter who will be a Tathāgata, Arhat, Completely Enlightened One in the future."

[From Chapter 26: "The Inspiration of Samantabhadra," p. 385, lines 5–15:]

Then, I, the lord, spoke again to the Bodhisattva Samantabhadra for the purpose of establishing those laymen, laywomen, monks, and nuns of the assembly in the teaching of the Dharma, the *Lotus Sutra:* "Good son, when a woman[15] has four qualities, she will have the teaching of the Dharma, the *Lotus Sutra*. What are these four qualities? (1) She will be subject to the power of the lords who are Buddhas.[16] (2) She will have cultivated virtuous habits. (3) She will be committed to the group which is confirmed [to the truth].[17] (4) She will awaken to the thought of Perfect Enlightenment for the purpose of saving all beings.

"Good son, when a woman has these four qualities she will have the teaching of the Dharma, the *Lotus Sutra*."

B. Introduction to "Sadāprarudita and the Merchant's Daughter" from *The Sutra of the Perfection of Wisdom in Eight Thousand Verses*

The *Prajñāpāramitā* or *Perfection of Wisdom* texts are a body of literature developed over a period of approximately 1,300 years. The oldest of these texts, *The Sutra of the Perfection of Wisdom in Eight Thousand Verses,* is also most likely the oldest of the Mahāyāna Buddhist texts, emerging about 100 B.C. in or near the Āndhra district of southeast India where matriarchal societies were believed to have existed. This basic text was expanded into editions of 18,000 verses, 25,000 verses, and 100,000 verses, among others, from approximately A.D. 100–300.

Abridged sutras and sutras in metaphorical verse form appeared from A.D. 300–500. The most popular are the *Heart Sutra (Prajñāpāramitāhṛdaya-sūtram)* and the *Diamond Sutra (Vajracchedikāprajñāpāramitā-sūtram)*. The last period of Perfection of Wisdom literature was composed about A.D. 600–1200 and is Tantric in orientation. All of these texts have both verse and prose sections, which have been interpolated and amended through centuries of development. The present Sanskrit texts have both old and new sections as verified by the Chinese translations.

In *The Sutra of the Perfection of Wisdom in Eight Thousand Verses*, the glorification of the supreme and ultimate wisdom and the characterization of the Bodhisattva practice are the central themes. No distinction is made between the secular and religious world, for both were viewed as Emptiness by those in deep meditative states. The distinctions and classifications of phenomena made by the monastic order in early Buddhist sects were philosophical abstractions which the mystics rejected, believing that the true meaning of the Buddha's teaching could not be reached by intellectual analysis but only through deep meditative states. These Buddhists who experienced meditative insights played a key role in the composition of the *Perfection of Wisdom*. During the state of deepest meditation (samādhi), the subject and object faded away. All perceptions and cognitive activities ceased. Everything became silent, quiet, and boundless in time and space.

Because of the esoteric quality of the *Perfection of Wisdom* sutra and in order to account for its development 500 years after the Buddha's appearance, the Buddhist legend arose that the Nāgas, serpentlike beings, were the first to hear the most sublime teaching of the Buddha in their kingdom under the sea. Only when the appropriate time occurred for other beings to be mentally receptive to the teaching, did the Nāgas entrust to Nāgārjuna (ca. A.D.

150–250), the greatest of Buddhist philosophers, the *Prajñāpāramitā-sūtram.*

Lokakṣema's Chinese recension of "Sadāprarudita and the Merchant's Daughter," translated from A.D. 179 to 180, is the oldest Chinese translation of *The Sutra of the Perfection of Wisdom in Eight Thousand Verses* and has, therefore, been selected instead of the Sanskrit recension partly because of its antiquity[18] but principally because of the dramatic style in Lokakṣema's rendition as compared with the more placid and rather tiresome account which has been preserved in Sanskrit.

Sadāprarudita, the main character in the story, is a beginner Bodhisattva who is striving to realize the Bodhisattva career. The Buddha is telling the story of Sadāprarudita to Subhuti. When the Bodhisattva Sadāprarudita was sleeping one night a long time ago, he had a dream in which a voice cried out: "Go and seek the Dharma." The Bodhisattva then woke up to look for the Buddha and to hear the Dharma of the *Perfection of Wisdom* sutra, but he searched in vain. Being dejected and frustrated, the Bodhisattva wept for days at a time. The gods in heaven saw him weeping and gave him the name "Forever Weeping" (Sadāprarudita) before his entire family and friends. He dreamed a second time and a voice cried out that there is a Bodhisattva named Dharmodgata who will help him. Bodhisattva Sadāprarudita immediately left his home for the mountains but did not see the Bodhisattva Dharmodagata nor hear the sutra. He again wept, and a voice cried out from the heavens that there was a great Dharma called the Perfection of Wisdom which, after Sadāprarudita heard it, would enable him to become a Buddha, if he went east and remained focused on the objective of learning the Dharma.

There is a series of weeping episodes and periods of doubt, depression, and revelations, which eventually reinforce Sadāprarudita to embark on his journey to see the Bodhisattva Dharmodgata and to attain the Perfection of Wisdom.

"Sadāprarudita and the Merchant's Daughter"* from *The Sutra of the Perfection of Wisdom in Eight Thousand Verses (Aṣṭasāhasrikāprajñāpāramitā-sūtram),* Chapters 28–29.[19] T. v. 8, n. 224, pp. 470–77.[20]

[T. v. 8, n. 224, pp. 472 a 29–474 a:]

The Bodhisattva Sadāprarudita then embarked on his journey and found the land Māra's Delights en route. In a garden on the outskirts of the city, the Bodhisattva Sadāprarudita stopped for the night and thought to himself: "The Buddha's sutras are truly difficult to obtain! How much more difficult are they to hear! I should revere them exhaustively as if they were my teacher. Now I am only one individual and furthermore, I am destitute. I do not have any expensive or beautiful things or flowers, incense, or other offerings with which to pay reverence to my teacher. Since I have nothing whatsoever, I would like to sell my own body as an offering for my teacher." With this intention he then entered the city streets and cried out: "Who would like to buy me?"

Then Māra [the Evil One], who had been living on the outskirts of the city while cavorting with fifty thousand lewd women, spied the Bodhisattva and heard him crying out to sell himself. Then Māra thought to himself: "This

*This English translation is by Diana Paul.

Bodhisattva Sadāprarudita who is going to sell himself as an offering wishes to pay reverence to the Bodhisattva Dharmodgata in order to become a Buddha. This man will leave my realm to free many people. Now I must destroy him!"

So, he prevented all the men and women in the land from seeing him or from hearing his voice. Now when the Bodhisattva Sadāprarudita tried to sell his body, he could not sell it. He then threw himself on the ground, writhing, weeping, and wailing out loud: "I want to sell myself as an offering in order to pay reverence to my teacher, yet no one wants to buy me."

Just at this time, Śakra, lord of gods, saw the stamina of Bodhisattva Sadāprarudita from his heaven and thought to himself: "I will go and test him. Then I will know if he truly will become a Buddha and is not merely giving lip service."

Then Śakra, lord of the gods, descended [from heaven] and appeared as a Brahman. He asked the Bodhisattva Sadāprarudita: "Good son, why do you undergo such pain? For what purpose do you writhe and weep?"

The Bodhisattva Sadāprarudita responded: "You must not ask." But the Brahman traveler [Śakra] asked three times: "Please tell me what you wish to have done because I would like to help you." The Bodhisattva Sadāprarudita responded: "What you wish to know, traveler, is that I want to sell my body in order to pay reverence to my teacher."

The Brahman spoke to the Bodhisattva Sadāprarudita: "Sir, [if] it is because you wish to pay reverence to your teacher, I now wish to make a great sacrifice. I wish to have human blood, flesh, marrow, and a human's heart. If you can give these to me, I will give you many benefits and wealth."

Then Bodhisattva Sadāprarudita, enraptured, spoke: "I wish to give to you." Then the Bodhisattva Sadāprarudita took out a knife and sliced off his two arms. The blood spurt out while he held them to give to Śakra. Then he sliced off his two thighs and the back flesh, giving them to him. Then he broke his bones to take out the marrow to give to him. He even wished, in addition, to slice off his chest when the daughter of a merchant saw him from a high tower. She saw him and was struck with pity and compassion for him. Then the merchant's daughter with her five hundred women attendants and entourage of musicians followed the Bodhisattva Sadāprarudita and asked: "Good son, you are so young and so good-looking. Why do you mutilate your body?"

The Bodhisattva Sadāprarudita responded: "Because I wish to pay reverence to my teacher. For that purpose I have cut out my blood, flesh, and marrow, wishing to sell them as offerings to pay reverence to my teacher."

Then the merchant's daughter asked the Bodhisattva Sadāprarudita: "If you pay reverence to your teacher, what kind of merits will you gain? What is your teacher's name and where does he live?"

Sadāprarudita [replied]: "My teacher lives in the East. His name is Dharmodgata, and he will teach the Perfection of Wisdom for my benefit. When I hear it, I will practice and uphold it. Because of this, I will become a Buddha. My body will have the thirty-two marks, eighty ancillary marks, ten superpowers, the four superknowledges, the four fearless powers, and the eighteen special characteristics [of a Buddha].[21] I will be able to turn the Dharma wheel and will be able to save people in all directions."

Then the merchant's daughter spoke to the Bodhisattva Sadāprarudita: "Good son, if what you say is true, then you have no equal on heaven or earth. You should not injure yourself in this way. I will give you gold, silver, and many precious jewels. I will follow you with my five hundred women attendants. I also would like to pay reverence to the Bodhisattva Dharmodgata and would like to hear the sutra."

Just at that time the Brahman spoke to the Bodhisattva Sadāprarudita: "Excellent, excellent, good son. Your stamina is difficult to match. Do you wish to know me? Good son, I am the lord of the gods, Śakra, king of heaven. Because I came to test you, I want to give you whatever you wish, sir."

The Bodhisattva Sadāprarudita spoke to Śakra, the king of heaven: "If you pity me, then make my body the same as it was."[22]

Then the Bodhisattva's body was the same as it was, and Śakra, lord of the gods, left for home.

At this time the merchant's daughter spoke to the Bodhisattva Sadāprarudita: "Let us return together to my mother and father's house. I will give you silver, gold, and many precious jewels. When we have reported to my mother and father we may leave."

So the Bodhisattva Sadāprarudita went to her mother and father's house. When the girl had returned, she completely explained to her mother and father what had happened. The mother and father responded to their daughter, saying: "What you have explained to us is extremely rare and difficult to understand. We also would like to go with you, but because of our old age, we cannot go. Please tell us what you wish and it will be yours."

The daughter: "I would like to have gold, silver, and precious jewels."

The parents: "Daughter, take whatever you want."

The daughter then took gold, silver, and many precious jewels, covering them with sandalwood, well-known incense, and other varieties of powdered jewels, honey, and numerous perfumes. She carried them herself into five hundred carriages assisted by her five hundred attendants.

Then the five hundred women attendants went to report

to the merchant daughter's mother and father: "We wish to accompany our lady in following the Bodhisattva."

Having reported to them, they all left. Then the Bodhisattva Sadāprarudita, the five hundred women attendants, and the merchant's daughter embarked on their journey. From a distance they saw the land of Incense (Gandhavatī) with its many banners, like the hanging banners of the heaven of the thirty-three gods. From a distance they heard musical notes from the land of Incense. From afar they saw the land of Incense and seven layers of seven-jeweled silks on the city walls. Below these there were seven layers of seven-jeweled canopies. Between each layer there were small bells hanging. Seven rows of seven-jewel trees encircled the outside of the city walls. There were play-theaters[23] outside the city walls where men and women played[24] and had pleasure. Among them were those who rode in carriages and who were talented in pleasures. Among them there were those who walked about and were talented in pleasures. A perfumed breeze diffused in the four directions, pervading them. There were none who did not experience it, for it was like heaven's perfume. Therefore, this land was called Incense.

At that time the Bodhisattva Sadāprarudita and the five hundred women attendants along with the merchant's daughter entered the city gates from the west. The Bodhisattva Sadāprarudita entered the city gate from the rear and beheld a high terrace engraved with gold and silver and painted with the five colors and the darkest yellow-gold. The brilliant radiance [of the terrace] glimmered. The terrace was four-sided and square, and all [sides] had plumes fanning toward the shade, having suspended canopies and banners as well. The musical notes were in perfect harmony. Having seen all of this from a distance, he asked a man who was coming from the outskirts of the city: "What kind of terrace is this with canopies and seven-jeweled textiles of priceless beauty?"

The man responded to Sadāprarudita: "Worthy one, don't you know? On this [terrace] is a Bodhisattva named Dharmodgata. He is the most honored in humanity, and there is no one who does not revere and honor him. This Bodhisattva has constructed this terrace for the Perfection of Wisdom. On this [terrace] there is a seven-jeweled box tied with gold with 'Perfection of Wisdom' carved on it. Inside the box there are hundreds of thousands of varieties of well-known incenses. The Bodhisattva Dharmodgata reveres [the Perfection of Wisdom] daily. He offers various flowers and well-known incenses, lamps and banners, flowered umbrellas and various jewels, and hundreds of thousands of different musical pieces for the purpose of revering the Perfection of Wisdom. The other Bodhisattvas pay reverence to the Perfection of Wisdom in a similar way. The gods in heaven three times throughout the day and night each bring the flowers of the coral tree[25] and huge flowers from that tree to revere the Perfection of Wisdom three times in this way."

The Bodhisattva Sadāprarudita and the five hundred women attendants, along with the merchant's daughter, heard this and were extremely excited and enraptured. All of them went to the terrace of the Perfection of Wisdom. Taking gold threaded robes, some of them covered it with them. Some among them took the robes and made them into thread. Some took the robes and made couches and screens. Some among them took the robes and gave them as alms. Then the Bodhisattva Sadāprarudita and the five hundred women attendants along with the merchant's daughter, having paid reverence to the Perfection of Wisdom, proceeded to the high throne in the great assembly where the Bodhisattva Dharmodgata was. They were not far from the high throne where the Bodhisattva Dharmodgata was sitting when they saw a young, very handsome man who was radiant. He was teaching the Perfection of Wisdom to a group of many multitudes.

Having seen the Bodhisattva Dharmodgata, the Bodhisattva Sadāprarudita and the five hundred women attendants, along with the merchant's daughter, were extremely excited and enraptured, taking varieties of flowers and incense to scatter on the Bodhisattva Dharmodgata. They took thousands of jewels to scatter on him and hundreds of varieties of colored jeweled robes to cover the Bodhisattva. They paid homage to the Bodhisattva Dharmodgata and circumambulated him eight hundred times saying: "We would also like to have the holy sutra in this way."

Then the Bodhisattva Dharmodgata held the profound sutra, the good text, and spoke to the Bodhisattva Sadāprarudita and to the five hundred woman attendants, along with the merchant's daughter:

"Hello and welcome. I hope you are not tired. If there is anything you wish or need, please do not hesitate to ask me. I am the teacher who saves humanity and who cares for them without exception."

The Bodhisattva Sadāprarudita humbly spoke to the Bodhisattva Dharmodgata: "When I originally searched for the Perfection of Wisdom, I wept profusely on a desolate mountain. In the sky an image of a Buddha with the thirty-two marks appeared to me. His golden-colored body emitted thousands of millions of brilliant rays of light. At that time this Buddha image praised me: 'Excellent, those who yearn for the Perfection of Wisdom should be like you.' Again he spoke to me: 'Go east for twenty thousand leagues to a land called Incense. It is 480 leagues square and has many jeweled canopies and fabrics like those in the palatial mansions in the heaven of the thirty-three [gods]. There is a Bodhisattva named Dharmodgata who is the most honored in humanity. He continually and repeatedly teaches people. You should go to him and hear the Perfection of Wisdom. In former lives for thousands of millions of generations he was always your teacher. When you first awakened to the thought [of enlightenment] he was your teacher. Now you have heard the teacher's name.' I was extremely thrilled beyond compare. Because of my joy, I realized the Concentration [samādhi] which sees the Buddha in all ten directions.

"Then all the Buddhas praised me: 'Excellent, those who yearn for the Perfection of Wisdom should be like you. When we originally yearned for Buddhahood, we yearned for the Perfection of Wisdom like you. When one realizes the Perfection of Wisdom, one will achieve Buddhahood for oneself.' After the Buddhas had taught this sutra for my benefit, I no longer saw them. I thought to myself: 'Where did the Buddhas come from and where did they go?' Take this case, teacher, for I wish you would explain it to me. Where did the Buddhas come from and where did they go?"

Then, the Bodhisattva Dharmodgata answered him: "Sir, listen carefully."

Sadāprarudita [replied]: "Yes, I will listen carefully."

[Then] Dharmodgata [spoke]: "Emptiness originally does not come from anywhere, nor does it go anywhere. The Buddhas are also similar in this respect. Nonconceptualization originally does not come from anywhere nor does it go anywhere. The Buddhas are also similar in this respect. Absence of a basis originally does not come from anywhere nor does it go anywhere. The Buddhas are also similar in this respect. . . ."[26]

Then the Bodhisattva Sadāprarudita heard the Buddha's profound facts about the Dharma which were as incomparable, inconceivable, and infinite as the great Dharma itself. Then, while in his seat, he realized the sixty thousand gates to Concentration. What are these gates to Concentration?

1) The placeless Concentration,
2) the fearless Concentration without one's hair standing on end [from fear],
3) the fearless Concentration freed from Māra,

4) the Concentration freed from the source of desire,
5) the Concentration freed from the dangers of warfare,
6) the inconceivable Concentration of turning toward [Enlightenment],
7) the infinite Wisdom Concentration like the great sea,
8) the adornments and merits Concentration on Mt. Sumeru,
9) the Concentration which sees the formlessness of the five psychophysical elements [skandhas] and six sensory realms [āyatanas],
10) the Concentration which enters the Buddha realm,
11) the Concentration in which all the Buddhas are seen,
12) the Concentration in which the Bodhisattvas protect the path,
13) the Concentration which teaches that the Dharma in all sutras is originally formless,
14) the precious jewel-adornment Concentration,
15) the Concentration in which all learning enters like a precious jewel,
16) the Concentration of mindfulness toward all Buddhas,
17) the Concentration in which the Bodhisattvas are exalted,
18) the Concentration of the truly irreversible turning of the Dharma wheel,
19) the adorned Buddha-merits Concentration,
20) the impeccable and pure Concentration,
21) the Concentration in which all things are heard like the great ocean,
22) the Concentration in which nothing is obtained or renounced,
23) the Concentration in which the happiness of the sutra's sounds are all-pervasive,

24) the Concentration of the Dharma of the sutra which finally reveals its banner,
25) the Concentration in which the formless body of the Tathāgata enters,
26) the Concentration in which the formless Dharma of the sutra is all-pervasive,
27) the Concentration on the Bodhisattva's symbolic hand gestures [mudrā],
28) the Concentration on the Tathāgata's vision,
29) the Concentration on all the illuminating Buddha realms which are the completion of one's vows,
30) the Concentration which frees all people everywhere from hardship,
31) the Concentration which faces the majesty of Buddhahood,
32) the Concentration on the varieties of multicolored flowers,
33) the many precious jewels Concentration,
34) the Concentration in which the Dharma wheel eternally turns,
35) the Concentration in which even distant sounds are included,
36) the Concentration which enters into the source of all humanity,
37) the Concentration which pervades the Triple World,
38) the Concentration which possesses all merits,
39) the Concentration in which there can be no transgression of the six perfections,
40) the Concentration in which the web of unorthodox views is destroyed when the Bodhisattva sits under a tree,
41) the Concentration on the Tathāgata who appears to be flying,
42) the Concentration on the majesty of the immeasurable merits,

43) the Concentration on the merits of the precious jewel of wisdom,
44) the Concentration on the stage of omniscience,
45) the Concentration on all causes for purity,
46) the Concentration which is the all-pervasive light,
47) the Concentration in which wisdom emerges from the roots of the human condition present in everyone everywhere, and
48) the Concentration which is equal to the past, present, and future.

Equivalent to these [Concentrations], the Bodhisattva Sadāprarudita attained the sixty thousand entries to Concentration. Then the Bodhisattva Dharmodgata arose [from his throne] and entered the palace.

[T. v. 8, n. 224, pp. 474 b–475 a 6:]

Then the Bodhisattva Sadāprarudita quietly came out of his meditational state and went to Dharmodgata's palace gate together with the five hundred women attendants and the merchant's daughter. Standing outside the gate he thought to himself: "Today, for the purpose of the Dharma in the [*Perfection of Wisdom*] sutra, I have come to my teacher who is inside. I cannot sit or lie down. My teacher must come out and sit on his high throne to teach me the Perfection of Wisdom." And so he sat with the five hundred women attendants and the merchant's daughter, who likewise followed the Bodhisattva Sadāprarudita's posture.

At that time the Bodhisattva Dharmodgata was teaching a suitable doctrine to the women in the palace.[27] Having explained the path described in the sutra, he bathed and put on clean clothes. Taking a seat on the terrace where the Perfection of Wisdom was, he concentrated and entered various trances of meditation, without moving or stirring for seven years. Then the Bodhisattva Sadāprarudita and the five hundred women attendants, along with the merchant's daughter, also spent seven years without sitting or lying down.

After the seven years had passed, the gods in heaven proclaimed: "In one week the Bodhisattva Dharmodgata will come out of his meditational state." Then the Bodhisattva Sadāprarudita heard the voices of the gods and thought to himself: "Today I must sweep the throne for my teacher so it will be pure." Then Sadāprarudita and the five hundred women attendants, along with the merchant's daughter, together went to the place where the sutra would be taught. When they had prepared the throne for the Bodhisattva Dharmodgata, the five hundred women attendants removed their outer clothing to drape over the throne.

Just at that time, Māra, the Evil One, thought to himself: "This has never happened before! I've never seen such a thing! This Bodhisattva Sadāprarudita prepares this throne for the Bodhisattva Dharmodgata in order to pay reverence to him and to become a Buddha. He has stamina and courage without respite. Those who realize the path leave my realm to free incalculable numbers of people. Today I must destroy him while he is in the middle of the path."

Then Māra, the Evil One, upset the seats of the Bodhisattvas by turning them over. He deluged them with sand, pebbles, rocks, thorns, and dried bones. When the Bodhisattva Sadāprarudita and the five hundred women attendants, along with the merchant's daughter, saw that the seats were turned over and were filthy, they thought to themselves: "Today the Bodhisattva Dharmodgata will sit here to teach the sutra, and his disciples will sit here to listen. Now we should sweep and readjust the remaining seats."

After they had swept and readjusted the remaining seats, they thought to themselves: "Today, the ground is very dirty. We're afraid that our teacher and all the Bodhisattvas will be covered by this dirt. So we must go together and fetch water to sprinkle over them." But they could not find any. Why couldn't they? Because Māra, the Evil One, took care of that.

They thought to themselves: "Now we have looked for water but couldn't find any. We should take the blood from our bodies to sprinkle over them." Then the Bodhisattva Sadāprarudita and the five hundred women attendants, together with the merchant's daughter, each pierced themselves with knives and used the blood which spurted out to sprinkle the ground because they cherished the Dharma in the [*Perfection of Wisdom*] sutra.

Then Śakra, lord of the gods, thought to himself: "The world has such people in it as these! They have stamina and respect because they cherish their teacher and the sutra."

Then Śakra, lord of the gods, went to Sadāprarudita and praised him saying: "Excellent, sir, who can truly compare in stamina with you! Because you have stamina and cherish your teacher, today you will hear the Perfection of Wisdom without further delay. Sir, if there is anything else you need or desire, please tell me. As for your companions, I will also give them whatever they wish."

At that time the Bodhisattva Sadāprarudita spoke: "Śakra, lord of the gods, you already should know what I want."

Then Śakra, lord of the gods, covered the ground with precious jewels. On top of these was golden sand. Śakra, lord of the gods, restored the bodies of the Bodhisattva Sadāprarudita, the five hundred women attendants, and the merchant's daughter to their previous state. Around all four sides of their seats he created lakes of lapis lazuli. Surrounding the lakes were seven-jeweled stairways with precious jeweled banisters. On both sides of the stairways were trees studded with precious jewels of hundreds of varieties which were arranged beautifully on them.

Then Sadāprarudita, the five hundred women attendants, and the merchant's daughter collected the rain water from the heaven while the flowers from the coral trees and other celestial flowers rained down amounting to over four thousand times one hundred pounds.[28] Śakra, lord of the gods, picked up these [flowers] to give to Sadāprarudita and said: "Take these flowers to pay homage to the Perfection of Wisdom and scatter them over Dharmodgata and all the Bodhisattvas. Drape these five hundred celestial robes over Dharmodgata's throne. Take them to him."

The Bodhisattva Sadāprarudita accepted all of them and again fervently vowed. Dharmodgata came out of his meditational state after seven years time and approached his throne accompanied by forty thousand multitudes of Bodhisattvas who also sat down. Throngs of people were seated in front of him. Then Sadāprarudita, the five hundred women attendants, and the merchant's daughter all scattered flowers on them and took sandalwood powdered incense, and sweet powdered incense of all sorts and finely crushed jewels to scatter on Dharmodgata and all the other Bodhisattvas.

After they had prostrated themselves at his feet, circumambulating him three times, they then stood at a distance. With the subtlest deference they glanced at the Bodhisattva Dharmodgata. At that time the walls in Dharmodgata's great assembly, measuring forty leagues on each side, were brimming with people. Then Dharmodgata, gazing at those in the assembly on all sides, saw that Sadāprarudita, the five hundred women attendants, and the merchant's daughter desired to realize the Dharma in the sutra. For the benefit of the Bodhisattva Sadāprarudita he began to teach the Perfection of Wisdom.

[T. v. 8, n. 224, pp. 475 c 11–476 a 17:]

For Sadāprarudita's benefit the Bodhisattva Dharmodgata taught the scope of the Perfection of Wisdom both day and night for one week. Those who listened to the sutra exclaimed: "The time passed as if we were sitting down to a meal!" Why is that? It is because of Dharmodgata's power and kindness.

When Sadāprarudita heard the teaching of the Perfection of Wisdom, he was thrilled and jumped with joy. The five hundred women attendants and the merchant's daughter together gathered the celestial robes and eight hundred precious varieties of gems to pay reverence to the Bodhisattva Dharmodgata. Śakra, lord of the gods, gathered celestial flowers from the coral trees and scattered them on the Bodhisattva Dharmodgata and on the other Bodhisattvas in order to increase his merit and virtues. Then, in the entire Buddha realm all the trees—herbal, fruit, and jeweled—all leaned toward the Bodhisattva Dharmodgata in tribute to him. The sweetly perfumed flowers rained down from heaven. The perfume from these flowers was sensed throughout the entire Buddha realm. All who smelled the perfume from these flowers saw Dharmodgata on his throne teaching the sutra together with the Bodhisattva Sadāprarudita, the five hundred women attendants, and the merchant's daughter. All the people were weak with joy. From afar they came to pay tribute to the Bodhisattva Dharmodgata. Throughout the land the earth quaked. At that time many thousands of multitudes realized the infinite Dharma in the [*Perfection of Wisdom*] sutra. The numberless Bodhisattvas attained the stage of irreversible Bodhisattvahood.

The merchant's daughter and her five hundred women attendants humbly spoke to the Bodhisattva Sadāprarudita, saying: "We attendants wish to become the servants of our teacher. We give you our lives. We wish to serve our teacher. Together we take these five hundred carriages containing precious jewels for you. Why? Today, our teacher has undergone enormous suffering for our benefit. We consider our teacher as no different from a Buddha. We have received great kindness from you and have been able to listen to the holy sutra. After we heard this sutra, there was no doubt in any of us, not even the slightest. Now we give ourselves in service to you. Even in thousands of millions of eons we could not repay one moment of your kindness toward us, because we have been able to listen to the holy sutra."

Then the Bodhisattva Sadāprarudita accepted the five hundred women attendants, the merchant's daughter, and the five hundred carriages containing precious jewels in order to give [them] merit along the path. After he accepted them, Sadāprarudita wished to give them to his teacher. He humbly spoke to the Bodhisattva Dharmodgata: "I wish to give myself to you as well as these five hundred women attendants, the merchant's daughter, and these five hundred carriages containing precious jewels, for you are a great teacher. Pity us. We want you to accept these. You should help us earn merit." Because the Bodhisattva Dharmodgata wanted Sadāprarudita to earn merit, he accepted all five hundred of the women attendants, the merchant's daughter, and the five hundred carriages, which contained precious jewels. After he accepted them, he returned them to the Bodhisattva Sadāprarudita: "Take these five hundred women attendants and the merchant's daughter for your servants as well as the five hundred carriages containing precious jewels."

Then all those in the heaven of the thirty-three gods praised him, saying: "Excellent, excellent! The Bodhisattva Sadāprarudita has given everything to his teacher. Such a mind is difficult to find." Then the thousands of millions of gods and men came together to listen to the Bodhisattva Dharmodgata explain the sutra. Sadāprarudita was thrilled and jumped with joy, attaining entry into the sixty thousand states of meditation. . . .[29]

Then all the Buddhas gave the Bodhisattva Sadāprarudita his prediction: "When you become a Buddha you will come into the world as a Buddha,[30] the Tathāgata, Arhat, Completely Enlightened One. When you become a Buddha, you will be called by this name. Then the five hundred women attendants and the merchant daughter will very gradually become Buddhas."

So when Dharmodgata the Bodhisattva was in the world, the five hundred women attendants were magically transformed into men.[31] Throughout their many lifetimes they were never separated from the Buddha lands. Sadāprarudita and the five hundred [women][32] attendants from generation to generation always were outstanding, and they always would teach everyone in the world.

The Buddha said to Subhuti: "If a Bodhisattva wishes to become a Buddha, if he sees the present Buddha, or if after the Buddha's final Nirvana he wishes to realize the Perfection of Wisdom, then he must always be energetic and always pay respect to the Perfection of Wisdom just like the Bodhisattva Sadāprarudita."

General Introduction to "Āśā," "Prabhūtā," and "Vasumitrā"* from *The Harmony of the Young Sapling Sutra*

In the following selections from *The Harmony of the Young Sapling Sutra,* three good friends—a young girl, a woman lay disciple, and a prostitute—each aids the Bodhisattva Sudhana and instructs him in the Bodhisattva practice.

*All introductions to these texts are by Frances Wilson.

Although only two guides, Mañjuśrī and Maitreya, in *The Harmony of the Young Sapling Sutra,* are named as Bodhisattvas, the concluding paragraphs of all the episodes are equivocal. Each good friend denies complete knowledge of the Bodhisattva conduct, coursing, and life. Consequently, each directs Sudhana to another good friend to learn the Bodhisattva life. Five of these good friends are women, not goddesses and no longer children. They live by themselves (sometimes with a retinue of multiple facsimiles) in vast jeweled palaces and parks.

Three women figures in the *Gaṇḍavyūha* are associated with nurturing, being patient, and quieting the passions. In the following chapters, Āśā ("Hope"), Prabhūtā ("Bountiful"), and Vasumitrā ("Excellent Friend") represent the religious ideals of nurturing (dāna), being patient (kṣanti), and quieting the passions (virāga), respectively. In the process of portraying feminine figures as religious ideals, the author has divorced the woman of his secular world from the ideal for which she was the partial model. The result is that it is not possible to identify historically the women of early India with the religious ideals in the *Gaṇḍavyūha.* But if the *Gaṇḍavyūha* can be used as a source book for the cultural history of women in India, it will be associated with other source books in the manner given in the paragraphs and chart below.

The prologue opens at Śrāvastī where a congregation of Bodhisattvas, disciples, and gods surround the Buddha. The Bodhisattvas important to this sutra are Samantabhadra, Mañjuśrī, and Maitreya. Mañjuśrī is the first in the series of good friends, and Maitreya, the last good friend, is the teacher in the culminating episode. The story of Sudhana's quest for enlightenment is a parable of Samantabhadra's meditations or inner religious life. When Sudhana realizes his identity with Samantabhadra—and all the other Bodhisattvas—the literary form of the sutra has taken the form of the uniquely Sanskrit rhetorical figure in which the thing to be compared (Samantabhadra) is identical with the thing to which it is compared (Sudhana). If the text is taken as an allegorical representation of the meditation of the Bodhisattva Samantabhadra, the good friends are figures of allegory, representing the components of fifty-three meditations, some relating to the six perfections.

The *Gaṇḍavyūha* is a sutra in that category which endeavors to reveal the Mahāyāna tradition which asserts: "The Buddha is omnipresent, and this world is essentially the ideal world, if one will recognize it as such."[33] The *Vimalakīrti* sutra is another such sutra. The difference between the *Gaṇḍavyūha* and the *Vimalakīrti* is that the *Gaṇḍavyūha* describes this world in terms of the ideal religious world (dharmadhātu), and the *Vimalakīrti* sutra describes the ideal world in terms of this world. Vimalakīrti, the hero of the sutra, only points out that the two worlds are the same. The following chart is a comparison of the *Gaṇḍavyūha* and the *Vimalakīrti* with reference to the identity between the ideal religious world and the secular world.

Ideal world (dharmadhātu)		This world (lokadhātu)	
		socially ideal	*satirically "real"*
Heaven	1	4	7
Earth	2	5	8
Hell	3	6	9

Such a scheme is somewhat oversimplified, especially if one were to strictly categorize the *Gaṇḍavyūha* and the *Vimalakīrti* solely in the above manner. The scheme is useful, however, for pointing out that heaven is not the same as the ideal world of a Buddha land or Pure Land. Even the creatures of hell participate in the ideal world. Otherwise, the scheme declares what this author considers to be the metaphorical literary devices that forward the themes of the *Gaṇḍavyūha* and the *Vimalakīrti*.

The *Gaṇḍavyūha* presents the religiously ideal world (1, 2, 3). *Vimalakīrti* presents this world of secularism as satirically "real" (7, 8, 9). Finally, the *Law Books of Mānu (Mānavadharmaśāstra)* present the socially ideal (4, 5, 6). These are non-Buddhist brahminical texts which have been included in the above chart as a referent for the social ideals of "this world" of secularism in India 600 years after the birth of the Buddha.

The epic cosmology to which the *Law Books of Mānu* refer is the same used by the Buddhists. The extensive chapters on law were the common social law justified by the cosmology. The *Law Books of Mānu* are a convenient reference for the customs of Indian communities described in the *Gaṇḍavyūha*. Unlike the *Gaṇḍavyūha* and the *Vimalakīrti*, the *Law Books of Mānu* are not concerned with the identity between the ideal world and this world of secularism but with the social conduct of this world and the appropriate models exemplified by given deities. The assumption in the *Gaṇḍavyūha-sūtram* is that "this world" and its social roles are identical with the "ideal world" and its religious roles for those who understand the Buddha's teaching.

C. Introduction to "Āśā" ("Hope"), the eighth good friend whom Sudhana encounters

The author of the *Gaṇḍavyūha* refers to the good friend Āśā (Hope) as a lay disciple. Āśā, because her special attainment (vimokṣa) is a Bodhisattva attainment, is by implication, a Bodhisattva. Āśā says: "Bodhisattvas produce a resolution to enlightment for *all* beings." She emphasizes that her vows must "have as a conclusion that which is the end of the defilement residues of all beings." It will not be until this conclusion that she herself will awaken to Supreme, Perfect Enlightenment. She is sustained by the presence of the Tathāgatas. If Prabhūtā is the embodiment of giving, Āśā is the embodiment of patience (kṣānti). As a socially ideal type in this world, she would be the Indian mother whose celestial prototype is the Goddess Earth (Bhū). Like Earth (Dṛdhā) in the *Suvarṇaprabhā-sūtram* she dwells ever at the feet of the Tathāgatas.[34] She is thereby a support for their preaching.[35]

From the description of Āśā, one may conclude that she exemplifies the virtues of the wife in the ideal world in this world. Exemplifying the prototypical wife, it is natural that Āśā is associated with a prototypical father figure (Bhiṣmottaranirghosa), to whom she directs the pilgrim-hero.

"Āśā"* from *The Harmony of the Young Sapling Sutra (Gaṇḍavyūha-sūtram).* Sanskrit text in Vaidya.

[P. 79, line 1, to p. 85, line 25:]

Then Sudhana, the merchant's son, honoring the qualities of the good friends, directing his thought toward the good friends, possessed by a desire to see the good friends, being aware of the instructions of the good friends, remembering the words of the good friends, filled with love for the good friends, seeing the persons of the good friends as appearances of the Buddha, seeing the good friends as revealing the qualities [dharmas] of the Buddha, seeing the good friends as teaching the qualities [dharmas]

*This first English translation is by Frances Wilson.

of all-knowing, recognizing the good friends as endowed with the vision able to see the Buddha skies—in due course he went to Samantavyūha park in Samudravetālī province. He viewed Samantavyūha park surrounded by walls wrought from all the precious metals and gems, adorned with rows of trees wrought from all precious metals and gems, and filled with bright flowers wrought from all precious metals amd gems. The trees gave forth fragrance in all directions and were laden with a rain of garlands wrought from the various metals and gems. The grounds of the park were made beautiful, lavish, brilliant with gems from trees wrought from all royal gems. The entire area was well-arranged and pleasant, shaded with shawls of all colors and flowers from the tree of wishes. The wind brought forth music from woodland instruments. It was sweeter than that from celestial woodlands. . . .

And, you know, in that great park of Samantavyūha there were ten one hundred thousands of crores of pavillions adorned with harmonies of turrets wrought from all the precious gems and metals. . . . There were apartments, . . . palaces, . . . [and] lotus ponds. . . . And in the middle of Samantavyūha park was a great palace, named Colorful Banner [Vicitradhvaja]. It was like the Kaustubha jewel churned from the ocean onto the surface of the earth. . . . And in Colorful Banner Palace were arranged countless seats, lotus seats, wrought from star-jewel, sun-jewel lotuses. . . . The many turrets of Colorful Banner, wrought from uncounted jewels, were a harmony of brilliant gems and metals composing pleasant forms from the lights of uncounted colors. And from far above, Samantavyūha park was shaded by ten hundred thousand canopies. There were canopies of finest cloths, of woodland garlands, of flowers and flower garlands, of perfumes, gems, gold, diamonds, and canopies magically wrought by the celestial nymphs of Rāvaṇa's Lañka. Also, there were ten hundred thousand nets of precious gems: Nets which rang from within the jeweled bells; nets of jeweled umbrellas. . . . nets of ocean-born pearls. . . . And the park was illumined with ten one hundred thousands of lights.

Āśā, the lay disciple, sat on an auspicious golden seat, wearing clothes of pearl and a crown. The harmony of her arms had golden bracelets and were bright with the light of her body's luster. Her locks were black, immaculate, adorned with jewels, and arranged with a net of precious gems. From the necklace at her throat hung a wish gem. Her body sparkled from the light, the jewel adornments, and one hundred thousand crores of beings did obeisance to her person. Whatever beings [mahābrāhmaṇas, . . . vaśavartins, . . . tuṣitakāyikas, . . . suyāmakāyikas, . . . devendras, . . . nāgas, āsuras, pretas, and men] would come from the eastern direction or the southern, western, northern, northeastern, etc., who are afflicted with various diseases, obsessed by defilements, clinging to various heretical views, stopped by the obstructions of past actions, they had all their afflictions quieted by the sacred vision of the lay disciple, Āśā. Their minds were freed of the stain of defilements. The thorn of wrong views is removed. The mountain of karmic obstructions is scattered. They enter the unobstructed pure circle where they purify their virtuous habits (roots) and nourish the moral-faculty sprouts and come to the omniscience-method-sea . . . and come to the all-meditations-ingress-method sea. Ingress to all vows and ingress to all conduct was begun. Ingress to the realization of all good qualities was purified. . . .

Then, Sudhana, the merchant's son, entered Samantavyūha park and looking all around saw Āśā, the lay disciple upon an auspicious seat. He went to where she was seated. He approached, reverently bowed his head, did several hundred thousand circumambulations, and said: "I, O reverend lady, have produced a thought to Supreme, Perfect Enlightenment. Even so, I do not know how to train in the conduct of a Bodhisattva. I do not know how to proceed. I have heard that your reverend ladyship gives the instructions and teachings of the Bodhisattvas. Therefore, tell me, reverend lady, how does a Bodhisattva train in the conduct of a Bodhisattva? How does he progress?"

She said: "I, good son, am a practitioner of the Bodhisattva salvation by the name of 'Banner of Safety and Good Luck' [Aśokakṣemadhvaja]. My vision is fruitful; so too is my audition, service, medical treatment, and my abiding presence. I do not come before the eyes of beings whose roots of welfare have not been planted, nor those not sustained by the good friends, nor those not devoted to Supreme, Perfect Enlightenment. After taking my sacred vision, beings are not to be turned back from Supreme, Perfect Enlightenment. You should also know that Tathāgatas come from the eastern direction, sit here on the precious-gem seats, and teach the Dharma. As they come from the eastern direction, so they come from the ten directions. I am never parted from their sacred vision, audition, or presence. Also eighty-four one hundred thousand crores of beings dwell in Samantavyūha park. Like me they are coursing to Supreme, Perfect Enlightenment and are not to be turned back. Some other beings, good son, dwell here. They are all irreversible to Supreme, Perfect Enlightenment. Bodhisattvas like me come together to form a congregation of those who are irreversible."

He said: "How long ago, O reverend lady, did you produce a resolution to Supreme, Perfect Enlightenment?"

She said: "I, good son, in a former life remember Dīpaṅkara, a Tathāgata, a fully enlightened Arhat. In his presence I practiced the chaste and holy life. I did honor to him and received the preaching on the Dharma from his presence. After him, there was a Tathāgata by the name of Vimala. I set forth from home for a holy life under his instruction, and I upheld the wheel of the Dharma. After him there was a Tathāgata by the name of Ketu. He was served by me. After him there was a Tathāgata by the name of Meruśrī . . . [a series of six more Tathāgatas are enumerated]. By this series I took entrance into the Buddha lineage. Remembering the Tathāgatas, the Arhats, I remembered those Tathāgatas who were like the sands of the Ganges, those Tathāgatas who were propitiated, served, worshipped, and honored, those Tathāgatas whose sermons were heard by me and under whose instructions I practiced the chaste and holy life. Thereafter, good son, as many Tathāgatas I served, there were more who professed their Tathāgatahood. Countless, good son, are the Bodhisattvas who produced the initial resolution because Tathāgatas go throughout all the Dharma realm. Countless, good son, are the Bodhisattvas with the method of great compassion because Tathāgatas go to all the worlds. Countless, good son, are the Bodhisattvas in the ten directions who are possessed of the great vows because Tathāgatas approach the limits of the Dharma realm surface. Countless, good son, are the Bodhisattvas with friendly love because Tathāgatas pervade the whole world. Countless, good son, are the Bodhisattvas with Bodhisattva conduct because Tathāgatas go through all eons to all fields. Countless, good son, are the Bodhisattvas with the power of meditative concentration because Tathāgatas do not withhold the path of the Bodhisattva. . . . Countless are the Bodhisattvas, good son, with the power of the supernatural knowledges because Tathāgatas produce the circle of the net of light suited to the disposition of each being. . . . Countless are the Bodhisattvas with pure body because the Tathāgatas pervade all the Buddha lands with their own body."

Sudhana said: "How long will it be until you are awakened to Supreme, Perfect Enlightenment?"

She replied: "I tell you, good son, Bodhisattvas produce

a resolution to enlightenment not for the sake of one being, that is, not for one person's training and maturation, nor for one hundred thousand beings . . . nor for the beings included in world systems equal to the atom dust of the great trichiliocosm [the thousand million world system], but, rather, Bodhisattvas produce a resolution to enlightenment for *all* beings included in *all* world realms having a remainder . . . without a remainder. . . . A Bodhisattva does not produce a resolution to enlightenment to do service to one Buddha, that is, to do service to their needs and to do honor to them. . . . Bodhisattvas desire to take vows in order to serve and do acts of worship in honor of all Buddha lineages included in all Buddha realms without remainder. . . . In brief, good son, the above are the first of the ten one hundred thousand of uncountable ingresses into the method of Bodhisattva conduct. These are to be accomplished by the Bodhisattva. I say to you further, good son, the conduct of the Bodhisattvas is associated with all phenomena [dharmas], that is, for the sake of approaching wisdom. The conduct of the Bodhisattvas is associated with all the [Buddha] lands, that is, for the sake of purifying them. I, who have such vows, have purification of the realm of desire as the certain conclusion. My vows must have that certain conclusion. My vows must have a certain conclusion which is the purification of the world realms. My vows must have as a conclusion that which is the end of the defilement residues of all beings."

He said: "What is your salvation called?"

She said: "It is called, good son, 'Banner of Safety and Good Luck.' I know this one salvation. How am I able to know or to tell the conduct of the Bodhisattvas whose minds are like the sea because they welcome all the Buddha dharmas? They are like Mount Meru because of the firmness of their resolute intentions. They are like the great healing medicine because they free all beings from diseases and defilements. They are like the sun because they dispel the darkness of delusion for all beings. It is impossible to demonstrate the teachings or to show an approximate idea of the infinitely various vows of the Bodhisattvas. Go, good son, to Nālayur country, by name, in Samudravetāḍī, South India. There lives a seer, Bhiṣmottaranirghoṣa, by name. Go to him and ask. He will teach about the Bodhisattva life."

Then, Sudhana, the merchant's son, bowed his head to the feet of Āśā, the lay disciple, did several hundred thousand circumambulations, did obeisance weeping with tears streaming down his face and steadily reflecting on the difficulty of gaining Supreme, Perfect Enlightenment, of serving the good friends, of producing the acquisition of moral faculties, of purifying the Bodhisattva disposition, . . . [and] he went forth from the presence of Āśā, the lay disciple.

D. Introduction to "Prabhūtā" ("Bountiful"), the sixteenth good friend whom Sudhana encounters

The author of the *Gaṇḍavyūha* refers to the good friend Prabhūtā as a lay disciple, dressed in the white clothes worn by the Buddhist laity. Prabhūtā, because of her special attainment (vimokṣa) is by implication a Bodhisattva. Her attainment is the provision (dāna) of food and of all other requisites, however luxurious they may be, to all beings. She is the embodiment of the perfection of giving. As a socially ideal type in "this world," she could be the Indian wife who should be like the goddess Lakṣmī in the *Law Books of Mānu*[36] "Prabhūtā" literally means "abundance" and is one of Lakṣmī's names. Like the goddess Lakṣmī (or Śrī) in the Buddhist sutra *Suvarṇaprabhā,*[37] she gives in extraordinary measure. Altogether, even aside from her primary function of giving, she seems to fulfill the requirements of the ideal wife. All the women in the *Gaṇḍavyūha,* except for the nuns, are described as beautiful with lustrous black locks and skin the color of gold. Prabhūtā is also beautiful, but her description is of greater length and quite different. Most significantly, she has the extraordinary beauty which comes with first youth, with nubility. (The prostitute, on the other hand, is described as beautiful as a virgin.) Unlike the other women and female children and unlike her many thousands of female attendants, who are otherwise very like her, she is unadorned by any jewelry. In fact, it is a worldwide convention with regard to women who are just nubile. Adornment to beauty such as theirs would be inappropriate.

From this description of her beauty and virtue, one may conclude that Prabhūtā exemplifies the virtues of the ideal wife. As the ideal wife, it is natural that Prabhūtā is associated with an ideal male householder Vidvān, to whom Prabhūtā directs the pilgrim-hero of the story.[38] The good friends seem to have a this-worldly association. Śiva, the god, directs Sudhana the pilgrim-hero to another deity. Śākyamuni's mother directs Sudhana to her daughter-in-law. In the same way, Prabhūtā directs the pilgrim to another householder. Not only does Vidvān provide food and other requisites for beings, but, first of all, he begets beings into the Tathāgata lineage, and, after feeding them, he teaches them. He functions as a progenitor, a provider, and a teacher. Prabhūtā functions as the latter two: as provider and as teacher. Only one mention, however, is made of her function as a teacher. The main emphasis with both Prabhūtā and Vidvān is their provision of goods for all beings. This is really their special attainment. As householders, they are indeed the pillars of society and the support for all other beings.

The method of their providing is interesting—and contrasts the styles of their two methods. Prabhūtā provides for all beings with one small bowl placed in front of her. Especially she provides for Bodhisattvas ready for enlightenment. She and her retinue offer food upward and outward. Vidvān, on the other hand, provides for only his sons, recently born into the Tathāgata lineage. He reaches up for food and confers it downward. After giving food, he preaches.

"Prabhūtā"* from *The Harmony of the Young Sapling Sutra (Gaṇḍavyūha-sūtram).* Sanskrit text in Vaidya.

[P. 104, line 24, to p. 109, line 5:]

Then, Sudhana, the merchant's son, seeking the cloud of instruction from good friends, was unsated like the sea after torrential rains from a great cloud. His five moral faculties [faith, energy, mindfulness, concentration, and wisdom] sprouted like shoots through the surface of the wholesome earth, and they matured in the sunshine of knowledge from good friends who were as the sun in the sky. His body and mind were refreshed by the moonbeams of instruction from good friends who were as the moon. Like a herd of deer scorched by the rays of the summer sun, he thirsted for the waters of instruction from good friends. He was like a lotus pond: His lotus thoughts were awakened by instruction from good friends who were as the waters of a Himalayan stream; his lotus thoughts opened as if at the touch of swarming bees. He was illuminated every moment by the play of the jeweled instruc-

*This first English translation is by Frances Wilson.

tion from good friends. He was like a jeweled island set with all manner of precious gems. Because of instruction from good friends, he was endowed with an accumulation of knowledge and merit just as a great Jambu tree is laden with fruits and flowers. After hearing the instruction from good friends, he became weighty with the equipment [merit and knowledge] of those destined for enlightenment; he became like a great rain cloud born from the divine-play war of Indra, the rain god, and the mighty serpent Vṛtra, the demon god of drought. Because of the instruction from good friends, he approached the pure radiant Dharma Peak like unto Citrakūṭa, the sacred peak, which adorns the thirty-three worlds. Like Indra surrounded by the host of thirty-three deities and crushing hosts of demon kings, he prevailed, undominated, surrounded by hosts of virtues arising from the instruction of the good friends. In due order he came to the town of Samudrapratiṣṭhāna and sought out the lay disciple Prabhūtā. People informed him: "O good son, the lay disciple, Prabhūtā, remains at home in the middle of the city where she has her own estate."

Then, Sudhana, the merchant's son, approached the residence of Prabhūtā, prayerfully folded his hands, and went up to the gate house. He views the lay disciple Prabhūtā's estate and its gateways to the four cardinal directions. It spread out long and wide, encircled with walls made of the precious metals and gems, an immeasurable harmony of uncounted jewels, and an outcome of the maturation of inconceivable merit. He entered the estate and looking about the grounds; he saw the lay disciple Prabhūtā upon a seat made of the precious gems and metals. She was a very young woman: beautiful, gentle, and fair to behold with the first touch of youth. Her flower garland was made of the ever-fresh globe amaranth. Her long tresses were let loose and flowing. Her limbs were without ornament. Her petticoats and sari were white.

Aside from the Buddhas and Bodhisattvas, no one comes to see her whom she does not overwhelm with her physical and mental superiority, the lustre of her spiritual fire, her exquisite complexion, and her beauty. And whoever might see the lay disciple Prabhūtā—be they gods or men—know her to be the teacher. On her estate there are ten thousand crores of seats arranged. They are superior to those of men and gods and are a result of the maturation of Bodhisattva deeds. Otherwise, on that estate a person sees no repositories of food and water, no stores of items such as clothes and ornaments—except for one small bowl put down in front of Prabhūtā. One saw ten thousand women standing before her. They were like the celestial women in their complexions, beauty, attitudes, gestures, articles, gracious conduct, fine cottons, limbs with the play of celestial ornaments, sweet speech, and perfect size. These young women, her attendants, acting at her word, stand ready in front of her, remain ready, alert, attentive, respectful, observant, obedient, prayerful, and doing homage. A fragrance wafts from their limbs which perfumes the whole city. Whoever smells the perfume becomes at heart without ill will, without hostility, without injurious intent, without envy and meanness, without sickness and deceit; well disciplined, nonretaliatory; not downcast and not puffed up; possessed of equanimity, friendly love, benevolence, restraint; and without murmuring at the acquisitions of others. And whoever hears their melodious voices becomes at heart gladdened, happy, and tranquil. And whoever sees them knows himself to be free of the passions.

Now, Sudhana, the merchant's son, bowed his head to the feet of the lay disciple Prabhūtā and afterward, with his right side toward her, walked around the lay disciple Prabhūtā several hundred thousand times, prayerfully folded his hands, and said: "I have produced a resolution to achieve the Supreme, Perfect Enlightenment. And I do not know how a Bodhisattva is trained in the Bodhisattva conduct, how he practices and acquires it. And I have heard that your reverend ladyship gives the instructions and the teachings of the Bodhisattvas. Therefore, tell me, reverend lady, how does a Bodhisattva train in the course of conduct of a Bodhisattva? How does he practice and acquire it?"

She replied: "I, good son, have obtained the Bodhisattva salvation by the name of 'Storehouse of Merit, an Indestructible Harmony' [Akṣayavyūhapuṇyakośa]. From this, I, good son, with one small bowl restore beings of varying tastes with the food each desires prepared by diverse cooks using diverse seasonings, colors, and aromatics. Therefore, I, good son, from one small bowl restore even one hundred beings with the food each desires. Even one thousand beings, even one hundred thousand beings, even a crore of beings, even one hundred crores of beings, even one hundred thousand crores of beings, even one hundred thousand hosts of crores of beings, even up to countless upon countless beings of varying tastes I restore with the food each desires. I restore, I refresh, I satisfy, I cheer, I elate, I fill with delight, and I make glad at heart. And the bowl is not empty, nor bare, nor insufficient, nor exhausted, nor reached an end, nor reached the bottom. In this way, good son, beings even as many as the dust atoms of Jambudvīpa, and in the same way even as many as the dust atoms in the four-continent world system, even as many as the dust atoms in the thousand world system, even as many as the dust atoms in the two thousand world system, even as many as the dust atoms in the great trichiliocosm [the thousand million world system], even as many as the dust atoms in up to countless upon countless Buddha lands—these beings of varying tastes come, and with the food each desires I restore, I refresh, I satisfy, I cheer, I elate, I fill with delight, and I make glad of heart. And the bowl is not empty, nor bare, nor insufficient, nor diminished, nor exhausted, nor reached an end, nor reached the bottom, nor been completely finished, nor been scraped clean. If, good son, all beings throughout the world systems of the ten directions would come to me with their varying tastes and likings, all these also I would restore with the food each desires to the extent that I would make them glad of heart. As with the varying foods, so with varying sorts of liquid refreshments, with varying exquisite elixirs, with varying couches, with varying garments, with varying garlands, with varying flowers, with varying perfumes, with varying incense, with varying unguents, with varying powders, with varying jewels, with varying ornaments, with varying jewel chariots, with varying umbrellas, with varying flags, with varying banners,with varying special foods I would restore them until I would make them glad of heart. Furthermore, good son, whoever are the disciples of Pratyeka-buddhas in one world system in the eastern direction, bearing their last and final body, who obtain the fruits of the disciple and the Pratyeka-buddha enlightenment, they all have previously partaken of my food. As in one world system of the eastern direction, so in one hundred world systems, in one thousand world systems, in one hundred thousand world systems, in a crore of world systems, in one hundred crores of world systems, in one thousand crores of world systems, in one hundred thousand crores of world systems, in world systems which are like the atom dust of India, which are like the atom dust of the four-continent world system,which are like the atom dust in the thousand world system, which are like the atom dust in the two thousand world system, which are like the atom dust in the trichiliocosm, whoever, . . . in the world systems of the eastern direction, which are like the atom dust in up to countless upon countless Buddha lands, as disciples or Pratyeka-buddhas bearing their last and final body, obtain the fruit of disciples or Pratyeka-buddha enlightenment, they have all previously partaken of my food. As in the eastern direction, so in the southern, the western, the northern, in the northeastern, in the southeastern, in the southwestern, in the northwestern, in the lower and the upper directions.

"Whoever, good son, are the bound-to-one-more-birth-only Bodhisattvas, they all have previously partaken of my food and afterward sat under the enlightenment tree, defeated Māra and his hosts, and awakened unto the Supreme, Perfect Enlightenment. As in one world in the eastern direction, so whoever in one hundred world systems, in one thousand world systems, in one hundred thousand world systems, in a crore of world systems, in one hundred crores of world systems, in one thousand crores of world systems, in one hundred thousand crores of world systems, in one hundred thousand hosts of crores of world systems, whoever in the world systems which are like the atom dust of India, which are like the atom dust of the four-continent world system, which are like the atom dust in the thousand world system, which are like the atom dust in the two thousand world system, which are like the atom dust of the trichiliocosm, whoever, . . . in the world systems of the eastern direction, as many as the dust atoms in up to countless upon countless Buddha lands, are the bound-to-one-more-birth-only Bodhisattvas, they have all previously partaken of my food and afterward sat under the enlightenment tree, defeated Māra, and his hosts, and awakened to the Supreme, Perfect Enlightenment. As in the eastern direction, so in the southern, the western, the northern, the northeastern, the southeastern, the southwestern, the northwestern, and in the lower direction. Whoever, good son, in the upper direction are bound-to-one-more-birth-only Bodhisattvas, they all have previously partaken of my food and afterward sat under the enlightenment tree, defeated Māra and his hosts, and awakened to Supreme, Perfect Enlightenment. As in one world system in the upper direction, so in one hundred world systems, in one thousand world systems, in one hundred thousand world systems, in a crore of world systems, in one hundred crores of world systems, in one thousand crores of world systems, in one hundred thousand crores of world systems, in one hundred thousand hosts of crores of world systems, in the world systems which are like the atom dust of India, the atom dust of the four-continent world system, the atom dust of the thousand world system, the atom dust of the two thousand world system, the atom dust of the trichiliocosm, whoever, . . . in the world systems of the upper direction, as many as the dust atoms in up to countless upon countless Buddha lands, are the bound-to-one-more-birth-only Bodhisattvas, they have all previously partaken of my food, and afterward sat under the enlightenment tree, defeated Māra and his hosts, and awakened to the Supreme, Perfect Enlightenment.

"Do you see, good son, my ten thousand women attendants?"

He replied: "I see them, reverend lady."

She continued: "Preeminent are they among the countless hundred thousands of women. Their actions are like mine. They have one vow, one root of welfare, one harmony for deliverance, and are kept pure by a path determined by one zealous concern. They are kept pure by a mindfulness like mine and by a route to salvation like mine. Their intelligence is immeasurable like mine and the sensitivity of their moral faculties, the pervasion of their thought, the scope of their sense spheres, their entry into the method of the Dharma, their doctrinal exegesis of meaning, their illumination of the meaning of the Dharma, the purity of their beauty, and their immeasurable powers. Undeterred and unconquered by the enemies, they, like me, speak of the Dharma. Their voices, like mine, are pure in the conventional expression suited to each being. Their virtues, like mine, are pure in their description and praise of infinite virtues. Their deeds and results, like mine, are pure in the purity which comes from the maturation of faultless deeds. They, like me, radiate loving friendliness in their protection of the whole world. They, like me, radiate great compassion in their zeal in effecting the maturation of the entire world. They, like me, have purity of action and body by their appearances which content each being according to her disposition. They, like me, are pure in the process of speaking as they give the conventional expression to the explanation of the sphere of religion. They, like me, attend the assembly circle of all the Buddhas. They, like me, go quickly forth to all the Buddha lands and have direct knowledge of how to serve and do worship to all the Buddhas in all the Buddha lands. They, like me, are pure in their conduct according to the method of the Dharma when they attain the levels of all the Bodhisattvas.

"These ten thousand women, good son, in one instant go throughout the ten directions specifically to offer food to the bound-by-one-birth-more-only Bodhisattvas from just this one small bowl. They go throughout the ten directions to offer alms food to those on the disciple and Pratyeka-buddha vehicle who are in their last and final birth. They go out and restore all the hosts of hungry ghosts. I, good son, from just this small bowl restore the gods with divine food, Nāgas with Nāga food, spirits [Yakṣas] with spirit food, Gandharvas with Gandharva food, antigods [Āsuras] with antigod food, birdlike spirits [Garuḍas] with birdlike spirit food, semihumans with semihuman food, great serpents with great serpent food, human beings with human food, and nonhumans with nonhuman food. All these I restore. Come for a time, good son, so that you will all witness."

Immediately upon these words of Prabhūtā, the lay disciple, countless beings enter the estate by the eastern gate; specifically they had been invited by the lay disciple Prabhūtā in accord with her previous vow. In the same way by the south, by the west, by the north gate to the estate countless beings enter specifically; they had been invited by the lay disciple Prabhūtā in accord with her previous vow. Prabhūtā, the lay disciple, has them sit down, and with the food each desires, prepared by diverse cooks using diverse seasonings, colors, and aromatics, she restores them. She restores, refreshes, satisfies, cheers, elates, fills with delight, and makes glad of heart. As with the varying food, so with varying liquid refreshments, with diverse exquisite elixirs, with varying seats, with varying couches, with varying vehicles, with varying clothes, with varying flowers, with varying garlands, with varying perfumes, with varying incense, with varying unguents, with varying powders, with varying ornaments, with varying jewel chariots, with varying umbrellas, with varying flags, with varying banners, with varying special foods she restores them until they are glad of heart. She restores the gods with divine food, the Nāgas, spirits, Gandharvas, antigods, birdlike spirits, semihumans, great serpents, the humans and the nonhumans. She restores each with suitable food. She restores them until they are glad at heart. And the bowl is not emptied, nor bare, nor insufficient, nor diminished, nor exhausted, nor reached an end, nor reached the bottom, nor been completely finished, nor been scraped clean.

Then, the lay disciple Prabhūtā said to Sudhana, the merchant's son: "I know the Bodhisattva salvation which is a storehouse of merit and an indestructible harmony. How can I know the conduct of the Bodhisattvas? Their merit is indestructible by the indestructibility of their sea of merit. They are fashioned like the firmament with the magnitude of their extensive and well-produced merit. They are like the jewel which is the king of wish gems in the completeness of their vow for the welfare of the whole world. They are like the Cakravāḍa mountain range surrounding the earth by their protection of the root of welfare for the whole world. They are like a great cloud of merit because they provide rains like those of the Bodhisattva Ratnapāṇi for the whole world. They superintend the great storehouse of merit by their guardianship of the door to the city of the Dharma. They illumine great merits with light for the darkness and poverty of the whole world. How can I know the Bodhisattva conduct? How can I tell its qualities?

"Go, good son. Right here in South India is a city by the name of Mahāsaṃbhava. There a householder by the name of Vidvān lives. Go to him and ask: "How is a Bodhisattva trained in the Bodhisattva conduct? How does he practice and acquire it?' "

Then, Sudhana, the merchant's son, bowed his head to the feet of the lay disciple Prabhūtā, and afterward, with his right side toward her, walked around her several hundred thousand times. After looking back again and again, he set forth from her presence although he was still unsated with the sacred vision of the lay disciple Prabhūtā.

E. Introduction to "Vasumitrā" ("Excellent Friend"), the twenty-sixth good friend whom Sudhana encounters

The author of the *Gaṇḍavyūha* refers to Vasumitrā as a Bhāgavatī. The meaning of this term is not clear. Edgerton notes that it might mean a female follower of Śiva, its usual meaning being "a female follower of Viṣṇu."[39] The only reference to Śiva is the mention of a Saivite incense. The Chinese Gaṇḍavyūha is said to describe Vasumitrā as a prostitute. The account in the Sanskrit version does not state this, but it describes her thus:

She teaches the Dharma through a glance, an embrace, a kiss. Altogether the chapter devoted to the Bhāgavatī Vasumitrā is brief. Without internal evidence or a good commentary, nothing can be said about Vasumitrā as a courtesan or a female religious aspirant. She is associated with a nun called Lion-yawn who had directed the pilgrim-hero to see her. Chapter 3 has a brief statement about the possible association of the nun with the prostitute in which the latter may be a female religious aspirant and nonfamily woman, as is a nun.

"Vasumitrā"* from *The Harmony of the Young Sapling Sutra (Gaṇḍavyūha-sūtram).* Sanskrit text in Vaidya.

[P. 154, line 8, to p. 156, line 10:]

Then, Sudhana, the merchant's son, his mind illuminated with the light of great wisdom, meditating on the insightful knowledge of all knowing [sarvajñānāloka], confirming himself in the way of formulae, a way which is a treasury of the signals and calls of all beings, extending the way of formulae thus maintaining the Dharma wheel of all the Tathāgatas, protecting the whole world, upholding the power of great compassion, conforming to purity of vows pervading the circle of the Dharma realm, . . . in due course came to the city of Jewel harmony (Ratnavyūha) in Durga country, seeking out the Bhāgavatī Vasumitrā.

The men there, who did not recognize her good qualities and did not know the method and range of her knowledge, were surprised and thought of Sudhana: "This is a

*This first English translation is by Frances Wilson.

person of tranquil and restrained senses. He is self-possessed, fully aware, unflurried, and his mind is undistracted. He looks ahead only the length of a yoke. His mind is not given over to feelings and sensations. He does not respond to superficial appearances in any form. His eyes gaze upward. His mind does not wander. His gestures are majestic and grand like the sea. His mind is independent and unruffled. What can Bhāgavatī Vasumitrā do for this person? Men like him are not those given to passion; their minds are not perverted. They are not those obsessed with foul ideas. They are not those who are slaves of lust. They are not those who are dependent on women. They are not those who move in the province of Māra. They are not those who frequent the realm of Māra. They are not those sunk in the mud of lust. They are not those bound by the snares of Māra. . . ."

But there were other men there who recognized the preeminent qualities of Bhāgavatī Vasumitrā and had witnessed in person the range of her knowledge. They said to Sudhana: "Wonderful, wonderful, good son! What you seek is easy to obtain. If you understand that Bhāgavatī is the right person to question, then for a certainty you seek enlightenment. For a certainty you desire to make yourself a refuge for all beings. For a certainty, you desire to pull out the thorn of passion in all beings. For a certainty you desire to establish wholesome perceptions and thinking. Bhāgavatī Vasumitrā remains at home in her estate just to the north of the central intersection of the city."

Then, Sudhana, the merchant's son, heard these words and became happy, delighted, glad of heart, and joyous, and his mind became filled with bliss. He viewed her estate. It spread out long and wide, enclosed by ten walls made of the precious metals and gems and ten rows of palm trees made of the precious metals and gems. There were ten moats with water delicately scented and covered with white day-blooming lotuses, white night-blooming lotuses, white night-blooming water lilies, red day-blooming lotuses, and blue night-blooming water lilies, all made of the celestial precious metals and gems. The water had the eight excellent qualities [limpidity and purity, refreshing coolness, sweetness, softness, fertilizing qualities, calmness, power of preventing famine, and productiveness]. The bottom of the moats was covered with gold sand. Stirred by gently scented breezes, the water was fragrant. The moats surrounded the estate on all sides and were adorned with several walls made of the precious metals and gems. Light shimmered in the jewels and gems of the banners, reflecting the multifaceted brilliance of the lion's cages, the half moons, and the cow-eyed lattices of the arches, turrets, and the well-proportioned heights of the towers on the mansions and palaces made of all the precious gems and metals.

The surface of the grounds was finished with necklaces of precious metals and gems in a mosaic with lapis lazuli. The grounds were adorned with innumerable walls made of the various precious gems and metals. The surroundings were scented with all wholesome celestial fragrances, especially the fragrance from the burning incense of Śiva's aloe wood. The surroundings were anointed with all appropriate unguents. The walls were topped with copings made of all the precious gems and metals. The turrets were covered with nets of Jambunada gold strung with the various precious gems and metals. From one hundred thousand nets of golden bells, sweet charming sounds were sent forth by the wind. There were adornments of flowers, made of the precious gems and metals, strewn about as if sent forth from a cloud of flowers made from all the precious gems and metals. The gatehouses were adorned with brilliant banners made from all the precious gems and metals. All the surrounding countryside was illuminated by the shimmering lights of all the many different jewels. Ten great parks were adorned with an indestructible treasure of one hundred thousand collections of treasure, brilliant with crystal and diamonds: These collections were the branches of trees alight with an abundance of jewels.

There he saw Vasumitrā, beautiful, serene, and fair to behold—appropriately garlanded with a superb garland of the ever-fresh globe amaranth. Her hair was very black and her complexion golden. Her form in every limb and all limbs together were well proportioned. The glorious beauty of her features, form, complexion, and color exceeded that of celestial and human beauty in all the realms of desire. The quality of her voice was superior to that of Brahmā. She knew the many mantras uttered by all beings. She was endowed with the skill in salvation named "Harmonic Circle of Words" [Cakrākṣaravyūha]. She was adept in the skills of all the arts. Her body was charming, covered with a translucent net of all the precious gems and metals. It shimmered, decorated with a harmony of ornaments made from uncounted celestial jewels. In her tiara was a wish gem, a great king of jewels. At her throat was a necklace of lapis lazuli strung with lion's [mystical] gems and diamonds. Her attendants were charming with vows identical with hers and conduct based on the same roots of virtue. She possessed a great treasure of stores, the indestructible equipment of merit and knowledge. He saw that whole estate, a harmony of palaces and mansions made of all the precious gems and metals. Vasumitrā illuminated it with an exalted light, lovely and producing happiness and refreshment to the body and zest and joy to the mind. The light originated from the very body of Vasumitrā.

Then, Sudhana, the merchant's son, bowed his head to the feet of Bhāgavatī Vasumitrā, prayerfully folded his hands and said: "I have produced a resolution to the Supreme, Perfect Enlightenment. Yet I do not know how a Bodhisattva trains in the course of Bodhisattva conduct, nor how he practices and acquires it. And I have heard that your reverend ladyship gives instructions and the guidance of the Bodhisattvas. Therefore, would your ladyship tell me: How does a Bodhisattva train in the coursing of an enlightenment being, how does he practice and acquire it?"

She replied: "I, good son, have obtained the Bodhisattva salvation named 'Limit of renunciation.' Because of the purity of my voice and complexion, I exceed the beauty of the celestial women [Apsaras]: their complexion, their shapeliness, and their perfect size. With this beauty I appear before the gods, who are resolute believers, according to their disposition. Thus for the Nāgas, spirits, Gandharvas, antigods, birdlike beings, semihumans, great serpents, humans, and nonhumans I appear before those who are resolute believers, according to their disposition with translucent purity of my voice and complexion which exceeds the beauty of a virgin: her complexion, her shapeliness, and her perfect size.

"And to the beings who come to me, their minds obsessed with passion, I teach the Dharma, good son, for the renunciation of passion. And after they have heard that Dharma, they accordingly obtain the state wherein passion is renounced, and they receive the Bodhisattva meditation by the name of 'Unattached Sense Spheres' [Asaṅgaviṣaya]. Some, when they see me, attain renunciation of passion and receive the Bodhisattva meditation by the name of 'Joy and Delight' [Pramodyarati]. And some, just by talking to me, attain the removal of passion and attain the Bodhisattva meditation by the name of 'Treasury of the Unobstructed Melodious Voices' [Asaṅgasvarakośa]. Some just by taking my hand obtain the state wherein passion is removed and receive the Bodhisattva meditation by the name of 'Firm Grounding in All the Buddha Lands' [Sarvabuddhakṣetrānugamanapratiṣthāna]. Some, just by dwelling in the same estate, obtain removal of passion and receive the Bodhisattva meditation 'Light of Renunciation' [Visaṃyogāloka]. Some, with only a look, obtain renunciation of passion and receive the Bodhisattva meditation by the name of 'Harmony of Calm Attitude' [Praśāntākāravyūha]. Some, just by my yawn, obtain removal of passion and receive the Bodhisattva meditation by the name of 'Dispelling False Teachings' [Parapravādivikṣobhaṇa]. Some, with only a blink, obtain a renunciation of passion and the Bodhisattva meditation by the name of 'Light of Buddha Sense Spheres' [Buddhaviṣayāloka]. Some, with only an embrace, obtain renunciation of passion and attain the Bodhisattva meditation by the name of 'Womb of Renunciation and Conversion of the Whole World' [Sarvajagatsaṃgrahaparityāgagarbha]. Some, with only a kiss, obtain renunciation of passion and attain the Bodhisattva meditation by the name of 'Contact with the Treasury of the Merit of the Whole World' [Sarvajagatpuṇyakośasaṃsparśana]. I establish all those beings who come to me in the Bodhisattva salvation by the name of 'Facing the Unattached All-Knowing Stage which Attains the Limit of Dispassion' [Virāgakoṭigata Asaṅgasarvajñatabhūmyabhimukha]."

He said: "Where, reverend lady, did you plant your roots of virtue? And what sort of deeds and results did you accumulate—you who have such wealth."

She said: "I remember, good son, in times past there was a Tathāgata by the name of Atyuccagamī. As a completely enlightened Arhat, he was born into this world, perfect in knowledge and conduct. He was a Sugata; no one surpassed him in worldknowing. He was a teacher of gods and men, a Buddha. Good son, the Tathāgata, while he was entering the capital city of Sumukhā [because he was compassionately moved for the plight of beings] and as he was approaching the gate, the whole city moved and quaked. A harmony of light was established. It was made from several of the precious gems and metals. It spread out long and wide and was strewn with flowers made of various types of the precious gems and metals. Melodies were played by many different celestial instruments. In the sky were clouds of the exalted bodies of countless gods. And I, good son, at this time was the wife of a merchant by the name of Sumati. At that time, I, impelled by this Buddha miracle, ran forth with my husband, and, as the Tathāgata approached the gate, I, overflowing with exalted serenity, gave the Tathāgata a jewel cowrie. Also, at that time Mañjuśrī, the youth, was serving upon the Tathāgata Atyuccagāmī. Through him I produced a resolution to Supreme, Perfect Enlightenment. I know this Bodhisattva salvation 'Limit of Renunciation.' How is it possible for me to know the coursing of Bodhisattvas who are established in infinite skillfulness in knowledge and means, whose extensive storehouse of merit is indestructible, whose sphere of knowledge is unassailable? How can I describe their qualities?

"Go, good son, right here in South India is a city by the name of Śubhapāraṃgama. In that city a householder by the name of Veṣthila performs acts of worship at a Tathāgata shrine [caitya] with a sandalwood throne. Go to him and ask: 'How does a Bodhisattva train in the life of a Bodhisattva? How does he practice and acquire it?' "

Then, Sudhana, the merchant's son, bowed his head to the feet of the Bhāgavatī Vasumitrā, did several hundred thousand circumambulations, and looked back again and again as he set forth from the presence of the Bhāgavatī Vasumitrā.

Notes

1. Early Buddhist literature also recognized that women were capable of being good friends. See the story of Mālinī, in *Mahāvastu,* tr. J. J. Jones (London: Luzac, 1949), I, 249–65.
2. An epithet for a Buddha, literally meaning "conqueror."
3. *The Large Sutra on Perfect Wisdom,* tr. Edward Conze (Berkeley and Los Angeles: University of California Press, 1975), p. 318.
4. Emptiness.
5. *The Large Sutra on Perfect Wisdom,* p. 14.
6. Ibid., p. 114.
7. Ibid., p. 367.
8. Ibid., pp. 439–40.
9. Awakening to the thought of enlightenment precedes the reception of a prediction to future Buddhahood. Prediction to future enlightenment is verification for entering the path to Bodhisattvahood. The profession of vows and instructing others in the Dharma immediately follow the prediction. See Chapter 5 for a more detailed account of the stages in a Bodhisattva's career.
10. See Chapter 6 for an explanation of the teaching of Emptiness.
11. Other texts mention Ekayāna (universal salvation): *Laṇkāvatāra-sūtram, Śrīmālādevīsiṃhanāda-sūtram (The Sutra of Queen Śrīmālā Who Had the Lion's Roar),* and the *Bodhicaryāvatāra (Entering the Path to Enlightenment).*
12. See Chapter 3, text a: "Nuns: The Stating of the Matter."
13. The story of a young princess who becomes a Bodhisattva, described in the *Lotus Sutra,* is translated in Chapter 5, text b: "The Nāga Princess."
14. Sanskrit: *Bhaiṣajyarāja,* the name of a Bodhisattva.
15. Kumārajīva's translation mentions good sons and good daughters instead of only women (T. v. 9, n. 262, p. 61 a 28). Dharmarakṣa mentions women (fu-jen), not good daughters (T. v. 9, n. 263, p. 233 a 26).
16. Kumārajīva: "She will be protectively mindful to the Buddhas." Dharmarakṣa: "She will be protected by all the Buddhas who see her."
17. The Saṃgha or Buddhist community is implied here.

18. For a detailed study and concordance of the age of the various layers of textual passages from the time of Lokakṣema's recension through the middle period of the Chinese texts and the late period in the Sanskrit and Chinese, see Lewis R. Lancaster, "An Analysis of the Aṣṭasāhasrikāprajñāpāramitā-sūtra from the Chinese Translations," unpublished dissertation, University of Wisconsin, 1968. Also see Lewis R. Lancaster, "The Story of a Buddhist Hero," *Tsing Hua Journal of Chinese Studies,* X(2) (July 1974), 83–89.
19. These chapters on Sadāprarudita from the Chinese correspond to Chapters 30–32 of the Sanskrit recension.
20. Portions of the chapter with long lists of states of concentration (samādhi), descriptions of the Perfection of Wisdom, or events of Sadāprarudita without mentioning the merchant's daughter have been omitted for the sake of brevity. These omissions are indicated in the text.
21. This list delineates the technical attributes of a Buddha.
22. In the Sanskrit recensions, the Bodhisattva Sadāprarudita wishes to have the supreme qualities of a Buddha instead. Edward Conze, tr., *The Perfection of Wisdom in Eight Thousand Lines* (Bolinas, Ca.: Four Seasons, 1973), p. 286.
23. Chinese: *hsi-lu.* This compound could suggest a brothel.
24. Chinese: *yü-le.* Sexual overtones to "played" may be implied.
25. Sanskrit: *Mandārapuṣpa,* i.e., flowers from the coral or thorn-apple tree believed to be one of the five kind of flowers present in heaven.
26. The same statement is made regarding the placeless, formless, illusory, mirage, the person one dreams about, Nirvana, and imagination. A somewhat different statement is made regarding the unproduced, the nonadvancing (ungrown), the absence of a place to go, space, the conclusions in the sutra, and the fundamental causes. All of these are said to be similar to the desire to know the Buddha.
27. The women have a private lesson with the Bodhisattva Dharmodgata. Although such a favor would be highly treasured by the faithful Buddhist, it is not clear whether or not the "suitable doctrine" is the same Perfection of Wisdom which Sadāprarudita so intensely and passionately desires to learn or a different variation of the text. The separation of women from men for purposes of instruction was a common practice in the Buddhist community of monks and nuns.
28. *Tan* is a Chinese measure approximately equivalent to 133

pounds. The statement "over four thousand times one hundred pounds" is an approximation of 4,000 *tan*.

29. After a list of twenty-four states of meditation are enumerated, Dharmodgata compares the voice and body of the Buddha to a lute, a pipe, an image, a drum, a painting, a celestial palace, an echo, and a magically created man. All of these metaphors illustrate the complex constituents of the Buddha's body, which is manifested under many conditions and causes but which is ultimately empty, like a magically created man.
30. The name of the Buddha is transliterated *Chia-mo-chia-t'i-t'o-p'o-lo-yeh-heng*, but no Sanskrit equivalent corresponding to the transliteration is found in the Sanskrit edition which omits the name of this Buddha.
31. Sexual changes are discussed below in Chapter 5.
32. Variation in the manuscripts. One manuscript reads women (nü); two others read human (jen). See T. v. 8, n. 224, p. 477, footnote 17.
33. Edward Conze, *Buddhism: Its Essence and Development* (New York: Harper Torchbook, 1959), p. 157.
34. *The Sutra of Golden Light*, tr. R. E. Emmerick (London: Luzac, 1970), pp. 51–55.
35. According to the *Laws of Mānu* the ur-progenitors were seers (ṛṣi) *(Manavadharmaśāstra,* no. 1.34–41 (George Bühler, tr., *The Laws of Mānu* [Oxford University Press, 1886], reprinted in Delhi by Motilal Barnarsidass, 1964, pp. 14–15), Āśā is a mother figure, and Bhiṣmottaranirghoṣa, the seer, is the father figure. Specifically, in the *Gaṇḍavyūha*, Āśā is married to the prince Suprabha, not to a seer.
36. *Mānavadharmaśāstra*, ed. V. N. Mandlik (Bombay: 1886), p. 1229 (9.26).
37. R. E. Emmerick, tr., *The Sutra of Golden Light* (London: Luzac, 1970), pp. 48–51.
38. Prabhūtā and Vidvān are human householders just as Śiva and the devatās are deities. A specific relationship between Prabhūtā and Vidvān is not asserted.
39. Franklin Edgerton, *Buddhist Hybrid Sanskrit* (Delhi: Motilal Banarsidass, 1970), p. 408.

CHAPTER 5

The Bodhisattvas with Sexual Transformation

The path of salvation of the Bodhisattva is a complex one and varies markedly in presentation from sutra to sutra within the Mahāyāna tradition. The Bodhisattva is the spiritual assistant to the Buddha, the hero or heroine in Mahāyāna Buddhist literature. As an immensely compassionate person, the Bodhisattva comforts and teaches all beings, postponing his or her enlightenment but destined in the future to become a Buddha. This Buddha-to-be is characteristic of Mahāyāna Buddhism and distinguishes Mahāyāna from Theravāda or Hīnayāna, the "Lesser Vehicle." The notion of the Bodhisattva, however, does appear in the *Jātaka* tales,[1] or birth stories, in which the Buddha, in his former lives, that is, in his pre-Buddha past, performs many meritorious and self-sacrificing acts of compassion and love.

For the Mahāyānist, all devout followers of the Buddhist Dharma should aspire to be Bodhisattvas and eventually Buddhas. For the Theravādin believer, the Buddha was so infinitely superior in wisdom that only a very small proportion of the population could ever become a Buddha. Instead, the monastic order in particular, as well as the exceptional laity, both male and female, were urged to strive for sainthood or Arhatship. In contrast to the Theravādin ideal of Arhatship, from the Mahāyānist perspective, one ought to endeavor to realize the ultimate in spiritual attainment, namely, Buddhahood itself. The early Buddhist idea that the Buddha had passed into extinction with his final Nirvana was replaced, in the Mahāyāna tradition, by the idea that the Buddha remained in a Buddha land and that there were innumerable Buddhas and celestial Bodhisattvas[2] populating the entire universe.[3]

The Mahāyānists portray the Arhat in an unfair manner, due in part to the Mahāyānists' intention to establish their own teaching as orthodox. The Arhat is viewed by Mahāyāna as living in a self-centered spiritual state, in an existential vacuum, which has no religious vitality because there is no concern for the spiritual well-being of others. In contrast to the Arhat, the Bodhisattva or Buddha-to-be goes out to teach the masses out of tremendous compassion and love in the same way that Siddhārtha Gautama went out to teach others after he had awakened under the Bodhi tree. The Arhat is viewed as an introverted, contemplative scholar without an audience. The Bodhisattva, on the other hand, is the masterful teacher with tremendous charisma who soothes the aches and pains of all those he or she meets.

The religious significance of the Bodhisattva ideal was in its mass appeal for the common people as a heroic, merciful being, forever waiting compassionately to assist and comfort. By faith and supplication to the Bodhisattvas, the average person could feel solace and release from the anxieties of his or her everyday existence. In addition, the Bodhisattva ideal introduced the belief in the transference of merit which would give hope to many. All the merits from the good actions which the Bodhisattva has earned are given to others in order to help them. As a result of the transference of merit, the individual with a low degree of self-acceptance and motivation could still aspire to be a Buddha by acquiring merit and power given by the Bodhisattva. Since the Bodhisattva gives others his or her merit, the recipients would no longer be held responsible for the consequences (karma) of their own actions. The law of karma would be negated.

All Bodhisattvas have a great loving heart whose infinite love and compassion is extended to all living beings. This is the essential nature of a Bodhisattva. He or she assumes the suffering of others in order to eliminate their hardships. These Bodhisattvas serve as models for the faithful in showing the way to enlightenment and in struggling themselves to attain the wisdom of the Buddha. Several outstanding Buddhist philosophers throughout history have been regarded as Bodhisattvas. Although the powers of the celestial Bodhisattva are supranormal, every living being is considered a potential Bodhisattva.

The path of the Bodhisattva is strenuous and difficult, requiring an enormous length of time spanning many generations of rebirths. This journey toward Buddhahood begins with a mental resolution to become a Bodhisattva and an announcement of this aspiration in the presence of a Buddha. Known as Awakening to the Thought of Enlightenment,[4] this profound state of mind propels the person into new insights and to an unshakable conviction to aspire to the Supreme, Perfect Enlightenment. The Awakening to the Thought of Enlightenment transforms the ordinary human being into a Bodhisattva. External evidence which verifies the experience of Awakening to the Thought of Enlightenment includes: (1) an increasing desire to become a Buddha in order to help all beings, (2) a good friend who teaches the Buddha's Dharma, (3) recitation of ten Bodhisattva vows, (4) a visualization and appearance of a Buddha with a subsequent conversation between the neophyte Bodhisattva-to-be and the Buddha, and (5) miracles such as flowers falling from heaven, the gods singing praises, and the earth quaking.

In early Mahāyāna literature such as the *Perfection of Wisdom in Eight Thousand Verses (Aṣṭasāhasrikāprajñāpāramitā)*, the *Lotus Sutra (Saddharmapuṇḍarīka)*, and the *Pure Land Sutra (Sukhāvatīvyūha)* ca. 100 B.C. to A.D. 100, the awakening experience is not described in detail. Between ca.

A.D. 100 and A.D. 300, the path of the Bodhisattva became increasingly elaborate in the *Ten Stages Sutra (Daśabhūmika-sūtram),* the *Bodhisattva Stages (Bodhisattva-bhūmi),* and later Perfection of Wisdom literature.

With the advent of the awakening, the Bodhisattvas were considered members of the Buddha's family. They acquired superpowers, and the law of karma was replaced by the transference of merit. These powers enabled the Bodhisattva to continue on the course to spiritual enlightenment through helping all beings whom he or she would meet.

Mahāyānist sutras which depict the woman's role as a Bodhisattva may be classified according to three types: (1) denial of a woman's entrance into Buddha land, (2) acceptance of women as lower-stage Bodhisattvas, and (3) acceptance of women as advanced Bodhisattvas and imminent Buddhas.

In the first class of sutras, the *Pure Land Sutra* is the most notable. This sutra is not a metaphysical statement concerning the correct perception of this world as the ultimate reality. Rather, it is a social contract made by a Bodhisattva so that Pure Land[5] might come into existence in which all living beings will practice Mahāyāna Buddhism. This world for the Buddhist sect known as Pure Land is in no way ultimate reality. This sect looks forward to a Pure Land, a heaven of conditioned reality, that will obtain as the result of Bodhisattva vows. The famous thirty-fourth vow indicates the desired state for women in the Pure Land:

> "O Bhagavan [lord], if, after I have obtained Bodhi [enlightenment], women in immeasurable, innumerable, inconceivable, incomparable, immense Buddha countries on all sides, after having heard my name, should allow carelessness to arise, should not turn their thoughts toward Bodhi, should, when they are free from birth, not despise their female nature; and

> if they, being born again should assume a second female nature, then may I not obtain the highest perfect knowledge."[6]

The vow does not (nor does any other vow or statement in the sutra) preclude the possibility of woman's progress in the Bodhisattva vehicle. Even so, the implication points to the necessity of a male nature for such progress. In order to be born in the land of Amitābha, one must have a male nature. Because of the Bodhisattva's vow, there was the acknowledgment that women could be reborn as men in the next life and then realize spiritual growth.

The model of sexuality presented in the *Agañña-suttanta* assumes that a perfected being is desireless and hence asexual, resulting in a variety of portrayals of the Bodhisattva. We find a set of androgynous figures with a peculiar and sometimes bizarre fluidity of sexual identification. This presents problems of interpretation with regard to the path of salvation of Bodhisattvahood for women.

The majority of Mahāyāna sutras fall into the second category. While women are acknowledged as spiritual assistants to the Buddha, on the one hand, they are relegated, on the other hand, to a lower stage of development than their male counterpart.[7] This subordination of the woman's authority to that of the man's reflects both the social order of India at that time and the monastic hierarchical structure of the community wherein even the most senior nun must be deferential to the youngest novice monk. The majority of sutra literature is representative of this group, but one concession is made, however, to those advocating an egalitarian view toward all human beings. A narrative theme known as the "transformation of sex" (parivṛttavyañjana) plays an important role in advocating a more equitable sociopolitical order. If a woman's virtues and merits are extraordinary and her capabilities cannot, in justice, be ignored, she may become a Bodhisattva and even a Buddha within her present life which was begun as a female. Unlike the *Pure Land Sutra,* in which a woman was subjected to waiting for another existence as a male in order to be a Bodhisattva and eventually a Buddha, in this second class of sutras a woman may undergo a sexual change. The translations below from *The Sutra of the Perfection of Wisdom in Eight Thousand Verses,* the *Lotus Sutra, The Collection of Jewels,* and also *The Sutra of the Dialogue of the Girl Candrottarā* describe the lower-stage female Bodhisattva who sexually transforms into a male prior to imminent Buddhahood. Female Bodhisattvas who do not undergo any sexual change are presented in Chapter 6.

The motif of sexual change is found in many instances of folklore as a literary device for enhancing the narrative of the folktale. Buddhist literature is no exception.[8] The notion of sexual change or transformation occurs in a wide variety of Buddhist genres, however. For example, sexual changes are mentioned in: (1) the disciplinary rules *(Vinaya Piṭaka),* which regulate the religious communities of Buddhists; (2) in sutra literature which is highly symbolic in language; and (3) in treatises dealing with theories of physical and mental constituents of perception, such as the *Aṭṭhasālinī* and the *Abhidharmakośa.* Since sexual change is discussed both as a symbol and as an actual situation requiring legal statutes and philosophical analysis, it is necessary to investigate the concept and process of sexual change in these three types of texts.

First, a literal interpretation of sexual change as a physiological process will be analyzed before investigating the legal and symbolic aspects of sexual change. The early Buddhist text *Aṭṭhasālinī* claimed that sexuality first occurs at the moment of conception.[9] Sexuality appears as a primary organ or "power"[10] which is conditioned by past actions or karma. The secondary sexual characteristics,[11] which are controlled by the sexual power, consisted of physical traits (genitalia, hair, and breasts) and behavioral traits (walking, sitting, and daily tasks) which appeared during birth and childhood. These physiological characteristics and behavioral patterns were ineluctably entwined; choosing dolls as toys, for example, was part of a female's physiological composition. Sexuality was both mental, as the power conditioned by past actions and intentions, and physical, as indicated by the secondary traits of genitalia, breasts, and other characteristic features. According to the *Aṭṭhasālinī* "the features of men and women are perceived both by the eye and the mind."[12] The sexual power was unchangeable, but the secondary sexual characteristics were subject to change.

The *Abhidharmakośa,* a late fourth-century Sarvāstivādin account of metaphysics, states that the sexual powers or organs of masculinity and femininity may lead to either disequilibrium and delusion or to liberation and purification through control and desirelessness.[13] If one controls the sexual power or organ, the secondary characteristics, particularly the genitalia, would cease to function.

The relationship of the masculine sexual power to the feminine sexual power is not consistently treated in the *Abhidharmakośa.* Some textual passages imply that the feminine sexual power relegated women biologically to weakness of will,[14] preventing women from entering the soteriological path to spiritual growth. A woman's sexuality, her physical body, biologically determines her mental growth as severely limited. Her physical and her psychological structure are incapable of fulfilling the ultimate religious potential as Bodhisattvas. Women were like "soil saturated with salt where one cannot grow either corn or common herbs."[15] Other passages claim women do have the ability to strengthen their will against desires.[16] Weakness of will or inattention to moral precepts is associated with one's sexual power. For example, the state of bisexuality, defined as the possession of both masculine and feminine sexual powers, was considered unfortunate, that is, not conducive to spiritual growth. Because of the excessive sexual power of both masculinity and femininity, the bisexual individual had weakness of will or inattention to moral precepts.[17]

Destruction of the feminine sexual power was believed to change the physical character of future rebirths. Birth as a female was unfortunate while birth as a male was auspicious. No Bodhisattva was subjected to poverty, physical imperfection, or female birth.[18] Abandonment of female birth was considered necessary for advanced spiritual attainment. Women who mastered the supreme spiritual qualities (dharmas), cultivated in one of the four penetrations of meditation, were said to be both male and female in body.[19] The actual body in which the women meditated was female (because of past karma), but the destined body in the next life was male because of present karma. Stated in another way, this might suggest that the Buddhist believed that the achievement of wisdom affects physiological and behavioral patterns. When the social roles are reversed, intelligence and physiology change. If a man acquired these same spiritual qualities, he was not destined to both a masculine and feminine body since these spiritual qualities had already destroyed the female sexual power. His female sexual power had been destroyed by past good karma during a previous lifetime. The implication is that the physical and mental character of the female sexual power could be changed through the practice of meditation. Destruction of the female sexual power and cessation of rebirth as a woman were requirements for spiritual advancement. In summary, the sexual power of the individual controlled one's ability to attain spiritual growth. Destruction of the female power through meditation, followed by the destruction of male sexual power, caused the cessation of rebirth as a woman to be followed by the cessation of rebirth as a man.

The corpus of disciplinary rules and precepts *(Vinaya Piṭaka)* by which the religious community was governed, is the second type of literature to mention sexual change. Rules and precepts of community life in the religious orders necessarily had to consider the sexual differences, real or perceived, of the members of the community. For example, the establishment of the nuns' discipline reflected the traditional subordination of women in society, as described in Chapter 3. Moreover, the nuns' disciplinary rules reinforced the attitude that women were more passionate than men. By requiring an additional probationary period for nuns, which was not required for monks, the assumption was that women had greater passion, demanding a longer period of discipline to eliminate that passion. An alternative explanation for the longer period of probation was that an appropriate period must be allowed for a woman to ascertain whether she was pregnant.[20] Potential conflicts between maternal duties and the duties of a nun were thus avoided by this requirement.

These community rules and regulations considered not only existing sex differences but also situations of sex changes. The book of disciplinary rules *(Vinaya Piṭaka)* describes a monk who undergoes a sexual change of genitalia (liṅga), requiring his removal from the community of monks to the community of nuns.[21] No explanation for the cause of the sexual change is given. Another case, cited in the same text, mentions the sexual change of a nun into a monk. Rules of the religious community were to be observed according to the most current sexual character of the individual member. When sexual changes occurred, changes in the prescribed rules and regulations followed. Disciplinary laws were written to take into consideration the various situations, including sexual change and intercourse with hermaphrodites, which community members could encounter. As a result it is possible to speculate that sexual transformations were considered as possible situations needing an explicit statement of legal and administrative policy.

Descriptions of sexual changes in metaphysical treatises, such as the *Aṭṭhasālinī* and the *Abhidharmakośa* and in legal accounts such as the *Vinaya,* are not as numerous as are accounts of sexual change as a literary theme found in sutra literature. In Hindu literature sexual transformation symbolized the transition between cycles of sexuality (feminine image) and asceticism (masculine image).[22] In Buddhist literature the theme of sexual transformation serves a somewhat different function. In a similar way to the Hindu motif of sexual change as a transition from sexuality to asceticism, the Buddhist motif suggests a transition from sensuality to meditation. The Buddhist considered the body itself as imperfect and degenerate, whether in ascetic or erotic engagement.[23] The body indicated imperfection and immorality, as indicated in the *Agañña-suttanta.* Corporeality, when associated with the feminine, suggested a more potent image for the antithesis of perfection. Since the feminine represented the deceptive and destructive temptress or "daughter of evil," the feminine body represented imperfection, weakness, ugliness,[24] and impurity. Transformation of sex represented a transition from the imperfection and immorality of human beings (the female body) to the mental perfection of Bodhisattvas and Buddhas (the male body). Maleness was an image for the perfection of the mind. The transformation symbolized a mental change in attitude from a sensual state of attachment to a desireless state of enlightenment.

According to the *The Sutra on Changing the Female Sex (Fo shuo chüan nü shen ching):*

> If women can accomplish one thing [Dharma], they will be freed of the female body and become sons. What is that one thing? The profound state of mind which seeks enlightenment. Why? If women awaken to the thought of enlightenment, then they will have the great and good person's state of mind, a man's state of mind, a sage's state of mind. . . . If women

> awaken to the thought of enlightenment, then they will not be bound to the limitation of a woman's state of mind. Because they will not be limited, they will forever separate from the female sex and become sons.[25]

The male state of mind, that is, the Bodhisattva and Buddha state of mind, understands the teaching of Emptiness. The transformation from female to male symbolized the state of transition from ignorance to the Perfection of Wisdom which is Emptiness. Perfection of Wisdom is the supreme wisdom of the Bodhisattvas that apprehends all phenomena as equal by virtue of their Emptiness. The basic force behind the Bodhisattva practice is the ability to perceive all sentient beings as equal, having no discriminating or distinguishing marks. As a result of the Perfection of Wisdom, the Bodhisattva can command the universe because of that wisdom.

The association of the Perfection of Wisdom with the sexual transformation is mentioned in the chapter, "The Goddess of the Ganges," from *The Sutra of the Perfection of Wisdom in Eight Thousand Verses,* translated below. The sexual change of the goddess is associated with her understanding of the teaching of Emptiness, the Perfection of Wisdom. Because of that understanding, she experiences sexual change, rebirth as a male in her next lifetime.

Later texts, however, mention sexual changes within one lifetime and associate that sexual transformation process with an act or rite of truth which could be enacted only when one's religious duties had been perfectly performed. At that time one was believed to control the universe through the performance of an act or rite of truth.[26] On a popular level the act or rite of truth had the force of a magical formula that could produce supernormal wonders such as sexual change, flowers from heaven, and healing the sick. The efficacy of the rite of truth to produce these changes of a miraculous nature was believed to reside in the performer or speaker of the truth act. The performer is the deity, the invoker of cosmic power. As a formalized act, which is often witnessed by the heavens or by a Buddha, the act or rite assumed a sacramental character. The transformation of sex from female to male represented part of that rite. Performance of the rite produced changes in one's spiritual powers, allowing the channeling of all kinds of forces, including one's sexual powers and mental states, to transform from female to male, with or without physiological changes.

In Buddhist sutra literature, the act or rite of truth is associated with the Perfection of Wisdom and the other perfections. When one's religious practice was perfected, the desired sexual change from female to male[27] would necessarily result. For example, a woman who had attained the perfection of giving used an act or rite of truth to change into a man.[28] Sexual change, then, represented a perfection of one's spiritual role. In the case of later Mahāyāna literature, the sexual change occurs when the mind seeks enlightenment through the practice of the Perfection of Wisdom, that is, when one enters the Bodhisattva path.

All of the texts in this chapter depict female Bodhisattvas who undergo some kind of sexual change. "The Goddess of the Ganges," an excerpt from *The Sutra of the Perfection of Wisdom in Eight Thousand Verses,* is from one of the oldest Mahāyāna sutras now extant. The goddess' sexual transformation is predicted by the Buddha for her next rebirth when she will be reborn as a male and will reside in the Buddha land of Akṣobhya. The interpretation of sexuality in this text coincides with that of the *Abhidharmakośa,* in which the female sexual power and the female body must be abandoned in the next rebirth in order to advance spiritually on the path.

In the episode, "The Nāga Princess," the sexual change

is not one of rebirth as a male. The sexual change occurs within one lifetime and is accompanied by an act or rite of truth. The mental transformation from a female, unenlightened state of mind to a male state of "immeasureable wisdom" is prefigured by the perfection of her generosity in giving her jewel and by the princess' act of truth: "If it were possible for me to have magical power, reverend Śāriputra, I would have realized Supreme, Perfect Enlightenment even more quickly [than the Buddha's receiving my jewel], and there would have been no receiver of this jewel." The world then witnesses her sexual change, from female "organ" or "power" to male, appearing as a Bodhisattva and then as a Buddha.

In the later sutras "Questions Concerning the Daughter Sumati" and *The Sutra of the Dialogue of the Girl Candrottarā,* sexual change from female to male is preceded by an eloquent discourse on Emptiness, demonstrating the fact that both Sumati and Candrottarā have practiced the Perfection of Wisdom. "Questions Concerning the Daughter Sumati," a more recent text than the *Perfection of Wisdom* and the *Lotus Sutra,* describes the prerequisites for attaining the Bodhisattva's state of mind. After Sumati explains the constituents of Bodhisattva practice, she makes an act or rite of truth to demonstrate that she fully understands the requirements for Bodhisattvahood, has the state of mind to seek enlightenment, and wishes to profess the Bodhisattva vows: "If I profess these vows truly and without error, I will be able to practice them to perfection. I vow that the three thousand great world systems will quake in six ways; a heavenly rain of miraculous flowers will fall, and divine musical instruments will ring forth." After these wondrous events occur, Sumati again proclaims a truth act after proclaiming the teaching of Emptiness: "If my words are not false, then this great assembly will be golden in color and my female body will change into a male's, that of a thirty-year-old monk who knows the

Dharma." The heavens witness her transformation, and the gods proclaim she will become a Buddha. The Buddha then predicts Sumati's enlightenment and her name when she becomes a Buddha.

The Sutra of the Dialogue of the Girl Candrottarā, like "Questions Concerning the Daughter Sumati," also incorporates many miraculous events in the narrative of the girl's path to Bodhisattvahood. After seeing Mañjuśrī, the Bodhisattva of wisdom, Candrottarā discourses on Emptiness after Mañjuśrī asks her why she did not change her sex. Candrottarā answers that the nature of Emptiness cannot be changed or altered, so how could a woman change her sex. After professing her Bodhisattva vows, she receives the prediction to Buddhahood and transforms her sex, from a female body to that of a young male.

The older texts, *The Sutra of the Perfection of Wisdom in Eight Thousand Verses* and the *Lotus Sutra,* mention a sexual change, either after rebirth or after an act of truth, when the goddess and princess, respectively, have already made the mental resolution to seek enlightenment, have professed their Bodhisattva vows, and have received the prediction to Buddhahood. In the more recent *Dialogue of the Girl Candrottarā,* this order of events is retained. However, the "Questions Concerning the Daughter Sumati" changes the ordering of the sequence. She receives the prediction to Buddhahood only *after* performing the act of truth and changing her sex. Changing one's sex becomes a prerequisite for receiving a prediction of Buddhahood. This may indicate that an advanced spiritual state of mind, a transformed state from female to male, is essential to receiving a prediction. The prediction of Buddhahood would then become a feature of more advanced Bodhisattva practice. This change in status of receiving the prediction would thus require a more advanced stage of spiritual development, symbolized as a transformation from female to male, as a prerequisite.

In Chapter 6 the interpretation of sexual change will be discussed in the context of sutras depicting female Bodhisattvas who claim the notion of sexual change is contrary to the teachings of Emptiness and who, consequently, refuse to undergo sexual changes.

A. Introduction to "The Goddess of the Ganges" from *The Sutra of the Perfection of Wisdom in Eight Thousand Verses*

Because of the Bodhisattva's pervasive commitment to save all living beings, regardless of their environment or temperament, the Bodhisattva must be truly courageous to face all future ordeals and hardships. Consequently, the Bodhisattva is described as an undaunted, fearless personality who is willing to confront all dangers in order to perform acts of compassion for others. With regard to the intrepid character of this religious hero or heroine, spiritual powers or martial arts are attributed to the Bodhisattva, often suggesting a soldier or warrior in imagery. The female Bodhisattva's imagery is not described in martial overtones. However, if she is to be an advanced Bodhisattva, the implication in many texts is that she must have the spiritual martial arts which are associated with male personalities. The warriorlike symbolism of the Bodhisattva, generally being incompatible with feminine imagery, may have contributed to the depiction of the advanced stages of the spiritual life of the Bodhisattva as exclusively male in many Mahāyāna texts.

In the following selection, the goddess of the Ganges River asserts her dauntless nature in front of an assembly of Buddhist disciples. The Buddha acknowledges her assertion with obvious pleasure and predicts her future Buddhahood, indicating that she is a beginning Bodhisattva. However, in accordance with the archaic tradition of forbidding women in the Buddha lands, the goddess must wait for her next lifetime when she will be reborn as a male and permitted to enter the Buddha land. As a Buddha, the former goddess will reside in a land without any of the usual fear-instilling circumstances such as beasts of prey, thieves, disease, and famine. As a woman, the implicit assumption is that she cannot, in her usual societal roles, overcome the impending fears of daily existence as the man can or is expected to be able to overcome. Additionally, in literature analyzed in Chapter 1, the woman was a source of fear as a daughter of evil with remarkably virulent powers. As an agent of evil, woman is strong and powerful, but as a potential Bodhisattva who works for the well-being of living beings in society, a woman needs to have the fearlessness of a man.

In the following account, the woman is acknowledged to be fearless by the Buddha and subsequently receives a prediction of her Buddhahood. Nevertheless, she must wait for rebirth as a male in order to be an agent who constantly overcomes the fears of daily life.

"The Goddess of the Ganges"* ("Gaṅgādevībhāginī") from *The Sutra of the Perfection of Wisdom in Eight Thousand Verses (Aṣṭasāhásrikāprajñāpāramitā-sūtram),* Chapter 19. Sanskrit text in Vaidya.

[P. 180, line 21, to p. 182, line 14:]

Then, a woman joined the assembly and sat down. Rising from her seat, she adjusted the upper part of her robe to her shoulder, circumambulated the lord, folding her hands and spoke: "Lord, I will not be afraid of such a place. No, I will not be frightened. Without fear, I will teach the Dharma to all beings."

At that very instant, I smiled beaming. Radiating light upon the endless, limitless world spheres, even to Brahma's world, the smile then returned and circumambulated me three times, disappearing into my head.

Immediately after I smiled, the woman gathered golden flowers and scattered me with them. Free-standing, these golden flowers were sustained in space.

Then Ānanda, rising from his seat, adjusted the upper part of his robe to his shoulder, circumambulated me, folding his hands, and spoke: "Why did you smile, lord? The Tathāgata, Arhat, Perfectly Enlightened One does not smile without a reason."

[I replied:] "Ānanda, in the future this goddess of the Ganges will be the Tathāgata named Golden Flower [Suvarṇapuṣpa], the Tathāgata, Arhat, Perfectly Enlightened One, endowed with knowledge and practice, the Sugata, Knower of the world, Trainer of men, Teacher of both gods and men, the Buddha, the lord. That Buddha will

*This English translation is by Diana Paul.

appear in the world during the starlike era and will realize Supreme, Perfect Enlightenment. This goddess of the Ganges, Ānanda, after her death, will change her sex from female to male and be born in the Buddha land called Delight [Abhirati], which belongs to the Buddha Akṣobhya. Then, he will observe the practice of holiness in the presence of Akṣobhya.

"When he has died, he will go from one Buddha land to another, without ever separating from the sight of the Tathāgata. He will go from here to there, from one Buddha land to another, without ever separating from the Buddhas, the lords. Ānanda, in the case of an emperor, he goes from palace to palace during his lifetime, yet the soles of his feet never touch the ground. Until and including his death, his feet never touch the ground. Ānanda, in the same way this goddess of the Ganges will go from Buddha land [to Buddha land], without ever separating from the Buddhas, the lords, until she realizes the Supreme, Perfect Enlightenment."

Ānanda [spoke]: "Those Bodhisattvas, the great beings, who will be in the presence of the Tathāgata Akṣobhya, should be recognized as the assembly of the Tathāgata."

Then knowing that my own train of thought was identical to Ānanda's, I spoke to him: "Yes, you are correct, Ānanda. Those Bodhisattvas, the great beings, who have crossed over the quagmire [of immorality] observe the practice of holiness in the Buddha land of Akṣobhya, the Tathāgata, Arhat, Perfectly Enlightened One. They should be recognized as having approached the culmination of enlightenment. Moreover, Ānanda, Buddha Golden Flower's assembly of disciples will be unlimited. Why? Because his disciples are so many they cannot be counted. They amount to such a high number they are 'immeasurable,' 'numberless.' Ānanda, at that time, in that Buddha land, there will be no wastelands inhabited by beasts of prey or by thieves, no deserts, no disease, no famine.

These and all other such offensive wastelands will absolutely neither exist nor be perceived at any time. So Ānanda, when the Tathāgata Golden Flower has realized the Supreme, Perfect Enlightenment, then such wastelands which instill fear and horror will absolutely neither exist nor be perceived at any time."

Ānanda [asked]: "Lord, in which Tathāgata's presence did the goddess of the Ganges nurture virtuous habits to cause the first awakening to the thought which leads to the Supreme, Perfect Enlightenment?"

[I replied:] "Ānanda, in Dīpaṅkara's presence the goddess of the Ganges nurtured virtuous habits to cause the first awakening to the thought which leads to the Supreme, Perfect Enlightenment. The Tathāgata Dīpaṅkara was strewn with golden flowers by her, when she desired Supreme, Perfect Enlightenment.

"When I had scattered the five lotuses over the Buddha Dīpaṅkara, I obtained the patience to understand nonarising phenomena. Then Dīpaṅkara predicted my Supreme, Perfect Enlightenment: 'In the future, young man, you will be endowed with knowledge and practice, the Sugata, knower of the world, trainer of men, teacher of both gods and men, the Buddha, the lord.' "

When this goddess heard the prediction, she thought to herself: "Oh, I should certainly have a prediction for the Supreme, Perfect Enlightenment like that young man." So Ānanda, in the presence of Dīpaṅkara, the goddess nurtured virtuous habits to cause the first awakening to the thought which leads to Supreme, Perfect Enlightenment.

[Then] Ānanda [spoke]: "Lord, this goddess of the Ganges who has received the prediction of Supreme, Perfect Enlightenment has certainly been well prepared and is accomplished."

B. Introduction to "The Nāga Princess" from the *Lotus Sutra*

The description of the good daughter and good friend in Chapter 4 was based, in part, upon selections from the *Lotus Sutra.* A woman's capabilities as a teacher and spiritual friend were recognized in accordance with the teaching of universal salvation.

The following selection depicts the realization of Bodhisattvahood by an eight-year-old princess who is a Nāga, a species of serpentlike beings with human faces but having lower extremities resembling a snake. Nāgas were believed to inhabit aquatic paradises, namely, the depths of rivers, lakes, and oceans, residing in luxurious aquatic palaces. Not only were they the guardians of all the treasures of the seas, these serpentlike beings were also the protectors of the source of life, symbolized by the waters in which they resided and by their self-rejuvenation, illustrated in the shedding and replacement of the skin of a snake. They were viewed ambivalently as equally destructive and beneficial but always as mysterious and alluring. According to tradition, the Nāgas were entrusted with the Buddha's most precious teaching, the *Prajñāpāramitā.*

The Nāga princesses were especially renowned for their beauty, wit, and charm and were claimed to be the female ancestors of some South Indian dynasties. They were delicate water-sprite creatures similar to mermaids. It was considered the highest compliment to say that one had the beauty of a Nāga princess.[29] Love stories between human heroes and Nāga maidens are common folklore[30] and are also included in Buddhist literature.[31]

The most well-known episode concerning a Nāga princess is found in the *Lotus Sutra,* in the chapter "The Appearance of a Stūpa." (I have entitled the extracted selection "The Nāga Princess.") When asked by the Bodhisattva

Prajñākūṭa if anyone were capable of truly understanding the *Lotus Sutra* and realizing Supreme, Perfect Enlightenment, the Bodhisattva Mañjuśrī, who was known for his great wisdom, responded that an eight-year-old princess of the Nāga king Sāgara was astoundingly intelligent and could comprehend the most abstruse and esoteric teachings. In addition, she was endowed with compassion and every other conceivable virtue as well as disarming beauty.

Appearing before the Buddha Śākyamuni to profess her faith, the Nāga princess is reminded by the haughty Śāriputra that "even a woman who does not falter in diligence for many thousands of eons, completely fulfilling the six perfections still does not realize Buddhahood." Women were believed to be unable to attain the five kinds of high status of Brahmā, Indra, a great king, an emperor, or an irreversible Bodhisattva.

Each Nāga princess was believed to carry a priceless jewel on her head which male Nāgas did not possess. Therefore, the female Nāga's jewel was associated with her sex. In the following episode, the Nāga princess offers her jewel to the Buddha as a sign of her commitment to the Buddha's teaching, giving up her female sex to become a male. Appearing first as a Bodhisattva and then as a Buddha with his thirty-two marks, the former Nāga princess was paid homage by all beings. Prajñākūṭa and Śāriputra were silenced.

In the following episode the transformation of sex from female to male is a prerequisite for the Nāga princess' entrance to the path of Bodhisattvahood, presumably at the irreversible stage (because of the five kinds of status excluding females). The final result for the Nāga princess is that, because of her exceptional spiritual qualities as a female, she can attain the highest level of spiritual development within the lifetime which she began in a female form. The sexual change also encompasses mental attitudes. Being a male in mental attitude meant being unattached to sexuality and having responsibility over one's actions whereas being a female in Indian society did not entail such detachment and personal responsibility, as illustrated by the following account of Gopikā's sexual change:

> There was, at Kapilavatthu, a daughter of the Śākyans named Gopikā, who trusted in the Buddha, the Dhamma, and the Order, and who fulfilled the precepts. She, having abandoned a woman's thoughts and cultivated the thoughts of a man, was, at the dissolution of the body after her death, reborn to a pleasant life, into the communion of the three-and-thirty gods, into sonship with us. And they knew her as "Gopaka of the sons of the gods."[32]

The princess in the following story also "abandons her woman thoughts" in order to practice the Bodhisattva course and become a Buddha.

"The Nāga Princess"* from the *Lotus Sutra (Saddharmapuṇḍarīkā-sūtram)*. Sanskrit text in Wogihara and Tsuchida.

[From Chapter 11: "The Appearance of a Stūpa" ("Stūpasaṃdarśana-parivartaḥ"), p. 225, line 17, to p. 226, line 11:]

Mañjuśrī: "In the sea I have proclaimed nothing but the *Lotus Sutra.*"

Prajñākūṭa: "This sutra which is profound, subtle, and abstruse has no equal. Is there any living being who is

*This English translation is by Diana Paul.

thoroughly capable of understanding this jewel of a sutra and of realizing Supreme, Perfect Enlightenment?"

Mañjuśrī: "Yes, good son, there is the eight-year-old daughter of Sāgara, the Nāga king. She is very wise and acutely perceptive, acting physically, mentally, and verbally with deliberation. Having comprehended the generic and specific meanings of all the Tathāgata's teachings, she has understood the incantations and the thousand meditations and reflections of all beings and things instantly. Without wavering from the thought of enlightenment, she professes extensive vows, loves all other beings as herself, and is outstanding in all virtues, lacking in none. Endowed with perfectly exquisite beauty, with a smiling face and a loving heart, she speaks compassionately. She is capable of realizing Supreme, Perfect Enlightenment."

Prajñākūṭa: "I have seen Lord Śākyamuni, the Tathāgata, while striving for enlightenment, perform many meritorious acts as a Bodhisattva for many thousands of eras without ever faltering in his diligence. In the three thousand million world systems, there is not even one spot on earth the size of a mustard seed where his body has not been relinquished for the welfare of living beings. Later he realized enlightenment. So, who can believe that she is able to realize Supreme, Perfect Enlightenment instantly?"

Then, at that instant the daughter of Sāgara the Nāga king appeared before them. Having prostrated herself at Buddha's feet, she stood and recited these verses:

"Your body, adorned with the thirty-two marks,
Is truly holy and inexhaustible, permeating all directions.
Having the [eighty] ancillary marks and receiving homage from all beings,
You are accessible to all living beings like a marketplace which is nearby.
The Tathāgata here is my witness. Because I wish enlightenment,

I will extensively teach the Dharma which liberates from suffering."

At that moment, the venerable Śāriputra spoke to the daughter of Sāgara, the Nāga king: "Good daughter, you have certainly not wavered in awakening to the thought of enlightenment and have immeasurable wisdom. However, the state of Supreme, Perfect Enlightenment is difficult to realize. Good daughter, even a woman who does not falter in diligence for many hundreds of eras and performs meritorious acts for many thousands of eras, completely fulfilling the six perfections still does not realize Buddhahood. Why? Because a woman still does not realize five types of status. What are the five types? (1) The status of Brahma, (2) the status of Śakra (Indra), (3) the status of a great king, (4) the status of an emperor, and (5) the status of an irreversible Bodhisattva."

At that time the daughter of the Nāga king Sāgara owned one jewel which outvalued the entire three thousand million world systems. She gave this jewel to the lord who compassionately received it. Then King Sāgara's daughter spoke to the Bodhisattva Prajñākūṭa and the Elder Śāriputra: "This jewel which I gave to the lord was quickly received, wasn't it?" The Elder spoke: "Yes, you quickly gave it to the lord and he quickly received it."

The girl spoke: "If it were possible for me to have magical power, reverend Śāriputra, I would have realized Supreme, Perfect Enlightenment even more quickly [than the Buddha's receiving the jewel], and there would have been no receiver of this jewel."

Then, at that instant in time, before the Elder Śāriputra and the entire world, king Sāgara's daughter's female organs vanished, and the male organ became visible. She appeared as a Bodhisattva. At that instant in time, he walked toward the south; sitting at the foot of the Bodhi tree made of seven jewels in the world system Vimalā [immaculate], he appeared as an enlightened one. Radiating a form having the thirty-two marks and all ancillary marks, permeating all directions, he began teaching the Dharma. On the earth, all beings saw the Tathāgata and all the gods and semidivine beings like the Nāgas, Gandharvas, . . . and nonhuman and human beings paid homage to him while he taught the Dharma. All who listened to the Tathāgata's teaching of the Dharma did not retrogress and realized the Supreme, Perfect Enlightenment. The world system Vimalā and the earth quaked through six stages of change. Three thousand beings in Śākyamuni's assembly attained patience in understanding nonarising phenomena. Three hundred thousand attained the prediction of Supreme, Perfect Enlightenment.

Then the Bodhisattva Prajñākūṭa and the Elder Śāriputra were silent.

C. Introduction to *The Sutra of the Dialogue of the Girl Candrottarā*

The Sutra of the Dialogue of the Girl Candrottarā was probably composed about the third or fourth century A.D., about the same time as the sequel to *The Sutra of the Teaching of Vimalakīrti,* which is known as *The Sutra of the King Who Was Annointed on the Head (Ting-wang ching* or *Kuan-ting-wang ching).*[33] The Chinese translation of the *Candrottarā* was undertaken by Jñānagupta of Sui, a North Indian monk from Gandhara, and by the Chinese monk Chih-te in 591. The Tibetan translation was begun in the ninth century by Jinamitra.

The text is mainly in prose with several long sections of verse. The *Candrottarā* has few discourses on Mahāyāna teachings, focusing instead on a series of dialogues between Candrottarā, Śāriputra, and various Bodhisattvas, not all of which have been translated below in their entirety. A noteworthy feature in the *Candrottarā* is the portrayal of Vimalakīrti as a rather weak individual who is afraid of threats from other men. In *The Sutra of the Teaching of Vimalakīrti (Vimalakīrtinirdeśa)* (see Chapter 6), on the other hand, Vimalkīrti is an immensely powerful Bodhisattva of unmitigated energy, who devastates the arguments of the monk Śāriputra. In *Candrottarā,* ("On top of the moon") Vimalakīrti's daughter, who is named Candrottarā, in an apparent reversal of roles with the Vimalakīrti of *The Sutra of the Teaching of Vimalakīrti,* has the same eloquence and incisive wisdom with regard to the Dharma as her father. The *Candrottarā* may be viewed as a sequel to the *Vimalakīrtinirdeśa.*

The opening scene is in a large grove in Vaiśālī where the Buddha is residing with a contingent of monks, Arhats, and Bodhisattvas. An immensely wealthy householder of the Licchavī clan named Vimalakīrti and his exceptionally beautiful and charming wife Vimalā had a daughter who was exquisite in form. Before her birth, they had awakened to the thought of enlightenment in the presence of the Buddha Kāśyapa. When their daughter was born, there was an intensely brilliant light which radiated everywhere. The earth trembled and flowers fell from heaven. Because whatever touched her body would shine brilliantly, her parents called her Candrottarā.

After she had barely been born, she grew to the height of an eight-year-old. Everywhere she walked, the earth would glisten, and perfume would pervade the air. The sons of the Kṣatriyan king and those of many Brahman noblemen had heard about this incomparable girl Candrottarā and passionately desired her as their wife. Promising jewels and magnificent gifts for her and threats of violence if rejected, these young men terrified Vimalakīrti.

Seeing her father crying, Candrottarā recited the following verses:

"Exhausting themselves pursuing me
In the end they cannot hurt me.
Compassion is not deflected by poisonous rods.
Water and fire also are ineffectual.

Do not fear the pangs of death
Nor those who curse you.
The compassionate are resolute and do not hate
Nor do they fear others.

I have compassionate thoughts
Of protecting the world as my own life.
I do not cause another's pain
So who can harm me?

Desireless, I have no thoughts of desire.
I am compassionate without hate or jealousy.
I have no desire to hate or for foolishness.
So no one can harm me.

I see all living beings
As if they were my parents.
For only the world's compassionate
Will never be deceived by others.

As if the sky could sink in the earth
Or Mt. Sumeru enter a mustard seed
Or cow hoof prints in the four seas
So nothing can befall me."

She consoles her parents and asks them to bear with her. Candrottarā then announces at the crossroads to Vaiśālī that she will choose a husband within seven days. In the interim she has a visit from one of the Buddha's messengers after she had promised to observe the moral precepts for the laity. She desires to learn about the Buddha's teaching and flies through the air to meet the Buddha in Vaiśālī. In the presence of the Buddha and various

Bodhisattvas she eloquently explains the most profound dimensions of the Dharma and presents a brief statement about the irrelevance of sexual transformation from the perspective of viewing the world as Empty.

Receiving the prediction that she will become a Buddha, Candrottarā, nevertheless, changes her sex, in spite of the discourse she has just delivered, perhaps as a concession to the fact that rejection of marriage in society at that time was virtually impossible for a woman unless she entered the religious order of nuns. Restrictions upon a woman because of family responsibilities to marry and to become the mother of sons resulted in restrictions upon a woman's religious roles. Candrottarā changes into a male to avoid these restrictions.

The Sutra of the Dialogue of the Girl Candrottarā (Candrottarādārikāvyākaraṇa-sūtram).* T. v. 14, n. 480, pp. 615–23.

[T. v. 14, n. 480, p. 617 a 13–23:]

Six days afterward, on the fifteenth day when the moon was full, Candrottarā accepted the eight precepts [for Buddhist laymen and laywomen]. That night a bright light glowed in the tower chamber [where she was staying] and passed by. Because of the Buddha's sustaining powers, suddenly a single lotus appeared in her right hand. The stalk was gold and the petals were silver white. The stamen was of cat's eye and the anther was emerald. In this flower there was a statue of the Tathāgata sitting in a full lotus position and reflecting its golden color. Its immense brilliance illuminated the tower. This statue had the thirty-two

*This first English translation is by Diana Paul.

marks of the great person and the eighty majestic physical attributes. The rays of light emitted from this statue of the Tathāgata illuminated the entire interior of Candrottarā's house. After having seen this flower suddenly appear in her own hand, Candrottarā looked reverentially at the statue of the Tathāgata and rejoiced, completely ecstatic with regard to its incomparable form. . . .

[After Candrottarā praises the beauty of the statue and the virtues of the Tathāgata, the statue speaks to her and explains that he is a messenger of Śākyamuni and describes the attributes of a Buddha. Candrottarā then yearns to see the Buddha and goes to her parents, grasping the lotus and the image of the Buddha. On the seventh day a great crowd gathers, and the young men start clamoring for Candrottarā. She suddenly flies into the air and proclaims that those who have desires cannot be liberated.]

[T. v. 14, n. 480, p. 618 c 27 to p. 619 a 7:]

Then, after she had finished reciting these verses the earth quaked. In the sky there were countless gods who raised their voices shouting, dancing, and singing unlimited and countless tunes. Hundreds and thousands of flowers rained from heaven. The music produced was entirely inexpressible.

After the great crowd had listened, they immediately turned away from thoughts of desire to thoughts which were extraordinary and marvelous [concerning the Dharma]. Then even to the ends of their body hair there was no thought of desire, no hatred, no hostility, no greed, no delusion, no anger, no jealousy, no envy, no contentiousness. Nor was there any defilement or other anguish. All of them were suffused with joy. Each individual hoped his parents, brothers and sisters, and superiors would give up all defilements. Then each prostrated themselves before Candrottarā.

[Candrottarā decides to seek the Buddha, traversing

through the sky to Vaiśālī, where the Buddha and five hundred monks are staying. Because the earth quaked wherever she placed her feet, the crowd of eighty-four thousand could follow Candrottarā's tracks. En route, she discusses with Śāriputra the teaching that all phenomena are nondiscriminative and ineffable. In the presence of the Buddha Candrottarā engages in a dialogue with Mañjuśrī.]

[T. v. 14, n. 480, p. 620 b. 1–c 8:]

Then the youth Mañjuśrī spoke to Candrottarā: "In the past where did you relinquish your body to be born here? When you relinquish this body where will you be born?"

Candrottarā: "Mañjuśrī, why do you think in such a way? I am holding a statue of the Tathāgata seated in a lotus. Where did this relinquish its body to be born here? Now, if it should relinquish this body, where will it be reborn?"

Mañjuśrī: "This [statue] is fabricated. When something is said to be fabricated, there is neither a place to relinquish its body nor afterwards is there birth."

Candrottarā: "Yes, Mañjuśrī, so it is. All phenomena, in their essential nature, are fabricated. I do not see when these phenomena are to be relinquished nor when they arise."

Then the Bodhisattva Amoghadarśana[34] spoke to Candrottarā: "Candrottarā, one cannot become a Buddha while being a female. Why don't you change your female sex now?"

Candrottarā: "Good son, the nature of Emptiness cannot be changed or altered. This is also true for all phenomena. [Consequently] how could I change my woman's body?"

Then the Bodhisattva Dharaṇīmdhara[35] spoke to Candrottarā: "Have you unequivocably seen the Tathāgata?"

Candrottarā: "Good son, I see the Tathāgata as if he

were the fabricated Buddha [statue] in my hand for the Tathāgata is no different from this [statue]."

Then the Bodhisattva Pratibhānakūṭa[36] asked Candrottarā: "Have you presently discussed the meaning of the Dharma?"

Candrottarā: "Good son, the nature of the Dharma realm is ineffable, and abstraction through language cannot express it."

Then the Bodhisattva Pratisamvit[37] asked Candrottarā: "In the past, when you were at the Buddha's place of residence, what kind of teaching did you learn?"

Candrottarā: "Good son, now look up to the sky. The Tathāgata's teaching of the Dharma is equal to this sky and not different from it. Those who listen to him are also like that [sky]. Good son, the attributes of the Dharma are like the sky, being without difference or distinction."

Then the Bodhisattva Ākāśagarbha[38] spoke to Candrottarā: "In the past, in a place given to the Buddhas, why did you give [to others] and why did you transfer merits?"

Candrottarā: "Good son, I gave to the Buddha and Saṃgha in this statue of the Buddha which is fabricated. How are there virtuous actions to attain?"

Ākāśagarbha: "But this Buddha is fabricated. In giving to it there is no attribute of virtue."

Candrottarā: "Good son, in the past I also was in the Buddha's presence, performing acts of giving and transferring merits. These also produced attributes, and there was transference of merit."

Then the Bodhisattva Prāṇātipātavirati[39] spoke: "Now how can you be equally compassionate toward all living beings?"

Candrottarā: "Good son, because these living beings are equal and without difference."

Prāṇātipātavirati: "Then why do these living beings act in certain ways?"

Candrottarā: "The actions of living beings are neither

past, present, or future, and the compassionate mind is also neither in the past, present or future but is ineffable. Good son, the actions of the compassionate mind also [are timeless and ineffable]."

[After Candrottarā engages in further conversations with the Bodhisattvas, Śāriputra, and Ānanda, she professes her ten Bodhisattva vows, each vow preceded by the miraculous appearance of a lotus. Then the Buddha predicts her imminent Buddahood.]

[T. v. 14, n. 480, p. 623 a 29–c 29:]

When Candrottarā had heard the Buddha give her prediction, she was ecstatic, leaping in the air countless times to the height of seven Tāla trees. Resting on the seventh tree, the girl changed her female body, transforming into a boy. Then the earth quaked. Great sounds rang out and flowers rained down from heaven.

A brilliant light illuminated the world. Then the Bodhisattva Candrottarā, while remaining in the sky, praised the Buddha in verses, saying:

"Today I have the prediction of enlightenment.
The Dharma wheel is turned without distinction
As the lord's teaching of the Dharma.
I have listened for one hundred eons.

My merits are for the eight groups of beings[40]
And for the four groups of religious.[41]
The countless Bodhisattvas
Have no doubts toward you and other Buddhas.

All will be without discrimination,
Because they will definitely be enlightened.
All phenomena are fictitious.
The Buddhas say they are dreams.

Here there is no one nor any support
For 'fate' of living beings or for personality.
The original nature of all phenomena
Is no different from space.

I formerly had a female body.
Having the nature of Emptiness, it was not real.
Its nature was not real but Empty.
The nature of Emptiness is nonsubstantive and incomprehensible.

Contrary views of that body arise from discrimination.
Discrimination is a bird's flight through the air.
Those who desire to be an enlightened Buddha
Desire the hindrance of the four evils.[42]

Those who desire, in the three thousand worlds,
The turning of the profound Dharma wheel
Will intensely awaken to the thought of enlightenment,
Revering and worshipping the lord.

In a short time they will be virtuous,
Being identical and inseparable from the nature of truth.
Virtuous monk and holy man,
At your feet I prostrate myself.

If I give what I love, I always will love.
If I give the Dharma's wealth, I will be free.
The Buddha is the basis for happiness and gives happiness.
He can subdue tyranny and evils.

I praise and should praise such holiness.
I praise those who are free without envy.
The places which I see in my thoughts
Are those of the inconceivable Buddhas.

Shine today, Śākya lion.[43]
I want to know the ten regional Buddhas.
All are identical to knowing the one Dharma.
In Suchness, there is nonduality.

Countless living beings are the true limit.
Those who have this patience will be Buddhas. . . ."

Then, after the boy left home, twelve thousand people attained the Supreme, Perfect Enlightenment. When he taught the foundation of the Dharma according to the Buddha, seventy hosts of gods avoided impurity, manifesting the pure vision among all phenomena. Five hundred monks attained liberation, having minds free from passionate impulses, partaking in the unconditioned. Among two hundred nuns and twenty thousand men, some have not yet attained the Supreme, Perfect Enlightenment. They will awaken to the thought of enlightenment. After the Buddha taught this text, the Bodhisattva Candrottarā, the venerable Ānanda, the assembly of Bodhisattvas, gods, men, Gandharvas, and the rest of the eight kinds of beings joyfully practiced his teaching.

D. Introduction to "Questions Concerning the Daughter Sumati"[44] from *The Collection of Jewels*

The thirtieth tale which is incorporated in *The Collection of Jewels* is "Questions Concerning the Daughter Sumati." This Sumati episode had been translated previously as an independent text first by Dharmarakṣa (265–308) and then by Kumārajīva (402–412). Bodhiruci of T'ang translated the text in 693 and inserted it in *The Collection of Jewels* anthology between 708 and 713.

The episode takes place in Rājagṛha where Sumati, daughter of Ugra,[45] the mayor of the city, asks the Buddha ten questions, reciting them in verse form. The Buddha then proceeds to answer each question, enumerating four conditions necessary for the resolution of each question, totaling forty conditions.[46] Sumati vows to undertake all forty conditions in order to realize the Bodhisattva practice, but the monk Maudgalyāyana is skeptical. In order to demonstrate her commitment, Sumati requests evidence that her vows are true. As a sign of her sincerity, the heavens provide auspicious signs.

Mañjuśrī then questions Sumati and raises the issue as to why she does not transform her female sex. Like *The Sutra of the Dialogue of the Girl Candrottarā,* Sumati denies the existence of any innate female characteristics on the one hand, yet undergoes a sexual transformation into a male, on the other. The necessity of transforming from female to male is retained in this text as a prerequisite for the advanced stages of Bodhisattvahood which will culminate in Buddhahood. The prediction of Buddhahood occurs after the sexual transformation. In contrast with the Nāga princess Jewel Brocade and the goddess in the *Vimalakīrti* sutra who present the argument that sexual transformation, as a form of discrimination, is counterproductive to understanding the nature of Emptiness, Sumati uses the argument that, since all phenomena are void of innate characteristics, sexual transformations are possible and support the teaching that all phenomena are Emptiness.

"Questions Concerning the Daughter Sumati"* ("Sumatidārikāparipṛcchā") from *The Collection of Jewels (Mahāratnakūṭa),* assembly 30. T. v. 11, n. 310, pp. 547–49.

Thus I [Ānanda] have heard [from the Buddha who preached this sermon to me]:

At one time I, the Buddha, was residing on Vulture Peak in Rājagṛha with 1,250 monks and ten thousand Bodhisattvas, those great beings. At that time the mayor of Rājagṛha[47] had a daughter named Sumati, who had just turned eight years old. She was of exceptional beauty, refined, and captivating in form. Those who saw her attributes were exalted. In her past she had been close to the countless Buddhas, paying homage to them and acquiring many good habits.

Then his daughter went to visit me, prostrating herself at my feet, circumambulating me three times, then knelt down and folded her hands to recite the following verse:

"The Supreme, Perfect Enlightenment
Is the illuminating lamp of the world.
I only wish you will listen to me
Concerning the Bodhisattva practice."

I spoke to Sumati: "Now you may ask. I will explain so you will sever the web of doubts." Then Sumati, in my presence, recited the following verses:

"How can one attain the absolutely perfect
Auspicious and blessed body?
Again, what are the causes
For not separating from one's followers?

*This first English translation is by Diana Paul.

How can one experience for oneself
Spontaneous generation[48]
Upon a thousand lotuses
With face uplifted toward you, the lord?

How can one attain
The self-actualizing superpowers,
Omnipresence in innumerable lands,
And reverence to all the Buddhas?

How can one be free from hate
To accept the words of the faithful,
Removing obstacles to the Dharma
And forever parting from bad karma?

How can one, at death,
Have a vision of the Buddhas
And listen to the pure Dharma
Without enduring pain?

Supreme lord of great compassion,
I only wish you will teach me."

Then I spoke to the daughter Sumati: "Excellent! You are able to ask about these profoundly abstract principles. Listen well and pay close attention. For your sake, I will teach you."

Sumati humbly spoke: "Yes, lord, I wish to listen."

I explained: "The Bodhisattvas accomplish four acts to accept an absolutely perfect body. What are the four? (1) They have no hate toward evil associates; (2) they have great compassion; (3) they deeply desire the true Dharma; and (4) they construct images of the Buddha."

Then I recited this verse:

"Hate destroys virtue, preventing its growth.
The compassionate seek the Dharma, making Buddha images.
If one decorates [the image's] body
All living beings will forever see it.

"Next, Sumati, the Bodhisattvas accomplish four acts to attain an auspicious and blessed body. What are the four? (1) On proper occasions, they practice charity; (2) they are not lazy; (3) they rejoice in giving; and (4) they do not seek rewards."

Then I recited this verse:

"On proper occasions they practice charity without laziness.
They rejoice and give without seeking [rewards].
Because of these actions, they will always practice
And be reborn in a wealthy position.

"Next, Sumati, the Bodhisattvas accomplish four acts to attain nonseparation from their followers. What are the four? (1) They abandon divisive language; (2) living beings with erroneous views are made to see correctly; (3) they cause the true Dharma to continue for a long time even though it is on the verge of destruction; and (4) they teach living beings to approach the enlightenment of the Buddha."

Then I recited this verse:

"Abandoning divisive words and erroneous views
They protect the true Dharma on the verge of destruction,
Granting peace to living beings through enlightenment,
They never will part from their followers.

"Next, Sumati, the Bodhisattvas, accomplish four acts to accept spontaneous generation upon lotus seats in front of me. What are the four? (1) They offer lotuses and powdered incense, scattering it on the [statues of the] Tathāgatas and in the stūpas; (2) they will never inflict injury on others; (3) they construct statues of the Tathāgatas resting on a lotus; and (4) they have a deep and pure faith in the enlightenment of the Buddhas."

Then I recited this verse:

"Flowers and incense are scattered on the Buddhas
and in the stūpas.
They do no injury to others but together make statues
They have a deep faith in the enlightenment
And will be born before the Buddhas on lotuses.

"Next, Sumati, the Bodhisattvas accomplish four acts to follow from one Buddha land to another. What are the four? (1) They see others practicing good without the obstacle of defilement; (2) others who teach the Dharma no longer have doubts; (3) they light lamps in reverence to the Tathāgata's stūpa; and (4) in meditation they always practice diligently."

Then I recited this verse:

"Seeing others practicing good and teaching the true
Dharma
Without slander or evil hindrances;
In my stūpa they offer lights
Meditating and roaming in Buddha lands.

"Next, Sumati, the Bodhisattvas accomplish four acts to reside in a world without hate. What are the four? (1) Without flattering, they are close to good friends; (2) they are not jealous of others' accomplishments; (3) when others attain fame they are always happy; and (4) they are never negligent toward the Bodhisattva practice."

Then I recited this verse:

"Without flattering they are close to good friends
And never jealous of others' accomplishments.
When others attain fame they rejoice.
The Bodhisattvas, without slander, have no hate.

"Next, Sumati, the Bodhisattvas accomplish four acts which are said to pertain to the faithful. What are the four? (1) They always respond appropriately in speech and action; (2) they never conceal evil from their good friends; (3) when listening to the Dharma they make no errors; and (4) they bear no malice toward those who teach the Dharma."

Then I recited this verse:

"In speech and action they appropriately respond
Hiding no evil from their good friends.
Listening to scripture they make no human errors
But accept faithfully all the words.

"Next, Sumati, the Bodhisattvas accomplish four acts which enable them to avoid obstacles to the Dharma and to become pure. What are the four? (1) With intense mental resolve, they accept the three disciplines [of morality, meditation, and wisdom]; (2) they listen to the most profound scriptures without abusing them; (3) seeing Bodhisattvas who have recently awakened to the thought [of enlightenment], they experience omniscience; and (4) they are equally compassionate toward all living beings."

Then I recited this verse:

"With intense mental resolve they accept the disciplines
Listening and understanding the most profound scriptures.
They respect the recently awakened mind as if it were mine,
Showing compassion, and thoroughly eliminating all obstacles.

"Next, Sumati, the Bodhisattvas accomplish four acts which enable them to separate from Māra, the Evil One. What are the four? (1) They completely know the equality of nature in all phenomena; (2) they manifest diligence; (3) they always are mindful of me; and (4) all their good merits are transferred [to others]."

Then I recited this verse:

"Knowing the equality of nature in all things
They always are diligent and mindful of me.
Transferring all their good merits,
No evil can affect them.

"Next, Sumati, the Bodhisattvas accomplish four acts which cause them, in time of death, to have [a vision of] the Buddhas before them. What are the four? (1) They satisfy those who seek charity; (2) they have a deep faith in the good Dharma; (3) they pay respect to all the Bodhisattvas; and (4) they pay homage to the three jewels [that is, Buddha, Dharma, and Saṃgha]."

Then I recited this verse:

"Those who seek [charity] are satisfied.
They have faith in the profound and give up vanities.
They pay homage to the three jewels, the field of merit
And, at death, have the Buddha before them."

Then, the daughter Sumati, after having listened to what I had taught, humbly spoke to me: "I will practice according to what the Buddhas have taught about the Bodhisattva practice. Lord, if I omit and fail to carry out even one of the practices among the forty, then I have transgressed against your teaching and have deceived you."

Then the venerable Elder Maudgalyāyana spoke to Sumati: "The Bodhisattva practice is extremely difficult to practice. You must now profess the most excellent of vows. Wouldn't you, by these vows, attain self-actualization?"

Then Sumati spoke to me: "If I profess these vows truly and without error, I will be able to practice them to perfection. I vow that the three thousand great world systems will quake in six ways, a heavenly rain of miraculous flowers will fall, and divine musical instruments will ring forth."

When she had said this, flowers rained forth from heaven and divine instruments rang out. The three thousand great world systems quaked in six ways.

At this time Sumati very deferentially spoke to Maudgalyāyana: "According to my true words in the future I will become a Buddha. Like the present Tathāgata, Śākyamuni, in my land there will also be no evil, evil destinies, or the name of woman. If my speech is not false, then the assembly will have bodies which are golden in color." After she had spoken these words, the assembly all turned golden in color. Then, Maudgalyāyana rose from his seat, bared part of his right shoulder, and prostrated himself at my feet. He humbly spoke to me: "I have, for the first time today, paid respect to the Bodhisattvas who have just awakened to the thought of enlightenment and to the entire assembly of Bodhisattvas, those great beings."

Then Mañjuśrī, the Dharma Prince, spoke to Sumati: "In what Dharma do you reside, professing these vows?"

Sumati: "Mañjuśrī, that cannot be asked. Why? Because there is no residence in the Dharma realm."

Mañjuśrī: "How can one say there is enlightenment?"

Sumati: "Because nondiscrimination of phenomena is enlightenment.' Mañjuśrī: "How can one say there are Bodhisattvas?"

Sumati: "Because all phenomena are equal to space [that is, Empty], there are Bodhisattvas."

Mañjuśrī: "How can one say there is the practice to enlightenment?"

Sumati: "Because the practice to enlightenment is like a mirage or an echo."

Mañjuśrī: "On what mystery do you base such explanations?"

Sumati: "I do not see mysteries or nonmysteries in even the slightest thing among these."

Mañjuśrī: "If that is the case, then will every ordinary being become enlightened?"

Sumati: "You said there is no difference between the enlightened and the ordinary being. One must not hold that view. Why? Because everything is identical with the one Dharma realm, there is no adhering to or abandoning of anything without destruction."

Mañjuśrī: "How long did it take for you to be able to completely understand this principle?"

Sumati: "Living beings who have no illusions with regard to the boundary of mental phenomena [ideas] and the nonillusory mind can completely understand this principle."

Mañjuśrī: "Since illusion has no basis, how do the mind and mentals exist?"

Sumati: "The Dharma realm also neither exists nor does not exist. The Tathāgata also is the same."

Then Mañjuśrī spoke to me: "Lord, Sumati is exceptional. She is accomplished in the patience [to understand the nonarising] of phenomena."

I responded: "Yes, it is true, as verified by what she has said. In the past this girl awakened to the thought of enlightenment over a period of thirty eras. I have attained the Supreme, Perfect Enlightenment. Like her I have enabled you to abide in the patience to understand the nonarising [of phenomena]."

Then Mañjuśrī arose from his seat and bowed, humbly speaking to Sumati: "In previous numberless eras I worshipped, yet now I cannot say that I am able to approach you [in wisdom]."

Sumati: "Mañjuśrī, now you do not discriminate. Why? Because you are able to be patient in understanding the nonarising of phenomena through nondiscrimination.

Mañjuśrī: "Why don't you transform your woman's body?"

Sumati: "If a woman's innate characteristics are untenable, what is to be transformed?"

"Mañjuśrī, because of you I should now eliminate all my doubts because I have heard the truth. In the future, when I have become Supremely and Perfectly Enlightened, the assembly of monks under my teaching will listen, having renounced their homes to enter the path. In my [Buddha] land, all living beings will have golden bodies. Their clothing and wealth will be like those of the sixth heaven, with an abundance of food according to their needs. There will be no evil actions or destinies. There will not even be the name 'woman.' On seats made of seven jewels there will be jeweled nets and seven-jeweled lotuses with jewel curtains. It will not be different from the adornments in the Pure Land which belongs to you, Mañjuśrī.

"If my words are not false, then this great assembly will be golden in color and my female body will change into a male's, that of a thirty-year-old monk who knows the Dharma."

When these words were uttered, the great assembly turned golden in color, and the Bodhisattva Sumati transformed from a female into a male, that of a thirty-year-old monk who knows the Dharma. Then, all those in the heaven of the gods appeared and said these words: "Excellent! Excellent! When the Bodhisattva, the great being, Sumati attains enlightenment in the future, the pure Buddha land will have virtues like these."

Then I spoke to Mañjuśrī: "The Bodhisattva Sumati, in the future, will be perfectly enlightened. She will be named the Tathāgata 'Jewel Storehouse of the Most Excellent Virtues' and appear in the world."

When the Buddha had taught this sutra, thirty hosts of living beings turned toward the Supreme, Perfect Enlightenment without regressing [from this path]. Eighty hosts of living beings turned from impurity and attained the purity of the Dharma eye. Eight thousand living beings manifested wisdom [prajñā]. Five thousand monks practiced the Bodhisattva vehicle with minds turned away from desire. Because he saw the excellence of the Bodhisattva Sumati's intentions, good habits, and virtues, each individual removed the outer portion of his robe to give to the Tathāgata. Having given these to him, they professed:

"With these good habits, we remain committed to our vows until we attain the Supreme, Perfect Enlightenment." These good sons were turned toward the Supereme, Perfect Enlightenment because of their good habits. Transcending ninety eras of suffering in the cycle of existence, they will not regress from the Supreme, Perfect Enlightenment.

Then I made this prediction: "In the future, after having passed one thousand eons, in the eon 'Immaculate Light,' in the Buddha land 'Impatient with Illusory Realms,' during the span of one era, there will be Buddhas identical to the letter, called the Tathāgatas 'Eloquence and Majesty' who will appear in the world. Mañjuśrī, this teaching of the Dharma has great merits. It can cause Bodhisattvas, the great beings, and those of the disciple vehicle to attain great benefits. Mañjuśrī, there are good sons and daughters who seek enlightenment without skill-in-means, practicing the six perfections for one thousand eras. If someone passes a fortnight reading and writing the manuscript of this sutra, he will attain benefits which, compared with the former in virtue, are one hundred times, one thousand times, one hundred thousand hosts of times greater in number and cannot be compared to any other.

"Therefore, Mañjuśrī, this particularly profound teaching is the basis for the sutras on Bodhisattvas. I now confer this to you. You would uphold it and read it in the future, teaching it for others. If any emperor goes out in the world, seven treasures are presented in front of him. When an emperor dies, his treasures also perish. Similarly, if this particularly profound teaching is disseminated throughout the world, then the Dharma eye and my seven enlightenment attributes[49] will not perish. If this teaching is not disseminated, then the true Dharma will perish. Therefore, Mañjuśrī, the good sons and daughters should be diligent in seeking enlightenment. They will transcribe the manuscript of this sutra, upholding and reading it, propagating it for others. This is my teaching. Do not begrudge future generations." After I had taught this sutra, the Bodhisattva Sumati, the Bodhisattva Mañjuśrī, and the assembly of gods, humans, Āsuras, Gandharvas, and others heard what I had said and were exalted, having faith and resolving to practice.

Notes

1. *The Jātaka or Stories of the Buddha's Former Births,* ed. E. B. Cowell (London: Cambridge University Press, 1897); reprinted by Routledge & Kegan Paul, 1973, 6 vols. Other descriptions of the Buddha as a Bodhisattva are found in the *Mahāvastu,* tr. J. J. Jones; and in the *Buddhavaṁsa* and *Cariyāpiṭaka,* to be found in *Minor Anthologies III,* tr. I. B. Horner (London: Routledge & Kegan Paul, 1975).
2. See Chapter 7 for a description of the celestial Bodhisattva.
3. Even within the Theravāda, a cult dedicated to the coming of the future Buddha Maitreya had gradually developed. Maitreya is believed to be alive and waiting in the Tuṣita heaven (where all the future Buddhas reside before appearing on earth) to respond to the prayers of his worshippers. Just as the historical Buddha had communicated with previous Buddhas, Mahāyāna masters journeyed to the heaven of Maitreya during meditation to listen to him.
4. For a beautiful description of this awakening, see *Entering the Path of Enlightenment: The Bodhicaryāvatāra of the Buddhist poet Śāntideva,* tr. Marion L. Matics (London: Macmillan, 1970), pp. 153–61.
5. Pure Land is the abode of the Buddha Amitābha.
6. F. Max Müller, ed. and tr., *The Larger Sukhāvatīvyūha* (Sacred Books of the East, XLIX) (Oxford: Clarendon Press, 1894), p. 19.
7. The irreversible Bodhisattva of the eighth stage was represented only by the male although the good sons (kulaputrāḥ) and good daughters (kuladuhitāraḥ) are both potential Bodhisattvas. The *Mahāvastu* claims that a Bodhisattva is not born as a woman, but this must certainly mean the eighth-stage Bodhisattva and above since women are acknowledged as Bodhisattvas of a less advanced stage. Cf. Har Dayal, *The Bodhisattva Doctrine in Buddhist Sanskrit Literature* (London: Routledge & Kegan Paul, 1932); reprinted in Delhi by Motilal Banarsidass, 1970, p. 223. According to the *Bodhisattvabhūmi,* a Bodhisattva may be a woman during the first immeasurable term (asaṃkhyeya) of the path but not during the second and third terms. Cf. *Bodhisattva-bhūmi: A Statement of Whole Course of the Bodhisattva (Being Fifteenth Section of Yogācārabhūmi),* ed. Unrai Wogihara (Tokyo: Sankibō Buddhist Bookstore, 1971), p. 94, lines 3–9. Vasubandhu, a phi-

losopher of Buddhist idealism, declares that the first term includes the first through seventh stages of the Bodhisattva inclusive, agreeing with the position mentioned above, namely, that women cannot realize irreversible Bodhisattvahood. Cf. *L'Abhidharmakośa de Vasubandhu,* tr. Louis de la Vallée Poussin (Paris: Paul Guethner, 1925), III, Chapter 4, 224, footnote 1 (hereafter cited as *Kośa*).

8. Among the early sectarian Buddhist texts which discuss sexual transformation are *Milinda-panha* 267, *Divyāvadāna* 473, *Sphutārthā Abhidharmakośa-vyakhyā,* and the Yamaka section in the *Abhidhamma-piṭaka,* as cited in P. V. Bapat, "Change of Sex in Buddhist Literature," in *Sripad Krishna Belvalkar Felicitation Volume* (Benares: Motilal Banarsidass, 1957), pp. 209, 211–12.
9. The following discussion of the *Aṭṭhasālinī,* a commentary on the *Dhammasaṅgaṇi,* is paraphrased from Bapat, "Change of Sex in Buddhist Literature." See previous note.
10. Sanskrit: *indriya.*
11. Sanskrit: *vyañjana.*
12. Herbert V. Guenther, *Philosophy and Psychology in the Abhidharma* (Berkeley: Shambala, 1974), p. 165.
13. *Kośa,* iv, pp. 56, 105.
14. Sanskrit: *chanda. Kośa,* iv. 80a, p. 174.
15. *Kośa,* iv. 55c, p. 104.
16. *Kośa,* ii. 18d, p. 140.
17. *Kośa,* p. 104.
18. *Kośa,* iv. 108a–d, pp. 220–21, cites the *Vibhāṣā,* 176.14. The Bodhisattva has performed good actions and knows with certainty that he will be a Buddha. Abandoning unfortunate destinies includes the abandonment of a female body.
19. *Kośa,* vi. 2la–b, p. 171.
20. *Kośa,* iv. 14a, pp. 43–44.
21. *Vinaya Piṭaka,* iii, 35 (Pārājika 1.106); see I. B. Horner, tr., *The Book of the Discipline* (London: Luzac, 1962), part 1, p. 54.
22. See Wendy Doniger O'Flaherty, *Asceticism and Eroticism* (New York: Oxford University Press, 1973), for an analysis of the cyclical transitions between sexuality and asceticism in a variety of literary motifs. Also, see Norman W. Brown, "Change of Sex in a Hindu Story Motif," *Journal of the American Oriental Society,* 47 (1927), 1–27.
23. Melford Spiro, in *Buddhism and Society* (New York: Harper & Row, 1970), pp. 296–97, 367, describes the phobia Bud-

dhist monks frequently have toward the body in present-day Burmese communities.

24. The *Kośa,* iv, pp. 57, 150, refers to the Vaibhāṣika who claimed that the sexual organs are the cause of ugliness. Those born in the World of Form (Rūpadhātu) are beautiful and without sexual organs. In the *Agañña-suttanta* differences between beautiful and ugly human beings do not occur until sexual distinctions of male and female have been created.
25. T. v. 14, n. 564, p. 918 c 6–9, 12–13.
26. For an explanation of the act or rite of truth, see Norman W. Brown, "The Metaphysics of Truth Act (Satyakriyā)," *Mélanges d'indienisme à la mémoire de Louis Renou* (Paris: 1968), pp. 171–77; E. W. Burlingame, "The Act of Truth (Saccakiriyā): A Hindu Spell and Its Employment as a Psychic Motif in Hindu Fiction," *Journal of the Royal Asiatic Society,* July 1917, parts 1 and 2, pp. 429–67; and Alex Wayman, "The Hindu-Buddhist Rite of Truth: An Interpretation," *Studies in Indian Linguistics* (Poona: 1968), pp. 365–69.
27. In Brahmanic literature, in contrast to Buddhist texts, the change from male to female is not always undesirable. Since women were believed to have more pleasure in sexual intercourse than men, a change from male to female indicated an increase in one's capacity to enjoy sexual acts. Cf. Norman W. Brown, "Change of Sex in a Hindu Story Motif," p. 7.
28. *Avadānaśataka, Rukmavatyavadāna,* cited in Norman W. Brown, "The Metaphysics of Truth Act," p. 176, footnote 2.
29. In tribute to her beauty, Ilā, mother of Purūravas, was said to equal or surpass the Nāga princess. Cf. J. Ph. Vogel, *Indian Serpent-Lore, or The Nāgas in Hindu Legend and Art* (London: Arthur Probsthain 1926), p. 33.
30. In the *Mahābhārata* Arjuna marries the Nāga maiden Ulūpī. Hsüan-tsang reports in the *Hsi-yu-chi* of a Śākyan prince marrying a Nāga princess. Samuel Beal, tr., *Si-yu-ki: Buddhist Records of the Western World* (Delhi: Oriental Books, 1969), part 1, pp. 128–32.
31. See, for example, Horner, tr., *The Book of the Discipline,* p. 111ff.; H. C. Warren, tr., *Buddhism in Translations* (Cambridge: Harvard University Press, 1896), p. 401ff.; reprinted in New York by Atheneum, 1968.
32. *Dialogues of the Buddha,* trs. T. W. Rhys Davids and C. A. F. Rhys Davids, part 2, p. 306.
33. Sanskrit: *Mūrdhābhiṣiktarāja-sūtra.* T. v. 14, n. 477 and n. 478.

34. Amoghadarśana teaches the doctrine of the Tathāgata's eternal abiding as the supreme truth, capable of transformations which are Empty in nature. He goes through physical changes and asks Candrottarā to do the same. Consequently, the question he asks Candrottarā is appropriate. Cf. Mochizuki Shinkō, ed., *Bukkyō daijiten* I, 943 c.
35. Dharaṇīṃdhara is sometimes identified with the Bodhisattva Avalokiteśvara and Bodhisattva Kṣitigarbha.
36. This Bodhisattva's name means "eloquence," and he skillfully lectures on time and on the awakening of living beings from the dream of ignorance. Candrottarā's response to his question appropriately focuses on the limits of language with regard to the Dharma realm.
37. This Bodhisattva's name means "detailed knowledge." The Bodhisattvas acquire four detailed knowledges: (1) knowledge of the essential nature of all phenomena, (2) knowledge of the meaning of all phenomena, (3) knowledge of the linguistic expressions of all phenomena, and (4) knowledge of the elocution to express the attributes of all phenomena.
38. This Bodhisattva appears as various forms, e.g., disciple, Pratyeka-buddha, Nāga, monk, or nun to those who worship him, bestowing many benefits until they become enlightened.
39. This Bodhisattva's name means "noninjury to other living beings."
40. These beings are nonhuman and appear in Buddhist folklore: (1) devas (gods), (2) Nāgas (serpents), (3) Yakṣas (spirits), (4) Gandharvas (celestial males), (5) Āsuras (antigods), (6) Garuḍas (demonic birds), (7) Kiṃnaras (semihuman beings), and (8) Mahoragas (great serpents).
41. The four groups are monks, nuns, male novices, female novices.
42. The four evils are defilements, the five psychophysical forces which bind one to existence, the pangs of death, and the evils of the world of desire.
43. An epithet for the historical Buddha.
44. Sumati means "intelligence."
45. Several persons named Ugra are listed in the Pāli canon, but none is cited as a citizen of Rājagṛha. Cf. G. P. Malalasekera, *Dictionary of Pāli Proper Names* (London: Luzac, 1960), I, 332–34.
46. These forty conditions appear to be a variation of the thirty-seven aspects of enlightenment (bodhipakṣyā dharmāḥ) with

the addition of three aspects pertaining to stūpa worship, i.e., worship of the reliquary of the Buddha.

47. In the recension translated by Dharmarakṣa, the mayor's name is Ugra. In Kumārajīva's translation he is also called Ugra.
48. Spontaneous generation (upapāduka equals aupapāduka) is a type of conception and birth for exceptional human beings, especially for the Buddhaṣ, Bodhisattvas, and emperors. They are often seated on lotuses, which may also be spontaneously generated. Cf. Franklin Edgerton, *Buddhist Hybrid Sanskrit Grammar and Dictionary* (Delhi: Motilal Banarsidass, 1970), p. 162 b.
49. The enlightenment attributes (bodhyaṅga or sambodhyaṅga) are (1) mindfulness, (2) study of the Dharma, (3) diligence, (4) joy, (5) tranquillity, (6) concentration, and (7) equanimity or impartiality.

CHAPTER 6

The Bodhisattvas without Sexual Transformation*

By far the most liberal portraits of women's spiritual achievements—as advanced-stage Bodhisattvas—are to be found in an extremely small percentage of sutras, but in some of the most popular and influential texts in Mahāyāna scripture. Among these texts are the *Vimalakīrtinirdeśa* and *The Sutra of Queen Śrīmālā Who Had the Lion's Roar* (presented in Chapter 8). The common element in these sutras is the emphasis on a metaphysical statement of the "conditioned" and "unconditioned." The *Diamond Sutra (Vajracchedikā Prajñāpāramitā)* summarizes the metaphysics of these texts most appropriately in the following quatrain which concludes the sutra:

> As stars, a fault of vision, as a lamp,
> A mock show, dew drops, or a bubble,
> A dream, a lightning flash, or cloud,
> So should one view what is conditioned.[1]

In this sutra, which views the "conditioned," whether one is a man or woman is irrelevant. If all phenomena are impermanent and insubstantial, then there are no self-existent entities with inalienable and unchanging characteristics such as "maleness" or "femaleness." There is no male or female. All such characteristics are illusion. Understanding the teaching of Emptiness removes illusions

*This chapter was written by Diana Paul and Frances Wilson.

of sexuality. The Dharma and the path are neither male nor female.

The traditional attitudes toward women described in Chapters 1 and 2, however, defined the feminine as power, both destructive and maternal. Characteristics of "femaleness" were imposed upon women in describing the soteriological path of the nun who must be deferential to the monks and implicitly might weaken the structure of the family. The good friend, good daughter, and, especially, the female Bodhisattva who undergoes a sexual transformation were viewed as limited as long as they retained their association with the feminine.

All statements about persons setting out in the Bodhisattva vehicle are made with reference to both good sons and good daughters, that is, those of virtuous habits and practices throughout past lives. Both can achieve the enlightenment of a Buddha:

> And yet, Subhuti, those sons and daughters of good family,[2] who will take up these very sutras, who will bear them in mind, recite them, study them, and wisely attend to them, and will illuminate them in full detail for others, they will be humbled, and they will be very well humbled. And why? The impure deeds which these beings have done in their former lives, and which are liable to lead them into the states of woe, in this very life they will, by means of that humiliation, annul those impure deeds of their former lives, and they will reach the enlightenment of a Buddha.[3]

The only two conditions of reaching the "unconditioned" and of achieving enlightenment are (1) the opportunity of hearing the *Diamond Sutra* and (2) being a good son or good daughter.

There is the implication that a Buddha or Tathāgata is not necessarily male.

. . . Therefore a Tathāgatha is not to be seen by means of his possession of marks.

Further I, the lord, taught on that occasion these stanzas:

> Those who by my form did see me,
> And those who followed me by voice,
> Wrong the efforts they engaged in,
> Me those people will not see.
>
> From the Dharma should one see the Buddhas,
> For the Dharma bodies[4] are the guides,
> Yet the Dharma's true nature should not be discerned,
> Nor can it, either, be discerned.[5]

The tenth of the thirty-two distinguishing marks of a Buddha is the concealment of the private organ in a sheath, that is, the concealment of the male sex organ. The common interpretation of this distinguishing mark makes Buddhahood for women impossible. Another interpretation of the concealment of the male sexual organ is that the Buddha was asexual, that is, he had no desire for sexual intercourse. He concealed his male character; in other words, "maleness" was irrelevant. However, there is no textual evidence to support such an interpretation of this "distinguishing mark" of the Buddha. If the Tathāgata is not to be viewed literally according to these marks, as acclaimed in the *Diamond Sutra,* then women would not be excluded from attaining Buddhahood. Stated otherwise, no metaphysical claims put forth by the sutras would preclude women from attaining advanced Bodhisattvahood and eventually the ultimate spiritual experience of Buddhahood.

The Buddha, who had "concealed" his sexuality through the removal of his desires, had, in effect, eliminated his sexual powers. If the Tathāgata were not viewed as a sexual being, then both men and women could and must release themselves from sexuality in order to attain Buddhahood. Instead of using the motif of sexual change, sutras such as the *Diamond Sutra,* the *Vimalakīrti* sutra, and "Jewel Brocade" present asexuality as neither male nor female. The male image is not used as the representation of asexuality.

The texts which repudiate the theme of sexual change are repudiating the illusion that there are innate sexual characteristics. The implicit assumption in the following texts is that the use of the notion of sexual change entails a belief in innate sexual characteristics of female and male. In addition, the symbols of the male and female as spiritual perfection and sensuality, respectively, were viewed as latent forms of discrimination.

In the selections from *The Sutra of the Teaching of Vimalakīrti* and the story of Jewel Brocade from *The Sutra of Sāgara, the Nāga King,* the line of argument is in accordance with the *Diamond Sutra,* namely, that there is no dichotomy between male and female in the unconditioned. Attitudes repudiating a woman's capabilities are merely another form of discrimination which binds one to a profane level of existence. In the episode of Māra and his female companions from *The Sutra of the Teaching of Vimalakīrti,* the women are possessions of Māra, the Evil One, but awaken to the thought of enlightenment, in contradiction to the portrayal of the feminine discussed in Chapter 1, "Temptress: Daughter of Evil." Māra's female retainers are no longer viewed as daughters of evil but rather as fledgling Bodhisattvas.

In the second episode from *The Sutra of the Teaching of Vimalakīrti,* the attachment of the monks to false discriminations is symbolized by the attachment of the flowers to the monks' robes. In a similar way, Śāriputra, the spokesman for the monkish views toward women, is attached to the notion of sexual discrimination. After a lively exchange of counterarguments, the goddess in this tale changes Śāriputra into a female in order to reinforce her assertion that all things are neither male nor female when one views the world as Emptiness. Śāriputra's appearance as a female symbolizes his attachment to sexual discrimination, a parallel with the symbolism of the attachment of the flowers to the monks' robes. The masquerade or magical act of changing sex reinforces the teaching in Mahāyāna Buddhism that all phenomena are illusory.

The longest discourse on the illusion that all phenomena are substantial and possess innate characteristics occurs in the Jewel Brocade tale from *The Sutra of Sāgara, the Nāga King*. In an eloquent speech on the teaching of Emptiness, the Bodhisattva Jewel Brocade proclaims that the Dharma denies illusions such as sexuality. These two sutras, *The Sutra of the Teaching of Vimalakīrti* and the tale of Jewel Brocade, refute traditional views toward the feminine and toward women in a humorous and good-natured manner, provoking sympathy and subtle mockery at the sententious clergy, who often adamantly refused to recognize the spiritual needs and abilities of women.

A. Introduction to Selections from *The Sutra of the Teaching of Vimalakīrti*

This sutra is a humorous, often sardonic, exposition of the Mahāyāna teaching and has been especially admired by the Chinese since the fifth century and by the Japanese since the time of Prince Shōtoku. This text's basic doctrine is Emptiness as expounded by the Mādhyamikan tradition. The theories found in some of these liberal (Vaipulya) texts were systematized about the third century by Nāgārjuna, the foremost philosopher of Mādhyamika,[6] who often quoted *The Sutra of the Teaching of Vimalakīrti*.[7]

Seven Chinese translations were made, of which three are extant today; the present text was translated into Chinese by Kumārajīva in 406. Seng-chao (384–414), who was a great admirer of the Taoist masters Lao Tzu and Chuang Tzu, converted to Buddhism and became an eminent advocate of San-lun, the Chinese school of Mādhyamika, after having read the sutra. This text was so popular that it was recited at temple festivals as ballads and folk tales during the T'ang dynasty. Vimalakīrti, the wealthy lay Bodhisattva, was carved in many cave sculptures at Lung-men as well as in a famous painting by Ku K'ai-chih (345–411).[8]

The main tenets in *The Sutra of the Teaching of Vimalakīrti* are that all phenomena are without an innate nature, neither arising nor ceasing, that they are originally quiescent and naturally tending toward Nirvana, without distinct characteristics, and that they are inexpressible, and inconceivable, equal and nondual, that is, all phenomena are Empty.

Vimalakīrti is the principal teacher in the text. As a householder of considerable wealth, he nonetheless attains the wisdom of a Bodhisattva, far outstripping even illustrious monks such as Śāriputra in virtue and knowledge of the Dharma. He often pokes fun at the pedantic ways cherished by the monks and frequently intimidates the monks with his easy-going manner.

The text opens with Vimalakīrti becoming sick. The Buddha asks his disciples and various Bodhisattvas to visit him and inquire about his health. In a series of dialogues, one after another refuses the Buddha's request because of former interactions with Vimalakīrti which had proved embarrassing. Finally, the Bodhisattva Mañjuśrī goes to visit him.

The following two passages portray the attitude of monks and even of certain Bodhisattvas toward women in a humorous manner. In the first selection, the Bodhisattva

Jagatīṃdhara relates how he was tempted by Māra and a contingent of goddesses, only to be humiliated by Vimalakīrti's straightforward dealings with Māra. Māra's retinue of women become lower-stage Bodhisattvas, who propagate the Dharma in Māra's residence.

In the first passage, the episode of Māra and his female companions, the women are possessions whom Māra first gives to Vimalakīrti and then demands that they be returned to him. The women want to stay with Vimalakīrti, but he asks that they go with Māra, try to teach others, and change their spiritual environment. Implicitly, the female contingent is confined to societal roles which reduce women to possessions. The implication is that women should work from within the existing social structure and try to instruct others by their example, eventually resulting in the elimination of attitudes of possessiveness.

The second excerpt from *The Sutra of the Teaching of Vimalakīrti* focuses on a goddess who resides in Vimalakīrti's house. She playfully engages the eminent monk Śāriputra in a battle of wits. In contrast to the episode of Māra, the goddess presents a philosophical argument to indicate the absurdity of holding the position of innate distinctions among phenomena. In a delightfully engaging display of satire and illusion, the goddess eloquently wins her case without any mention of sexual transformation. Unlike the episodes in Chapter 5, the goddess does not feel the necessity to change her sex due to restrictions regarding the path of a female Bodhisattva.

*The Sutra of the Teaching of Vimalakīrti**(*Vimalakīrtinirdeśa*). T. v. 14, n. 475, pp. 537–57.

[From Chapter 4, T. v. 14, n. 475, p. 543 a 9 –b 27:]

I [the Buddha] spoke to the Bodhisattva Jagatīṃdhara. "Go ask Vimalakīrti about his illness."

Jagatīṃdhara said to me: "Lord, I can't ask him about his illness. You want to know why? I remember that, some time ago, while I was in meditation Māra, the Evil One, with his retinue of twelve thousand goddesses, disguised himself as Śakra [Indra], and playing music and singing, came to visit me. With his retinue, he prostrated himself, folded his hands out of respect, and then stood to one side. Thinking that this was Śakra, I spoke to him: 'Welcome, Kauśika. But if I have all these pleasures, I would not be able to restrain myself. You certainly know that sensual desires are ephemeral, that one tries to find something good in the body, in life, and in property which will be substantial.'

"Then Māra spoke to me: 'Righteous one, accept these twelve thousand goddesses as your housekeepers.' I spoke to him: 'Kauśika, do not offer them to me for I am a monk, a son of Śākyamuni, and these are not proper for me.' Before I could finish speaking, Vimalakīrti spoke to me: 'This is not Śakra but Māra who has come to tempt you.'

"Then Vimalakīrti spoke to Māra: 'These women should be given to me for I can accept them.'

"Māra was startled and thought to himself: 'I cannot let Vimalakīrti's questions torment me.' So he wished to dis-

*This English translation is by Diana Paul.

appear but he could not, even by his magical powers. Then, he heard voices from heaven: 'Māra, give these women to Vimalakīrti, and you can leave.' Because Māra was frightened, with averted eyes he gave them to Vimalakīrti.

"Afterwards, Vimalakīrti spoke to the women: 'Since Māra has given you to me, today all of you should awaken to the thought of the Supreme, Perfect Enlightenment.' Accordingly, he taught the Dharma which caused them to awaken to the path. Then he spoke again: 'Having awakened to the path, you are able to enjoy the pleasures of the Dharma. You will no longer find enjoyment in sensual pleasures.' The goddesses asked him: 'What are the pleasures of the Dharma?'

"He answered: 'There are the pleasures of (1) eternally believing in the Buddha, (2) listening to the Dharma, (3) paying respect to the Saṃgha, (4) separating from sensual desires, (5) seeing the five psychophysical elements as injurious, (6) seeing the four elements as poisonous snakes, (7) seeing the [twelve] bases of consciousness as an empty village, (8) protecting the thought to the path, (9) helping all living beings, (1) respecting one's teachers, (11) giving generously, (12) stalwartly maintaining morality, (13) being patient and gentle in the face of abuse, (14) diligently developing good habits, (15) meditating without disturbance, (16) attaining wisdom without defilement, (17) attaining enlightenment, (18) conquering all the evils of Māra, (19) eliminating all defilement, (20) residing in the pure Buddha lands, (21) possessing the characteristics [of a Buddha] because one has practiced all virtues, (22) possessing the adornment of practicing the path, (23) listening to the profound Dharma without fear, (24) penetrating the three gates to liberation without seeking them at the wrong time, (25) being near those who are friends, (26) having no aversion toward those who are not your friends, (27) helping the bad, (28) associating with the good, (29) having a pure and rejoicing heart, and (30) practicing the unlimited path.

" 'These are the pleasures of the Dharma which the Bodhisattvas possess.' Māra then replied to the goddesses: 'I want to return with you to our celestial palace.' The goddesses replied: 'We have been given to this householder. We now enjoy the pleasure of the Dharma and will never again enjoy sensual pleasures.'

"Māra spoke: 'You can abandon these women. The one who gives away everything he owns is truly a Bodhisattva.'

"Vimalakīrti spoke: 'I have already abandoned them. You can leave now. They have completed the vows to help all beings attain the Dharma.'

"The women asked Vimalakīrti: 'How can we return to Māra's palace?'

"Vimalakīrti spoke: 'Sisters, the teaching of the Dharma is the eternal lamp. You should study it. The eternal lamp is like a single lamp which lights one hundred thousand lamps. The darkness is entirely illuminated, and the light is never extinguished. Sisters, in the same way, one Bodhisattva teaches one hundred thousand living beings to awaken to the thought of Supreme, Perfect Enlightenment. Their thoughts of enlightenment will never be extinguished. The process of following the Dharma and perpetuating all good acts is the eternal lamp. Although you have lived in Māra's palace, use this eternal lamp to awaken the countless gods and goddesses to the thought of the Supreme, Perfect Enlightenment. With the Buddha's beneficence, promote the welfare of all beings.'

"Then the goddesses prostrated themselves at Vimalakīrti's feet and returned instantaneously with Māra to his palace and were seen no more."

[From Chapter 7, T. v. 14, n. 475, pp. 547 c 23 to p. 548 c 27:]

At that time, a goddess was residing in Vimalakīrti's house. After hearing the Dharma which the Bodhisattva

[Vimalakīrti] had explained, she presented herself to him. She scattered celestial flowers over the Bodhisattvas and the disciples. The flowers which landed on the Bodhisattvas fell off while those on the disciples did not. Even with all their magical powers, the disciples couldn't make the flowers fall off.

The goddess asked Śāriputra: "Why do these flowers fall off them [the Bodhisattvas]?"

Śāriputra: "Because flowers are not for the religious so they fall off."

Goddess: "Why shouldn't flowers be for the religious? These flowers are not objects of discrimination. Only you venerable monks conceive of such discrimination. Even though you renounce your homes for the sake of the Buddha's Dharma, if you make discriminations, you are not religious. If you make no discriminations, then you are truly religious. Look at these Bodhisattvas whose flowers do not remain on them because they have eliminated all discrimination. You are like frightened men who are seized by evil spirits. Disciples who are frightened by life and death are seized by sights and sounds, scents, tastes, and touch. Those who no longer are afraid have no sensual desires. Because you have not eliminated habits [of discrimination] which bind you [to sensual desires], these flowers remain on your bodies. When these habits which bind you are eliminated, the flowers will no longer remain on you."

Śāriputra: "How long have you been in this house, goddess?"

Goddess: "Venerable one, I have been in this house since the time you were enlightened."

Śāriputra ,"You have been here a long time?"

Goddess: "Have you been enlightened for a long time?"

Śāriputra was silent and did not answer.

Goddess: "Why are you, a venerable sage, silent?"

Śāriputra: "Enlightenment is ineffable. Therefore, I do not know what to say."

Goddess: "The words you say are a sign of enlightenment. Why? Enlightenment is neither internal nor external, nor in between the two. Therefore, don't stop using language to express enlightenment. Why? Because all phenomena are signs of enlightenment."

Śāriputra: "Well then, don't you think the elimination of lust, hate, and desire is enlightenment?"

Goddess: "The Buddha said that the elimination of lust, hate, and desire is enlightenment for those who have desires. For those who have no desires, the Buddha said the nature of lust, hate, and desire is enlightenment."

Śāriputra: "Very good, goddess. What have you attained and realized in order to have such eloquence?"

Goddess: "Because I have attained and realized nothing, I have such eloquence. Why? If one attains or realizes something, this is the Dharma of the Buddha for those who have desires."

Śāriputra: "Which of the three vehicles do you seek?"

Goddess: "With the teaching which I have heard, I convert living beings so I am a disciple. With the teaching of causation I convert living beings so I am a Pratyeka-buddha. With the teaching of great compassion I convert living beings so I am a follower of Mahāyāna. Just like someone who enters a forest having Campaka trees and smells only the fragrance of the Campaka flower and doesn't smell other fragrances, those who enter this house experience only the fragrance of the Buddha's virtues and do not desire the fragrance of the disciple's and Pratyeka-buddha's virtues.

"Śāriputra, Śakra, Brahmā, the four world lords, and the various gods and Nāgas who have entered this house to listen to this excellent man's teaching of the true Dharma desire the fragrance of the Buddha's virtues which produces the awakening to the thought of enlightenment. Śāriputra, I have been in this house for twelve years, and I haven't heard the teaching of the disciples or the Pratyeka-buddhas even once. I only have heard the inconceivable teaching of the Buddha, namely, his great compassion and kindness which are also the Bodhisattva's.

"Śāriputra, in this house there have always been eight miraculous and marvelous events. What are the eight? (1) In this house there is always a golden light which shines night and day without changing. One does not know if it is the sun or moon which is shining. This is the first miraculous and marvelous event. (2) Those who enter this house do not become defiled. This is the second miraculous and marvelous event. (3) In this house Śakra, Brahmā, the four world lords, and the Bodhisattvas of other lands never break off their relations with us. This is the third miraculous and marvelous event. (4) In this house the six perfections are always taught and there is no turning against the Dharma. This is the fourth miraculous and marvelous event. (5) In this house, the supreme music of the gods and of men always produces the countless sounds of the Dharma. This is the fifth miraculous and marvelous event. (6) In this house there are four immense treasures, overflowing with jewels without end, which are used to relieve the poverty of all who seek aid. This is the sixth miraculous and marvelous event. (7) It was in this house that the Buddhas Śākyamuni, Amitābha, Akṣobhya, Ratnaśrī, Ratnārcis, Ratnacandra, Ratnavyūha, Duṣprasaha, Siṃhakīrti, Sarvārthasiddha and all the other countless Buddhas in the ten directions first became aware of the virtuous state of mind and began to teach the profound mysteries of the Dharma of the Buddhas. After they had finished teaching [these mysteries], they returned [to their own Buddha lands]. This is the seventh miraculous and marvelous event. (8) All the magnificent celestial palaces and all the Buddha lands appear in this house. This is the eight miraculous and marvelous event.

"Śāriputra, in this house, the eight miraculous and marvelous events are always present. Who, after seeing these inconceivable events, would seek the teaching of the disciple?"

Śāriputra: "Why don't you change your female sex?"

Goddess: "I have been here twelve years and have looked for the innate characteristics of the female sex and haven't been able to find them. How can I change them? Just as a magician creates an illusion of a woman, if someone asks why don't you change your female sex, what is he asking?"

Śāriputra: "But an illusion is without any determinate innate characteristics so how could it be changed?"

Goddess: "All things are also without any determinate innate characteristics, so how can you ask, 'why don't you change your female sex?' "

Then the goddess, by supernatural power, changed Śāriputra into a likeness of herself and changed herself into a likeness of Śāriputra and asked: "Why don't you change your female sex?"

Śāriputra, in the form of a goddess, answered: "I do not know how I changed nor how I changed into a female form."

Goddess: "Śāriputra, if you can change into a female form, then all women [in mental state] can also change. Just as you are not really a woman but appear to be female in form, all women, also only appear to be female in form but are not really women. Therefore, the Buddha said all are not really men or women."[9]

Then the goddess, by her supernatural power, changed Śāriputra back into his own form. The goddess questioned Śāriputra: "Where are the female form and innate characteristics now?"

Śāriputra: "The female form and innate characteristics neither exist nor do not exist."

Goddess: "All things neither exist nor do not exist. The Buddha said there is neither existence nor nonexistence."

Śāriputra questioned the goddess? "After death, where will you be born?"

Goddess: "I will be born by the magical transformation of the Buddha."

Śāriputra: "But the Buddha's magical transformations neither are born nor do they die."

Goddess: "Similarly, all living beings neither are born nor do they die."

Śāriputra questioned the goddess: "How long will it be before you attain the Supreme, Perfect Enlightenment?"

Goddess: "When you become an ordinary man, I will attain the Supreme, Perfect Enlightenment."

Śāriputra: "There is no way that I will be an ordinary man."

Goddess: "There also is no way that I will attain the Supreme, Perfect Enlightenment. Why? Enlightenment is without a basis; therefore, there is nothing to attain."

Śāriputra: "What is meant then by the statement that all the Buddhas, more numerous than the sands of the Ganges, have attained, now attain, and will attain the Supreme, Perfect Enlightenment?"

Goddess: "When one speaks of the three states of time [past, present, and future], these are conventional expressions and measures. There is no enlightenment of the past, present, and future. Śāriputra, have you attained the path of the Arhat?"

Śāriputra: "Because there is nothing to attain, I have attained it."

Goddess: "Similarly, all the Buddhas and Bodhisattvas attain enlightenment because there is nothing to attain."

Then Vimalakīrti spoke to Śāriputra: "This goddess has already paid reverence to ninety-two million Buddhas. She easily handles the powers of the Bodhisattva, has completely professed the vows [of the Bodhisattva], has attained the patience to accept the nonarising [of phenomena], and will not revert [from the Bodhisattva path].[10] Because of her vows and according to her wish, she will teach and convert all living beings."

B. Introduction to "Jewel Brocade Receives the Prediction" from *The Sutra of Sāgara, the Nāga King*

The Sutra of Sāgara, the Nāga King is also known as *The Sutra of the Nāga King Sāgara Who Asked about the Incantations (Dhāraṇī)* and *The Sutra of the Accumulation of the Pure Dharma, the Dharma Jewel.* This sutra was translated into Chinese by Dharmarakṣa in A.D. 285 and is also extant in Tibetan.

The first half of the sutra takes place on Vulture Peak (Gṛdhrakūṭa), the latter half in the Nāga king's oceanic palace. The principal teachings of the text are the Bodhisattva practice and the inexhaustible Dharma of Mahāyāna. This sutra is divided into twenty chapters, the main exposition is in the fourth chapter, "The Inexhaustible Storehouse"[11] [of Bodhisattva practice] through the sixth chapter, "The Body of Incantations." The principal theme is that the Mahāyāna teaching is embodied in the incantation of the inexhaustible storehouse of merits which are accumulated by the Bodhisattva practice.

The Sutra of Sāgara, the Nāga King appears to have been greatly influenced by the *Prajñāpāramitā* but also suggests influence from the Pure Land school because of its reference to being born in the Buddha's land after hearing his name,[12] probably referring to the Buddha Amitābha and Pure Land. During the Nara period in Japan, this sutra gained immense popularity as a sacred text for the rituals of rain ceremonies because of the rain-giving faculty attributed to the Nāgas. The text was also used in rain ceremonies in China where sometimes as many as eleven hundred Buddhist priests attended the ritual.

Chapter 14, "Jewel Brocade Receives the Prediction," is strikingly similar to the Nāga princess episode in the *Lotus Sutra* and utilizes the same argument as the *Vimalakīrtinirdeśa* episode concerning the goddess.[13]

In the following episode, Jewel Brocade focuses on the key issue of the illusion of sexuality by arguing the case that all phenomena are equal in nature, that is, Empty, and should not be discriminated as being different in nature. The teaching of Emptiness is the fundamental and dominant theme in all Mahāyāna Buddhist literature. In accordance with that theme, the denial of innate sexual characteristics is a necessary corollary. *The Sutra of Sāgara, the Nāga King* is not the first text to conclude that there is no sexual discrimination if one accepts the teaching of Emptiness. In the *Ta-chih tu lun (Mahāprajñāpāramitā-śāstra),* the discriminative characteristics of men and women are analogous to the ignorant individual's perception of water in a mirage.[14]

> If the characteristics of men and women are [discriminated as] identical or different, their true nature is unattainable. Why? Because phenomena [Dharmas] are neither the ego nor belong to the ego; they are Empty. Because they are Empty, there is neither male nor female.[15]

The commentary cites an author who explains that:

> . . . although women have superficial knowledge, conditioned by their past karma, they are able to receive a prediction [of future Buddhahood]. Because they express such a desire in their hearts, the Buddha will listen to them.[16]

Like the serpent princess in the *Lotus Sutra,* Jewel Brocade also offers her most precious jewel to the Buddha as a sign of her commitment to learn about his teaching. She immediately awakens to the thought of enlightenment, which indicates that she is a beginner Bodhisattva of the first stage and asserts, with her companions, that she will become a Buddha. Mahākāśyapa, the spokesman for the conservative Buddhist attitude toward women, immediately reminds the princess of the female sex's limitations. Here we see a different response to the conservative Buddhist position with regard to women. Unlike the Nāga princess in the *Lotus Sutra* who defers to the monk by changing into a male, Jewel Brocade replies that the Buddha's teaching has no male or female qualities. The princess then engages in a discourse on Emptiness which denies discriminations of any kind.

The episode of Jewel Brocade not only illustrates in a humorous way the comment from the *Ta-chih tu lun* that the Buddha will listen to those who desire in their hearts to commit themselves to the Bodhisattva practice but also ignores the sexual change required of aspiring young female Bodhisattvas, which we have found in other Buddhist texts. The Dharma removes notions of sexuality for those practicing the Bodhisattva path.

"Jewel Brocade Receives the Prediction,"* ("Nü pao-chin shou-chüeh") from *The Sutra of Sāgara, the Nāga King (Hai-lung-wang ching),* Chapter 14. T. v. 15, n. 598, pp. 149–50.

Once upon a time the Nāga king, Sāgara, had a daughter who was called Jewel Brocade[17] because she never wore soiled brocades of any kind. She was highly respectable, had a beautiful face, and was simply captivating. She and the ten thousand Nāga queens each had a precious jewel on her right hand. With concentrated minds they meditated upon the Buddha, and within a wink, the Buddha whom they revered stood before them. Then Jewel Brocade and the ten thousand queens offered their precious jewels to the lord and in unison praised him:

"Today, with supreme contemplation, we have awakened to the thought of the Supreme, Perfect Enlightenment. We, in the future, will attain the true and perfect enlightenment because of you, the Tathāgata. We will teach the Dharma of the scriptures and will protect the entire Saṃgha in accordance with you, the Tathāgata, today."

Then the venerable Mahākāśyapa explained to the girl and all the queens:

"The Supreme, Perfect Enlightenment is extremely difficult to attain. One cannot attain Buddhahood within a woman's body."

Jewel Brocade spoke to Mahākāśyapa: "The practicing Bodhisattva whose mind is determined and originally pure attains Buddhahood without difficulty. Awakening to the

*This first English translation is by Diana Paul.

thought of enlightenment, he attains Buddhahood as if perceiving the palm of his hand. He becomes accomplished in the superpowers and in wisdom,[18] embracing the entire Dharma of the Buddha. You have said: 'One cannot attain Buddhahood within a woman's body.' Then, one cannot attain it within a man's body either. What is the reason? Because the thought of enlightenment is neither male nor female. The Buddha has said: 'The one who perceives through the eyes is neither male nor female nor are [the perceptions of] the ears, nose, mouth, body, and mind male or female. What is the reason? Because only the virtuous have eyes of Emptiness. The one who perceives through Emptiness is neither male nor female. The ears, nose, mouth, body, and mind are also Empty.

"Just as the stillness of space is neither male nor female, if one can understand completely the origin of the eyes, then one is said to be enlightened. The same holds true for the [origin of the] ears, nose, mouth, body, and mind. The one who perceives through enlightenment has the Dharma which is neither male nor female.

"Therefore, Kāśyapa, just as all phenomena are autonomous so the path is autonomous. I am also autonomous."

Kāśyapa asked the princess: "Are you enlightened?"

The girl answered: "Venerable elder, would you say that I do not have the path?"

Mahākāśyapa: "I do not have Buddhahood, but I am a disciple."

Princess: "Who converted you to the virtuous [life]?"

Mahākāśyapa: "The Tathāgata."

Princess: "Would it have been better if the Tathāgata had not achieved Supreme, Perfect Enlightenment but instead converted the elders?"

Mahākāśyapa: "No."

Princess: "Therefore, the virtuous should know if one resides in him then, because of the path, there is no unenlightened path."

Mahākāśyapa asked the girl: "Is the perverted [also] the path?"

Princess: "Yes, Kāśyapa, if there is the perverted then there is the path. Why? If one differentiates the originally pure which is knowable, the path has no comprehension of the perverted. The perverted and the originally pure then are the path. If Emptiness is originally without differentiation from the perverted, then there is the path. If all phenomena were united yet separate then there would be no path. When all phenomena are equal and exist as they are, then there is the path."

Mahākāśyapa: "Who gave you such eloquence?"

Princess: "The Lord has given me eloquence, Kāśyapa. Supposing you had not asked me what caused my eloquence. It would be as if you had no breath to call out. What conditions sound? If one does not ask the meaning of 'Bodhisattva' then there is no cause for eloquence."

Mahākāśyapa: "How long have you revered the Buddha?"

Princess: "As long as you have been eliminating impurities."

Mahākāśyapa: "I have not eliminated [all] impurities."

Princess: "Do the common people have impurities?"

Mahākāśyapa: "I also have no impurities which I do not eliminate."

Princess: "Are you fixed within impurities?"

Mahākāśyapa: "Neither arising nor ceasing, they [impurities] are also without fixation. To understand in this manner is [to understand] the originally nonproduced [that is, codependent]."

Princess: "Is the originally nonproduced better than the knowable?"

Mahākāśyapa: "No."

Princess: "Why do you say, 'That wisdom which is known as the path is not to be known in this manner?' If one understands the originally nonproduced, wisdom and the common people are equal."

Mahākāśyapa: "What you have said defies all speech."

Princess: "What I have not eliminated also is ineffable. Why? The Dharma realm is not eliminated. All explanations should be of the Dharma realm."

Mahākāśyapa: "Is it better that you and I and the common people have no misgivings concerning the Dharma?"

Princess: "If one is confirmed in the Dharma, which is the wisdom of the virtuous and the common people, then if each were different I would have misgivings. I mean that the virtuous is no different from the common man. Therefore there are no misgivings. If all phenomena are equal, then there are none[19] [which are different and cause misgivings]. These [phenomena] are equal."

Mahākāśyapa: "Are you and the common people equally virtuous?"

Princess: "I am not an ordinary person, but I am also not virtuous. Why? If I [thought I] were equal to the ordinary person, I wouldn't practice the Bodhisattva way. If I [thought I] were equal to the virtuous, I would be eliminating the Buddha's Dharma."

Mahākāśyapa: "If you are not equal to the ordinary person nor to the virtuous, then are you equal to the Buddha?"

Princess: "No. Why? The origin of my body is equal to the Buddha's Dharma."

Mahākāśyapa: "If you are equal to the Buddha's Dharma, then have you reached the Buddha's Dharma?"

Princess: "Venerable elder, do you believe that the Buddha's Dharma has a past, present, and future which are conditioned? That there are directions with residences of blue, yellow, red, white, and black?"

Mahākāśyapa: "The Buddha Dharma is without images."

Princess: "If the Buddha Dharma is without images, how can I seek it?"

Mahākāśyapa: "In what are you seeking the Buddha Dharma?"

Princess: "In the sixty-two visions I seek it."

Mahākāśyapa: "In what are you seeking the sixty-two visions?"

Princess: "In the Tathāgata's liberation I seek them."

Mahākāśyapa: "In what do you seek the Tathāgata's liberation?"

Princess: "In the five perversions, I seek them."

Mahākāśyapa: "In what do you seek the five perversions?"

Princess: "In knowing the perfections, I seek them."

Mahākāśyapa: "What do you mean by this?"

Princess: "There are no ties, no escape, no grasping, no abandoning in the originally pure. These are the profound teachings of the Dharma of which I speak. There is nothing else to say."

Mahākāśyapa: "What you say about the teachings are not in agreement with what the Tathāgata says!"

Princess: "My speaking the truth neither agrees with nor refutes the Tathāgata's teachings. Why? The path of the Tathāgata is not attained. It also cannot be sustained, nor can it be explained. All words are sounds [only]. Understand that the origin of the path is also soundless. Only the virtuous realize that the path is quiet and impressionless. By 'impression' is meant the impression of selfishness."

Mahākāśyapa: "If the path is impressionless, how can one compare its characteristics, saying one achieves the most supreme enlightenment?

Princess: "Neither from the body nor from the mind does one attain the most supreme enlightenment. Why? The mind and body naturally attain the path. Their naturalness is entirely without enlightenment. If I have the path, it is not because the path is the attainment of the most supreme enlightenment."

Mahākāśyapa: "If you have the path, why not turn the Dharma wheel?"

Princess: "I do turn the Dharma wheel."

Mahākāśyapa: "What kind of Dharma wheel do you turn?"

Princess: "The immovable wheel is separate from all extremes.[20] Because the Dharma wheel is the place of the Dharma realm, the originally nonproduced Dharma wheel is originally nonproduced. Therefore, the wheel which was not eliminated is the originally pure place. The wheel without attachment is the complete understanding of all phenomena. Because there is nothing to which one is attached, the wheel of nonduality is equal to all phenomena. The wheel which is like no other is steadfast in practice. The wheel of the ineffable Dharma transforms all sounds without conceptualization, entering into the homogeneity [of all phenomena]. The pure wheel is entirely without stain. The wheel which eliminates all discord neither attains the permanent nor the impermanent. The nonrebellious wheel clearly sees all benefits. The wheel which is true neither arises nor ceases. The nonwheel of Emptiness is without characteristics or aspirations. Kāśyapa, when the wheel is like this, then what is turned?"

Mahākāśyapa: "A woman's eloquence is not included in attaining the supreme, complete path to the most supreme enlightenment."

Princess: "When you have attained the most supreme enlightenment, I also will attain the most supreme enlightenment."

Mahākāśyapa: "I ultimately cannot attain the most supreme enlightenment."

Princess: "One who completely understands the Dharma body [knows] the path resides in nonresidence. One cannot attain or reach the most supreme enlightenment."

When the girl had finished speaking, five hundred Bodhisattvas attained patience in understanding the nonarising of phenomena. The Buddha praised her saying:

"Well done, well done indeed. You have joyfully explained this Dharma."

Then in the assembly the gods, Nāgas, Āsuras, spirits both good and evil, of sound and of smell, concentrated their minds and thought to themselves:

"When will this girl Jewel Brocade attain the supreme complete path to the most supreme enlightenment?"

The Buddha knew the minds of the gods, Nāgas, Āsuras, spirits of sound and of smell, and spoke to the monks:

"This girl Jewel Brocade, after three hundred immeasurable eons, will attain Buddhahood and be called Universal World,[21] the Tathāgata, Arhat, Completely Enlightened One. Her [Buddha] world will be called Radiance.[22] The era will be pure. The world of Radiance will be eternally luminescent with the rays of the Tathāgata. The Bodhisattvas will number ninety-two million. The Buddha's life will be ten short eons."

Then the ten thousand Nāgas [that is, the Nāga queens] humbly spoke to the Buddha:

"When the Tathāgata Universal World has become a Buddha, we wish to be born in that land."

The Buddha then predicted that they would be born there.

Notes

1. Edward Conze, tr., *Buddhist Wisdom Books* (New York: Harper & Row, 1958), p. 68.
2. "Sons and daughters of good family" is an alternate translation for "good sons and good daughters." The latter translation has been preferred because the meaning of virtuous men and women is more readily conveyed to the reader. In addition, "good son" and "good daughter" are literal translations from the Chinese.
3. Conze, p. 56.
4. "Dharma bodies" refers to the Buddhas in this context.
5. Conze, p. 80.
6. *L'Enseignement de Vimalakīrti,* tr. Etienne Lamotte (Louvain: Université de Louvain Institut Orientaliste, 1962), p. 37.
7. Kenneth K. S. Ch'en, *Buddhism in China: A Historical Survey* (Princeton: Princeton University Press, 1964), p. 382.
8. Ibid., p. 176; Erich Zürcher, *The Buddhist Conquest of China* (Leiden: Brill, 1959), p. 132.
9. Changes in appearance and mental states are being discussed. "Female forms" denotes the physical appearance; "woman" denotes the mental state of desire.
10. At the eighth stage, a Bodhisattva's enlightenment is imminent, being unable to revert to a lower stage of the path because of the accumulation of merit. Therefore, this goddess is an eighth-stage Bodhisattva.
11. Chinese: *wu-chin tsang.*
12. See also Chapter 1, "Practice," in *The Sutra of Sāgara, the Nāga King,* T. v. 15, n. 598.
13. The Jewel Brocade tale appears to have been influenced by the *Vimalakīrti* sutra, having been translated approximately sixty years after the first recension of the *Vimalakīrti* which is no longer extant.
14. T. v. 25, n. 1509, p. 102 b 2–4.
15. T. v. 25, n. 1509, p. 206 b 6–8.
16. T. v. 25, n. 1509, p. 591 c. 10–12.
17. Chinese: *pao-chin.*
18. *T'ung-hui* is an equivalent for *shen-t'ung* and *chih-hui,* according to Ui Hakujiu, *Bukkyō jiten* (Tokyo: Daitō shuppansha, 1971), p. 748.
19. *Jo-kan* signifies an indefinite number. I have construed *wu jo-kan* as "none."

20. *I-chu:* literally, "one-sided place."
21. *P'u-shih,* perhaps a nonstandard translation for *Samantāloka,* which may be the name of a Bodhisattva who "looks all around." Franklin Edgerton, *Buddhist Hybrid Sanskrit Grammar and Dictionary* (Delhi: Motilal Banarsidass, 1970), p. 563 b.
22. Chinese: *Kuang-ming;* Sanskrit: *Prabhā.*

KUAN-YIN STANDING ON THE WAVES. CH'ING DYNASTY (1644–1912). LIGHT GREEN JADEITE.

The Celestial Bodhisattva Kuan-yin was associated with the sea, serving as the patron and protector of sailors who faced calamities on the waves. (*Photograph by Dawn Hawk. Stanford University Museum of Art, gift of Mrs. Frank E. Buck*)

PART III

Images of the Feminine

SEATED WATER-MOON KUAN-YIN. LATE YÜAN OR EARLY MING DYNASTY. A.D. 14TH CENTURY.

This delicately slender feminine Bodhisattva, who bears a small image of the Buddha Amitābha on her crown, epitomizes the compassionate and tranquil dimension of Kuan-yin. (*Asian Art Museum of San Francisco, The Avery Brundage Collection*)

CHAPTER 7

The Celestial Bodhisattva: Kuan-Yin

Perhaps the most explicit and striking examples from Mahāyāna Buddhist sutra literature, which magnify the tensions between misogyny and egalitarian ideals, were the depictions of Bodhisattvas with sexual transformations. Interpretations of the accessibility of the Bodhisattva path for women ranged from fulfillment of this path only after rebirth as a male to a symbolic transformation of a woman's mental state from the profane, sensual world to the Dharma world. Texts which described Bodhisattvas without sexual transformations fully acknowledged the accessibility of this soteriological path to both sexes.

Chapters 7 and 8 discuss the exalted image of the feminine, exploring theoretical statements concerning the feminine nature of deities. In sharp contrast with Part I, the feminine here is associated with the sacred, the spiritual states of perfection, namely, the celestial Bodhisattva and the Buddha.

The advanced Bodhisattvas of the seventh stage and beyond were known as celestial Bodhisattvas, who had nearly mastered the superpowers of the Buddha. These celestial Bodhisattvas who acted exclusively out of consideration for others were not historical but mythical figures, who became the objects of cult worship throughout the history of India, China, Tibet, and Japan. The deification of Bodhisattvas became popular by the fifth century in India. Rulers were often considered to be manifestations of various celestial Bodhisattvas. In contrast to the lower-level Bodhisattva, the celestial Bodhisattva did not, strictly speaking, pertain to a soteriological path as did the Bodhisattvas described in Chapters 5 and 6. Bodhisattvas, as contrasted with celestial Bodhisattvas, were Buddhist men and sometimes women who were considered by the general populace to be very charitable and sensitive, demonstrating their compassion toward all without ever claiming to be Bodhisattvas. These earnest and committed Buddhists were respected and imitated by others as representing the personality of a Bodhisattva.

The celestial Bodhisattvas became deities in their own right, often being personifications of the highest Mahāyāna Buddhist ideals. In almost all cases the celestial Bodhisattvas were depicted iconographically as males. Their bodies were no longer believed to be constituted of gross material elements but were spiritual or "dharmic" in nature and were created at will under many different forms. Transformations of sex could easily and frequently did occur. The world was a magic show generated by the concentration of the celestial Bodhisattva who freely chose to perform good acts for all living beings (who were also participants in the magical panorama of events).

In many ways these celestial Bodhisattvas, who led living beings to enlightenment and who were the special assistants to the Buddhas, preempted the Buddhas in importance. The average lay Buddhist prayed to the Bodhisattva for assistance in becoming virtuous, for protection from catastrophes, and for material benefits. Since the celestial Bodhisattva was merciful, it was logical for the faithful Buddhist to assume that the Bodhisattva would be concerned with the wishes and needs of his or her followers.

The devotees to these celestial Bodhisattvas attributed names, spiritual and physical attributes, and specific functions to a given celestial Bodhisattva. Among the most famous celestial Bodhisattvas are Mahāsthāmaprāpta and

Avalokiteśvara (Kuan-yin), who are closely associated with the Buddha Amitābha in the *Pure Land Sutra (Sukhāvatīvyūha)* and Mañjuśrī, the eternally youthful Bodhisattva of wisdom, who is associated with the *Perfection of Wisdom.*

The meaning of the name Avalokiteśvara remains ambiguous. Various interpretations are "the lord who sees," "the lord whom we (that is, the world) see," and "the lord who hears the sounds of the world." The Chinese name Kuan-yin or Kuan-shih-yin signifies "looking at the sounds [of living beings]" and "listening to the world's sounds," respectively. Kuan-yin or Avalokiteśvara is usually represented iconographically by eleven heads, facing all directions (samantamukhā)[1] in order to save living beings.

Statues of Avalokiteśvara were common throughout India by the fifth century, according to the Chinese pilgrim Fa-hsien. Avalokiteśvara was the epitome of mercy and compassion who, as the chief assistant to the Buddha Amitābha, escorted the faithful to the Pure Land along with Amitābha's other chief assistant, the Bodhisattva Mahāsthāmaprāpta. Simply hearing the name of Avalokiteśvara would result in great happiness. Any of sixteen male appearances of Avalokiteśvara mentioned in the *Lotus Sutra* may be seen by the faithful who worship him. In the Sanskrit texts of the *Lotus Sutra, Gaṇḍavyūha, Karaṇḍavyūha,* and in other Indian accounts, the Bodhisattva Avalokiteśvara is a male. In China, however, the Bodhisattva who is known as Kuan-yin is usually represented as a female.

It is not at all evident how this intriguing transformation from male to female took place nor whether this change shows a varying assessment as to what feminine attributes are in the various cultures and subcultures in India, Central Asia, and China. One would have to know very nearly the exact time and place and the subculture in which the cult of Avalokiteśvara originated in order to account for the sexual change as recorded in both textual and iconographic representation.

Feminine deities, or more properly speaking, Bodhisattvas, were introduced into Mahāyāna Buddhism by the late fourth century,[2] radically dividing the Mahāyāna tradition from the early Theravādin tradition in which the Buddha was the father figure without an accompanying mother figure. Since Avalokiteśvara is one of the Bodhisattvas who is a construction of philosophers or Buddhist practitioners, one may consider this celestial Bodhisattva as an autonomous deity.[3] By "autonomous" is meant: (1) the deity's independent development outside the Buddhist tradition, being subsequently incorporated by Buddhist practitioners; or (2) a personification and deification of an abstract philosophical principle or ideal which was part of an earlier tradition, for example, the deification of the Perfection of Wisdom.

These autonomous deities entered the Buddhist pantheon as females because of the grammatical accident that they are feminine abstract nouns in the Sanskrit language. Sanskrit abstract nouns are predominantly feminine in gender. However, one could argue that the selection of nouns to express philosophic concepts could have intentionally been chosen in the masculine gender if attributing feminine qualities to a deity were extremely repugnant. Although Mahāyāna Buddhism gradually acknowledged the importance of the feminine, in general, the implications of the feminine and its relation to the masculine as part of the divine were ignored.

There is a possibility that even in some Indian tradition, Avalokiteśvara was known as a female Bodhisattva named Avalokitā. This feminine abstract noun Avalokitā means "the state of looking down [compassionately]." The evidence that Avalokiteśvara existed as Avalokitā is very sparse, if not nonexistent, however. There are some textual difficulties in the *Gaṇḍavyūha* which offer minimal clues that Avalokiteśvara was referred to in the feminine gender.

In China there are numerous images in the caves at Yün-kang and Lung-men which portray Kuan-yin as a male Bodhisattva who even has a moustache in some presentations. These portrayals date as late as the tenth century.[4] Beginning with the T'ang dynasty, that is, in the seventh and early eighth centuries, a delicately slender, white-clad female figure becomes the dominant portrait of this celestial Bodhisattva. She became the patroness of women who wanted children and of sailors who wished to have her protection from calamities at sea. Referred to as the "Goddess of Mercy" the white-clad (pai-i) Kuan-yin was transported to Japan where she was known as Kannon and performed the same functions as she did in China. The origin of the female Bodhisattva Kuan-yin is usually associated with the introduction of Tantric Buddhist texts into China, during the T'ang dynasty. When Kuan-yin emerged as a female celestial Bodhisattva in China, the Tantric Buddhist pantheon which included White Tārā, the female consort to Avalokiteśvara, had been well established in India and had been introduced into Tibet. This White Tārā, according to several scholars, had become assimilated with Avalokiteśvara by Chinese Buddhists who superimposed Tārā's qualities onto Kuan-yin, perhaps believing that the White Tārā was a lower stage manifestation of Avalokiteśvara. This alleged fusion of Tārā with Kuan-yin persisted and continues to predominate to this day throughout China and Japan. Other scholars have attributed the female representation of Kuan-yin to the fusion between Avalokiteśvara and the Taoist Queen Mother of the West.[5]

The scriptural reference to female forms of Kuan-yin appears as early as Kumārajīva's recension of Chapter 25 in the *Lotus Sutra,* which was translated into Chinese in A.D. 406. According to Kumārajīva's translation, Kuan-yin assumes thirty-three appearances, of which seven are female. The number thirty-three has been associated with Kuan-yin ever since by both devout Chinese and Japanese Buddhists. Since the Sanskrit recension refers to only sixteen appearances, all of them male, Kumārajīva's translation indicates that a female depiction of Kuan-yin could have been possible as early as 400 years before the introduction of Tantric texts and the goddess Tārā to China. Since many female Bodhisattvas changed into males in Buddhist literature, the precedent for sexual changes in Bodhisattvas had already been established so that female celestial Bodhisattvas could be a logical possibility.[6] The celestial Bodhisattva Kuan-yin is indicative of a highly successful and popular image of feminine deity for both male and female Buddhists.

Of the artistic representations of Kuan-yin, one of the most popular is the White-Robed Kuan-yin,[7] a slender, white-robed female figure who usually carries a white lotus in her left hand. Another female representation of Kuan-yin shows her with either a water jug or a small child in her arms or near her feet. It is primarily upon the iconography of the White-Robed Kuan-yin that the proponents of the assimilation of Kuan-yin with the White Tārā base their hypothesis.

By A.D. 828 there was a statue of Kuan-yin in every monastery throughout China, numbering over 44,000 statues in all. In Japan all sects of Buddhism still honor Kannon (Kuan-yin) directly or indirectly. In the following translations, due to the ambiguity of Kuan-yin's sex, the female gender is used if the text is Chinese and if it makes no reference to sex.

In the first selection, Chapter 25 of the *Lotus Sutra,* more popularly known in China as the "Kuan-yin sutra," the celestial Bodhisattva is the savior or savioress of the distressed world. As the eye-witness to suffering, Kuan-yin immediately relieves the sorrows of all who call out his or her name. The text displays the magnificent powers of the celestial Bodhisattva in times of need for those who pay reverence and call out the name Kuan-yin. Emphasis is placed upon the many male and female manifestations of Kuan-yin. The particular appearance is dependent upon the needs of the devotee. To men and women who are anxiety-ridden, Kuan-yin appears as a male and female, respectively. The seven female forms are a nun, a Buddhist laywoman, a woman, a housewife, an officer's wife, a Brahman woman, and a young girl. Any of these forms of Kuan-yin are pure, holy, and compassionate. In a sensitive and devotional climax, the text concludes:

> "Having all merits,
> The compassionate eyes which see all beings
> Are the sea of endless merits.
> Therefore, I pay homage to you."

In the second selection, *The Bodhisattva Kuan-yin [Who Explains] the Conditions to Be Born in Pure Land,* the celestial Bodhisattvas Kuan-yin and Mahāsthāmaprāpta are portrayed as small children in their pre-Bodhisattva past lifetimes. The tale is written in an informal Chinese style of popular, vernacular form. A family model of the highest class in Indian society, namely, the Brahman, is the structural framework for the story but overlaid with Confucian elements of filial piety. The father figure and head of the house is Śākyamuni Buddha. In a peculiar twist the mother figure is Amitābha, the Buddha of Pure Land wherein no female forms are allowed. The sons are the two celestial Bodhisattvas Kuan-yin and Mahāsthāmaprāpta, but Kuan-yin also is mentioned as a mother figure for those who have the need for a mother.

Amitābha, represented in this text by the tale of the forbearing and suffering mother, is the central figure in Pure Land Buddhism. In many instances in *The Bodhisattva Kuan-yin [Who Explains] the Conditions to Be Born in Pure*

Land the Perfection of Wisdom as mother of the Buddha is implicit in the description of Amitābha as a mother. The mother in the story of Kuan-yin suffers great pain because of the thoughts of her sons. Likewise, the Perfection of Wisdom, in the metaphorical representation as a mother, suffers pain because of the difficulty of the Bodhisattva practice and of the intense identification with all living beings.[8] The author of *The Bodhisattva Kuan-yin [Who Explains] the Conditions to Be Born in Pure Land* constructs a Buddha family in Pure Land where the Buddha Śākyamuni and the Buddha Amitābha are indispensable partners like a husband and wife, both caring for and instructing the Bodhisattvas. This is an unusual description of Pure Land in which the father figure is usually Amitābha and Śākyamuni is secondary. The maternal side of the Bodhisattva's personality is central to the story.

A. Introduction to the "Kuan-yin Sutra" from the *Lotus Sutra*

The most famous episode devoted to Kuan-yin or Avalokiteśvara is found in Chapter 24 (or Chapter 25 in the Chinese recensions) of the *Lotus Sutra,* entitled "The Universal Face" ("Samantamukhā"). In China this chapter was translated as a separate text by Dharmamitra between 424–441 and was known simply as the "Kuan-yin Sutra."[9] Devout followers of the Kuan-yin cult would recite the text daily for the purpose of receiving the "sea of merits" as well as material benefits promised in the text.

When mantras and Tantric Buddhism were introduced into China during the seventh and eighth centuries, the cult of Kuan-yin became exceedingly popular. By far the most popular and definitive edition is the translation by

Kumārajīva in 406, which is incorporated in his translation of the *Lotus Sutra,* an apparently late addition to the text.

Thirteen cases of calamities or stress are delineated in the text, each of which is an occasion to solicit the compassion of Kuan-yin. Fire is the first calamity, which will change into a cool pond when Kuan-yin's name is invoked. During floods, the second calamity, safety will be assured for those who worship the Bodhisattva. The sailor who sets out on the high seas in search of fortune but fearful of shipwreck and oceanic demons has no cause for concern, for if even one sailor calls out "Kuan-yin" the entire crew will be saved. Besides these environmental disasters, even rightly deserved punishments apparently will be dismissed for the prisoner who invokes the name of Kuan-yin. Ghosts and demons will not be able to see the person who is devoted to Kuan-yin. Little statues or images of Kuan-yin were and still are carried by her devotees as insurance against harm. Robbers who are hazardous to merchants will cease to be a threat. Kuan-yin will assume a merchant's form and dismiss the culprit.

The woman's concern with being childless and therefore considered unworthy of respect was apparently as great a source of fear to her as were the environmental and physical fears of her male counterpart. Kuan-yin would alleviate a woman's anxiety by ensuring that a "virtuous and wise son" or "an exceptionally refined daughter" would be forthcoming for the faithful devotee. Presumably, Kuan-yin would appear as a female with a child whom she often carries as White-Robed Kuan-yin since the sexual form of the Bodhisattva matched the sex of the individual who was paying reverence and seeking assistance.

In caves of Ajanta, Ellora, Aurangābād, and Kānheri, we can see several scenes of the Kuan-yin section of the *Lotus Sutra* depicted with Kuan-yin or Avalokiteśvara in the center of the drama. These eye-witness cave sculptures in India and China surely must have instilled fear of impending danger from both natural causes and from absence of devotion of Kuan-yin.

"Kuan-yin Sutra"* ("Avalokiteśvaraparivarta") from the *Lotus Sutra (Saddharmapuṇḍarīka-sūtram)*, Chapter 24. T. v. 9, n. 262, p. 56 c 2–58 b 7

Then the Bodhisattva Inexhaustible Knowledge [Akṣayamati] rose from his seat, circumambulated me with his hands folded, and said: "Lord, why is the Bodhisattva Kuan-[shih]-yin called Kuan-[shih]-yin?"[10]

I spoke to the Bodhisattva Inexhaustible Knowledge: "Good son, if the unlimited hundreds of millions of living beings who undergo great suffering hear the Bodhisattva Kuan-yin and with concentration call out the name Bodhisattva 'Kuan-yin,'[11] then they will experience that sound [of the name] and all will be liberated. If one retains the name of this Bodhisattva Kuan-yin, then even if thrown into an immense fire, one will not be burned because of this Bodhisattva's great power. If there is a great river which is raging and one calls out this name, one will reach a safe [shallow] spot. If the hundreds of millions of living beings who seek gold, silver, lapis lazuli, tortoise shell, agate, coral, amber, and other precious jewels embark on the great seas and meet with ominous gales which blow their ships, casting them down to the land of demons [Rakṣas], if even one individual in their midst calls out the

*This English translation is by Diana Paul.

name 'Bodhisattva Kuan-yin,' all will be saved from the demons. That is why this Bodhisattva is called 'Kuan-yin.'

"If there is someone who should be punished and calls out the name 'Bodhisattva Kuan-yin,' the one who holds the sword over him would have his sword destroyed and the person [to be punished] would be freed. If the three thousand great world systems were filled with spirits [Yakṣas] and demons [Rakṣas] who wished to torment them and these [Yakṣas and Rakṣas] heard the people calling out the name 'Bodhisattva Kuan-yin,' these evil spirits could not even see them with their evil eyes, let alone harm them. Supposing someone whether innocent or guilty, were handcuffed, chained, or bound, if one calls out the name of the Bodhisattva Kuan-yin these [bonds] will be broken and he will be freed.

"Supposing there is a thousand great world systems where there are robbers and there is a chief merchant who is in charge of the other merchants who carry precious jewels on a hazardous road. One person among them calls out, 'Good sons, do not be afraid. You should all concentrate and call out the name Bodhisattva Kuan-yin. This Bodhisattva can bring fearlessness to all living beings. You should call out the name and you will then be freed from these robbers.' All the merchants then called out, 'Praise to the Bodhisattva Kuan-yin!' Because they called this name, they will be saved.

"Inexhaustible Knowledge, the Bodhisattva Mahāsattva Kuan-yin's magnificent spiritual powers are like this. If living beings are intensely passionate and yet they always revere the Bodhisattva Kuan-yin, they will be able to give up their desire. If they are intensely hateful yet they always revere the Bodhisattva Kuan-yin, they will give up their hatred. If they are greatly disillusioned yet they always revere the Bodhisattva Kuan-yin, they will give up their disillusionment.

"Inexhaustible Knowledge, because of the immense benefits of the Bodhisattva Kuan-yin's power, living beings should always concentrate on this Bodhisattva. If a woman wishes to have a son and worships and pays homage to the Bodhisattva Kuan-yin, she will have a virtuous and wise son. If she wishes to have a daughter, again she will give birth to an exceptionally refined daughter who has past virtuous habits [from former lives] and whom everyone will cherish.

"Inexhaustible Knowledge, because the Bodhisattva Kuan-yin has such power that if living beings revere and worship this Bodhisattva, their favors will not be rejected, living beings should uphold the name of the Bodhisattva Kuan-yin. Inexhaustible Knowledge, if someone upholds the names of the Bodhisattvas numbering sixty-two times the sands of the Ganges and they tirelessly pay homage to the images, revering them and supporting them by donating food, clothing and medicine to all, how great do you think the merit is for those good sons and daughters?"

Inexhaustible Knowledge spoke: "Very great, lord."

I spoke: "If someone upholds the name of the Bodhisattva Kuan-yin for even one time, worshipping and paying homage, the merits of the two are exactly equivalent and without any difference, being inexhaustible for even a period of millions of eons. Inexhaustible Knowledge, upholding the name of the Bodhisattva Kuan-yin will bring unlimited and unending merits."

The Bodhisattva Inexhaustible Knowledge humbly spoke to me: "Lord, why does the Bodhisattva Kuan-yin move about in this secular world? How does this Bodhisattva teach the Dharma for the sake of living beings? How does the power of skill-in-means function?"

I spoke to the Bodhisattva Inexhaustible Knowledge: "Good son, in some lands, for living beings who are capable of being saved by a Buddha, the Bodhisattva Kuan-yin appears as a Buddha's body to teach the Dharma. For those who are capable of being saved by the Pratyeka-buddha, the Bodhisattva appears as a Pratyeka-buddha to teach the Dharma. For those who are capable of being saved by the disciple, the Bodhisattva appears as a disciple to teach the Dharma. For those who are capable of being saved by Brahmā, the Bodhisattva appears as Brahmā to teach the Dharma. For those who are capable of being saved by Indra, the Bodhisattva appears as Indra to teach the Dharma. For those who are capable of being saved by Lord Iśvara, the Bodhisattva appears as Lord Iśvara to teach the Dharma. For those who are capable of being saved by the Great Lord [Śiva], the Bodhisattva appears as the Great Lord to teach the Dharma. For those who are capable of being saved by an emperor, the Bodhisattva appears as an emperor to teach the Dharma. For those who are capable of being saved by Vaiśravaṇa,[12] the Bodhisattva appears as Vaiśravaṇa to teach the Dharma. For those who are capable of being saved by a minor king, the Bodhisattva appears as a minor king to teach the Dharma. For those who are capable of being saved by a merchant, the Bodhisattva appears as a merchant to teach the Dharma. For those who are capable of being saved by a householder, the Bodhisattva appears as a householder to teach the Dharma. For those who are capable of being saved by an officer, the Bodhisattva appears as an officer to teach the Dharma. For those who are capable of being saved by a Brahman, the Bodhisattva appears as a Brahman to teach the Dharma. For those who are capable of being saved by a monk, nun, layman, or laywoman, the Bodhisattva appears as a monk, nun, layman, or laywoman to teach the Dharma. For those who are capable of being saved by a woman, housewife, an officer's wife, or a Brahman woman, the Bodhisattva appears as a woman, housewife, an officer's wife, or a Brahman woman to teach the Dharma. For those who are capable of being saved by a young boy or girl, the Bodhisattva appears as a young boy or girl to teach the Dharma. For those who are capable of being saved by a Nāga, spirit, Gandharva, antigod, birdlike being, semihuman being, great serpent and others, the Bodhisattva appears as these to teach the Dharma. For those who are capable of being saved by Vajrapāṇi,[13] the Bodhisattva appears as Vajrapāṇi to teach the Dharma.

"Inexhaustible Knowledge, this Bodhisattva Kuan-yin has such attributes. By means of various appearances, this Bodhisattva moves about in various lands saving living beings. Therefore, you should concentrate and revere the Bodhisattva Kuan-yin. This Bodhisattva, a great being, can bring fearlessness to those who are in imminent danger and are frightened. Therefore, in this profane world all call this Bodhisattva the giver of fearlessness [Abhayaṃdada]."

The Bodhisattva Inexhaustible Knowledge humbly spoke to me: "Lord, today I will revere the Bodhisattva Kuan-yin." Then he unfastened a jewel necklace from around his neck, to the value of one hundred thousand gold pieces and offered it to the Bodhisattva, saying: "Kind one, accept this righteous gift of the jewel necklace." But the Bodhisattva Kuan-yin did not wish to accept it. The Bodhisattva Inexhaustible Knowledge again humbly spoke to the Bodhisattva Kuan-yin: "Kind one, because of your compassion for me and others, accept this necklace."

Then I, the Buddha, spoke to the Bodhisattva Kuan-yin: "You should be compassionate to this Bodhisattva Inexhaustible Knowledge and to the four classes [varṇa], the gods, Nāgas, spirits, Gandharvas, antigods, birdlike beings, semihumans, great serpents, and nonhumans. Therefore, accept this jewel necklace." Then the Bodhisattva Kuan-yin, having compassion for the four classes and for the gods, Nāgas, nonhumans, etc., accepted the jewel necklace and divided it into two. One half she gave to me, Sākyamuni, and the other she gave for the stūpa of the Buddha Prabhuratna.

"Inexhaustible Knowledge, the Bodhisattva Kuan-yin

has such spiritual power with which to move about in this secular world."

Then the Bodhisattva Inexhaustible Wisdom recited the following verses[14]:

"You, lord, endowed with profound marks
Today I would like to ask:
'Son of the Buddha, what are the reasons
For the name Kuan-yin?'

You with profound marks
Answered me:
'You listened to Kuan-yin's practices
Who responds well to all directions.

Professing vows as deep as the sea,
For immeasurable, inconceivable time
Serving many millions of Buddhas,
Kuan-yin professes great and pure vows.

I will briefly explain for you,
Hear the name and see the form.
Concentrate and do not err
And [Kuan-yin] will remove your sorrow.

If someone wishes to harm you,
Even if thrown into a great fiery pit,
Concentrate on the power of Kuan-yin
And the fiery pit will change into a pond.

If one is floating in the sea
With snakes, fish and various demons,
Concentrate on the power of Kuan-yin
And the waves will not drown you.

If someone on Mt. Sumeru
Is hurled down by another,
Concentrate on the power of Kuan-yin
And like the sun, you will stay in the sky.

If an evil man pursues you
And you fall down Mt. Vajra,

Concentrate on the power of Kuan-yin
And not even a hair will be hurt.

If one is surrounded by robbers
Carrying swords to stab you,
Concentrate on the power of Kuan-yin
And they will become kind.

If one meets an evil king who is offended
And according to law, wishes to execute you,
Concentrate on the power of Kuan-yin
And the sword will be shattered.

If one is imprisoned in chains
And hands and feet are bound,
Concentrate on the power of Kuan-yin
And you will be freed.

If one casts a spell on you with potions,
Desiring to harm you,
Concentrate on the power of Kuan-yin
And then you will part from him.

If one meets with a demon,
A poisonous Nāga or spirit,
Concentrate on the power of Kuan-yin
And then no one can harm you.

If one is surrounded by vicious beasts
With sharp hooks and claws which are frightful,
Concentrate on the power of Kuan-yin
And they will disperse in all directions.

If [one meets] snakes and dragons
With virulent and fiery venom,
Concentrate on the power of Kuan-yin
And the sound [of the name] will make them retreat.

If thunder and lightning
Bring down torrential rains,
Concentrate on the power of Kuan-yin
And then they will cease.

All living beings are distressed
And bear unlimited pains;
Kuan-yin's profound wisdom and power
Can save the world from pain.

Endowed with spiritual power,
Extensive knowledge and skill-in-means,
In all lands and all directions
There is no land which does not see Kuan-yin.

For all the deplorable destinies,
For those in hell and for animals,
Birth, old age, sickness and death
Will gradually cease.'

For the one who truly sees and sees purely,
Who sees with extensive wisdom,
Who compassionately and kindly sees,
I vow always to revere you.

Immaculate and pure light
Whose sunlike wisdom eliminates darkness,
You can conquer calamities of fire and storm
Illuminating the entire world.

Compassionate one, who regulates thunder,
Compassionate mind, subtle like a great cloud
Which moistens with the sweet dew of Dharma rain,
Extinguish the fire of defilement.

In times of strife which pass through the ranks
Among the frightened troops,
Concentrate on the power of Kuan-yin
And the enemy will retreat.

The subtle sound of Kuan-yin,
The sound of Brahma, the sound of the sea,
The excellent sound in all the world,
Therefore, I will always think of you.

Concentrate and do not doubt
The purity and holiness of Kuan-yin,

For all pain and death
Will end for those who depend [on Kuan-yin].

Having all merits,
The compassionate eyes which see all beings,
Are the sea of endless merits.
Therefore, I pay homage to you."[15]

Then the Bodhisattva Incantation Holder [Dharaṇīṃdhara] rose from his seat and humbly spoke to me: "Lord, if any living being hears the Kuan-yin chapter about the powerful actions of the one who faces all directions and sees the tremendous spiritual power, you should know that the merits of that person are not negligible."

When I had explained this chapter, everyone of the eighty-four thousand living beings in the assembly awakened to the thought of Supreme, Perfect Enlightenment, which is without equal.

B. Introduction to *The Sutra of the Bodhisattva Kuan-yin [Who Explains] the Conditions to Be Born in Pure Land*

As the title of the text indicates, the Bodhisattva Kuan-yin explains the conditions for being born in Pure Land in the presence of the Buddha Śākyamuni and the assembly. The old catalogues of sutra and commentary literature have no record of this text nor of its date of translation. In the appendix to the Indian compilation in the *Hsü tsang ching*, a Western Chin catalogue *(Hsi chin yüan)* is said to have an entry for it. It is a late composition in which the translator's identity has not been preserved, but the text is probably a Chinese rather than Indian composition. There is no recension in either Sanskrit or Tibetan. In terms of its content, the text discusses the popularity of the Pure Land teaching from a sectarian bias and reveals the past conditions of the Bodhisattva Kuan-yin who now resides on Mt. Potalaka.

The five principal characters in the text are the Buddhas Śākyamuni and Amitābha and the Bodhisattvas Dhāraṇīśvara, Kuan-yin, and Mahāsthāmaprāpta. The text opens with an assembly of monks, humans, and spirits gathering on Vulture Peak to hear the Buddha Śākyamuni who has just emitted a brilliant ray of light. A verse describing Kuan-yin is recited from within the rays of light. Because the assembly is bewildered, Śākyamuni directs the Bodhisattva Dhāraṇīśvara to go visit Kuan-yin and ask about the verse and the conditions for being born in Pure Land.

Kuan-yin narrates a tale concerning one previous rebirth as a little boy with his younger brother. The story is in the form of a flashback to a pre-Bodhisattva existence in which family tragedy influences the Bodhisattva Kuan-yin's commitment to vow to save all living beings and help them to be born in Pure Land. The compassion and love which Kuan-yin's mother embodied is the inspiration for Kuan-yin to save other beings and persevere in the Bodhisattva practice.

Filial piety is extolled; Kuan-yin vows never to part from the parents who were so good and virtuous. The family is ostensibly Indian but by implication represents the ideal Confucian model of the family. For example, on the mother's death bed she instructs her sons to awaken to the thought of enlightenment, embarking on the Bodhisattva career as a way to fulfill the four kindnesses to one's parents which are advocated by Confucianism:

> Now Quickly Separating, with a tender attitude, stretched out his two hands to reach the fine neck [of his mother]. In a high voice he wailed. Now Mānasārā [the mother] said to her two children: "You will arrive

> at the path without transgressing, awakening to the thought of enlightenment. Those who have the thought of enlightenment truly are compassionate. When you have reached a very old age, you will want to repay the four kindnesses [of your parents]. The thought of enlightenment will then benefit you."

Not only is Kuan-yin a representative of the feminine, maternal aspect of the Mahāyāna Buddhist ideal, but also Amitābha, Buddha of Pure Land, is represented as the compassionate dying mother who first inspired Kuan-yin and advised that the pursuit of the Bodhisattva career would be meritorious. In two separate metaphors Amitābha is the mother figure in the family model of the Pure Land, not the father figure. Kuan-yin follows Amitābha's example.

The following story is poignant and highly dramatic, written in a very flowing vernacular style in which the pace of the dialogues is rapid. There is much suspense which involves a fortune teller, a murder plot, and a wicked stepmother. The translator has found this particular story to be unlike any other tale in either Sanskrit or Chinese Buddhist sutra literature with regard to subject matter, style, and dramatization.

*The Sutra of the Bodhisattva Kuan-yin [Who Explains] the Conditions to Be Born in Pure Land**(Kuan-shih-yin p'u-sa wang-sheng ching-t'u pen-yüan ching)*. Chinese text in *Dai nihon zokuzōkyō*, part 1, 87.4.

Thus I [Ānanda] have heard [from the Buddha who preached this sermon to me]:

At one time, I, the Buddha, was residing at Rājagṛha on Vulture Peak with an assembly of monks, great Bodhisattvas, and various gods, Nāgas, humans, semihumans, and others comprising the eight categories of living beings who had come to pay reverence and were surrounding me for the purpose of [hearing] the teaching of the birth of the great Bodhisattva [Kuan-yin]. At that time a brilliant light radiated before me, illuminating southern India and gradually reaching other lands. Within this brilliant light, the following verse was recited:

Endowed with great compassion and the doors to liberation,
I eternally dwell on Mt. Potalaka in this world.
Day and night during the six changes [of time]
Kuan-yin's original vows cause benefits for all.

At that time the assembly saw this brilliant light and heard this verse. They never had such a thought and could not help but wonder. In succession they asked about the causes, but no one answered. Then, among the many Bodhisattvas was one great being, named Dharaṇīśvara-rāja, who rose from his seat and humbly spoke to me: "Lord, what are the causes for seeing this brilliant light? Who emitted it? We, in the assembly, have seen this brilliant light and have heard the verse, but yet we do not know

*This first English translation is by Diana Paul.

the cause. I wish, for our benefit, that you would explain the cause."

I spoke to Dharanīśvara Bodhisattva: "All right, listen well. From the west, passing Buddha lands more numerous than twenty thousand times the sands of the Ganges there is a world called the 'Pure Land' [Sukhāvatī]. In this land living beings do not have any suffering. They only experience happiness of all kinds. In this kingdom there is a Buddha named Amitābha. The holy ones of the Three Vehicles[16] completely fill his land. There is one Bodhisattva named Kuan-[shih]-yin who is bound to only one more rebirth [before Buddhahood]. For a long time during which various habits were cultivated, Kuan-yin accomplished the practice of compassion. Kuan-yin would like to come to this land now to reveal the fundamental causes for birth in the Pure Land. Displaying this brilliant light which illuminates the entire world, Kuan-yin will come here soon. You should ask Kuan-yin about the cause for this verse."

At that time the Bodhisattva Kuan-yin, the great being, and the assembly of one hundred thousand great Bodhisattvas had come together on Vulture Peak to pay homage to me. Having praised and worshipped me, they retreated to one side. Then Bodhisattva Dharaṇīśvara-rāja, through my sustaining power, went to Kuan-yin and they [the two Bodhisattvas] greeted each other. [Then Dharaṇīśvara-rāja] said to Kuan-[shih]-yin: "Good son,[17] from where was this brilliant light emitted? Please explain in detail the subtle and profound verse which I do not yet understand. What do you mean by fundamental cause?"

Then Kuan-yin spoke to Dharaṇīśvara-rāja: "Countless and inconceivable eons ago there was a kingdom in southern India called Maṇivatī. In this country there was a Brahman named Dīrghanakha, a householder, who was very wealthy. He had a wife named Mānasārā, who had not yet had a child. The husband and wife were always extremely disheartened: 'We have great wealth and property, yet we have no other thought but that we have no child. This is [a source of] great sorrow. Let us pray to the gods sincerely in expectation of a child.'

"His wife became pregnant in a short time, and when her time had come, she gave birth to a son whose handsomeness was incomparable. When he was three years old, she gave birth to another son. The Brahman [now] had two children and was ecstatic. He called in a fortune teller to see his two sons, but when the fortune teller saw [them], he became unhappy. After a long time he [the fortune teller] spoke [reluctantly] 'These children, although they are handsome, will separate from their parents shortly. The older son I will call Rapidly Separating. His younger brother I will call Quickly Separating.'

"Although they understood these words, the man and his wife together raised and cared [for their children] tirelessly. When Rapidly Separating turned seven years of age and when Quickly Separating turned five years of age, their mother was dying of a disease arising from the malfunctioning of the four elements in her body. Her physical appearance was pitiful and had deteriorated. Due to her extreme suffering and pain from the disease, she was unable to have a restful sleep. Water and food had been stopped, and she was at the threshold of death.

"The two children were to the left and right of their mother. They lifted their faces and eyes to her in sadness and loving compassion and cried. Their mother heard her children's compassionate voices and blood and tears flowed. From her sick bed she arose and touched the heads of her two children with her left and right hand saying: 'The destruction within the life-death cycle is inescapable. What the fortune teller stated is inexorably true. What is regrettable is that you, who have not yet reached the age of maturity, will leave and separate from me. What crime have I committed for this punishment? How unfortunate you are!'

"Then Rapidly Separating was resting on the side of her pillow. He swooned from extreme sorrow. After a long time he revived and cried out to heaven, wailing: 'We are now young and without knowledge. If we have no mother, who will show us the path? Heaven and earth are vast. Our spiritual welfare has no support. How can we part?'

"The compassionate mother soothed them with comforting words: 'Such are the ways of the world. What is born must cease like sailing a vessel which, in a short time, must come to rest. What you now hear of my sorrowful moanings is due to my illness.'[18]

"Now Quickly Separating, with a tender attitude, stretched out his two hands to reach the fine neck [of his mother]. In a high voice he wailed. Now Mānasārā [the mother] said to her two children: 'You will arrive at the path without transgressing, awakening to the thought of enlightenment. Those who have the thought of enlightenment truly are compassionate. When you have reached a very old age, you will want to repay the four kindnesses [of your parents]. The thought of enlightenment will then benefit you. For now, you must not cry for me although I am dying. You will live together with your father.'

"Then she called for Dīrghanakha and spoke to him: 'Now I have been with you like a wheel to a cart, like a feather to a bird. Then we had two children. I am dying and you are living. Your loving care will not be different from mine when I am no longer alive. If other circumstances arise, do not change your attitude [with regard to your care for our children].'

"The Brahman heard his wife's words and then fell with grief to the ground. When he revived, he cried out: 'A wagon without one wheel cannot advance one step. A bird without one wing cannot fly one foot into the air. When you enter death's door, who will care for our two children with me? The parting of a loving husband and wife is most sorrowful. I do not desire the world and will abandon my life in order to enter the door of death [with you].'

"Then his wife again spoke: 'You and I together gave birth to our two sons. Vow not to separate but to care for our two children.' Then she closed her eyes after saying this.

"Then the father and his two sons took [to heart] the words of the dying [mother]. They buried her and returned home.

"The older son sat on his right knee, longing for his mother. The younger son sat on his left knee, longing for food and sympathy [from his mother]. The Brahman, in his grief-stricken heart, thought to himself: 'I have no strength to seek another woman to be my wife who will care for and raise my young children.'

"Now there was a Brahman named Vīra who had a daughter who was virtuous at heart. When he [Dīrghanakha] took that woman for his wife, there was worldwide suffering from famine. The resources and crops had gradually been exhausted. The granary was empty. There was no means for making a living nor anything to rely upon. Dīrghanakha then spoke to his wife: 'I have heard that there is a mountain called Daṇḍaka in the north, about seven days travel from here. On this mountain there are sweet fruits. If I travel to that mountain and pick these exquisite fruits, I will be able to support you and the two children. After I return I will be able to provide for you.'

"The wife accepted what he said and supported the two children as would their natural mother. The husband went to the mountain alone for his mission and had been gone [now] for about twenty-seven days. When he had not returned, the wife had misgivings. She had these thoughts: 'Supposing Dīrghanakha does not return from that mountain. How could I support the two children? If he does pick fruits and comes home, although he has loving thoughts for his two children, what kind of share [of the fruits] will I have? Now I have a contingency plan to eliminate the two children.'

"Having had these thoughts, she spoke to a boatsman and set up a time. Then she told the two children: 'I have no strength to support you. Your father has not yet returned. Near this southern area there is an island on the seashore which is isolated. On the shore there are sweet fruits and on the banks there are beautiful vegetables. Together we should go to that isolated island.'

"They went to the boatsman's place. She and the two children rode together in the boat across the sea to the isolated island shore. She spoke to the two children: 'You two should descend first. You play on the banks and in the sand. I will remain on the boat to prepare the food. Step down from the boat and go look for fruits and vegetables.'

"Then the two children stepped down from the boat and ran around, playing without concern. Their stepmother secretively rode away in the boat, returning to her town. The two children returned to the river bank but they saw no boat. They did not know where their mother went. They ran to the seashore until they were exhausted and cried out: 'Mama.' But no one answered. The two children cried pitifully all day and night. The older brother Rapidly Separating then spoke: 'Our compassionate mother parted from us; having left, she will not return. Our compassionate father went to the Daṇḍaka mountain and did not return. Our stepmother placed us on this isolated island and secretively left. How can we continue to live?'

"Then he recalled his natural mother saying: 'I must awaken to the thought of Supreme, Perfect Enlightenment, become accomplished in the great compassion of the Bodhisattva, and practice the doors to enlightenment. First I must save others and then later I will become a Buddha. For those who have no parents, I will appear and serve as their parents. For those who have no eminent teacher, I will appear as their eminent teacher. For those who are poor, then I will appear as their benefactor. For kings and ministers of state, merchants, householders, rulers, and Brahmans, for the four assemblies and the eight groups [of living beings], for all the various kinds [of beings], there is none for whom I will not appear. I vow that I will always remain on this island. In all lands, in all directions, I will bestow peace and happiness. I will change[19] the mountains, rivers, land, the vegetation, five grains, and the sweet fruits to enable them [the living beings] to receive and make use of them, rapidly leaving the life-death cycle.'

" 'I vow that I will be born where my mother is and will not separate from where my father is. In this way I profess one hundred vows to the end of my life.'

"[Meanwhile] the father Dīrghanakha left Daṇḍaka mountain where he had picked the fruits and returned to his home. He first asked about his two children. The stepmother answered: 'Your children now are begging for alms and roaming about.'

"Their father then went to his friend's residence to ask about where the children were. The friend answered: 'After you left for over twenty-seven days, their stepmother set out and placed them on an isolated island in the southern seas. They certainly must have starved to death.'

"Then Dīrghanakha cried out in a severely self-rebuking way: 'Because I went to Daṇḍaka mountain to pick sweet fruit in order to support my two children, what kind of crime have I committed [to deserve this]? All of a sudden I have met with the misfortune of two separations. The first separation was difficult to endure. Now I have also separated from those to whom I gave birth and cannot bear it.'

"So he looked for a small boat and went to the isolated

island shore. He frantically looked for them in all directions, but there were only white bones heaped up in one spot. Clothing was scattered on the seashore. 'I know these are the bones of my dead children.' Embracing their clothing and bones, he wept and made a vow: 'I vow that I will save all evil living beings and realize Buddhahood. I will change the great land, the water, fire, and wind, the vegetation, and forests in order to support all living beings. I will change the five grains to increase the nourishment of others. As a god or human or spirit, in all worthy or unworthy shapes and forms, there is no land where I will not appear.'

"In this manner he professed five hundred vows. In addition [he said]: 'I will always remain in this mundane world to explain the Dharma and to teach and change [others].' During this time he did not eat and died. India quaked. The gods came, and the beasts compassionately cried out without rest. In the sky there were changes and dispersion [of the atmosphere]. They [the gods] made offerings to the white bones.

"The Brahman Dīrghanakha of that time is now Śākyamuni, the Tathāgata. The mother Mānasārā is now Amitābha, the Tathāgata. I was the older brother Rapidly Separating. Mahāsthāmaprāpta, the Bodhisattva, was my younger brother Quickly Separating. The friend is now Dhāraṇīśvara-rāja, the Bodhisattva. The mountain Daṇḍaka of former times is now Vulture Peak. The isolated island of former times is now Mt. Potalaka. When the [past] eon had come to an end, although the material world had been destroyed, when the [next] eon was formed, first there was a reciprocal returning [of elements] to that mountain. On its north face there was a cave. There was a great rock like a diamond called Ratnakarma. I always remain on that rock teaching with great compassion, practicing the doors of enlightenment and perfecting living beings.

"In the past, when I was Rapidly Separating, I professed

the vow to remain on top of the mountain. There is a seven-jeweled palace hall adorned in a rare and wonderful way. I always reside in that jeweled palace and reveal the teaching's benefits and joys. That was the place where I used to call [the name of] my parents. I depended upon that thought to be born in the Pure Land and to attain the [Bodhisattva] stage of irreversibility. Because I had the thought of abandoning my body, I remained on that mountain with various animals and beasts. In the past I converted them and presented vegetation to the place where I had abandoned my body, piling up leaves underneath. I should know that the verses from within that light [emitted at the beginning of the text] were also similar in circumstances throughout time."

Then I, Śākyamuni, the Tathāgata, praised Kuan-yin, the Bodhisattva, saying: "Excellent, excellent. It is truly as you have said. The conditions for being born [in Pure Land] are all like this. You and the others ought to know that, just as we do today, I and Amitābha each convert from the beginning to the end [of time]. Take the case of the mother and father who have one very young child who falls down to the bottom of a well. His father goes down to the bottom of the well to look for his child and to place him on the side ['shore']. His mother is on the side and embraces and cares for him. The close relatives help the mother care for him together with the assistance of friends. He [the child] does not return to the mud in the well. I am like the compassionate father. The five [kinds of] lowly ['muddy'] living beings are like the bottom of the well. Amitābha is like the compassionate mother who waits at the side which is like Pure Land. Kuan-yin Bodhisattva is like the friend who has realized irreversibility and does not return [to earlier stages of Bodhisattvahood].

"You ought to know that by entering this world in the middle of the five lowly [kinds of living beings], by teaching and changing the deluded and ignorant living beings in the six evil destinies, you cause them to be born in the Pure Land. Amitābha draws you out and does not abandon you. Kuan-yin and Mahāsthāmaprāpta protect and cause the irreversibility and nonreturnability of all [Bodhisattvas and others] who depend upon past conditions for professing their vows."

Then Amitābha, the Tathāgata, among countless hundreds of thousands in the holy assembly, manifested himself in the sky and recited the following verses:

"Excellent Śākyamuni,
Who resided among the lowly beings to benefit them.
Those who hear your name and see you
Will be steadfast in the path to Buddhahood.

Because of one's past conditions
Now one will see you in the sky.
Desiring to be born where I am,
You must go to the west."

Then Śākyamuni Buddha praised Amitābha in the following verses:

"Excellent, perfect lord,
You can bring benefits to this world.
Manifesting the truth, the Dharma,
Your compassion is given to all.

If there are karmic obstacles
Causing one not to be born in Pure Land,
Carried by the power of Amitābha,
They must be born in Pure Land.

If there are those who commit many crimes,
They would fall into hell.
Just hearing your name 'Amitābha'
The fierce fire will be cooled.

If one is mindful of you, Buddha Amitābha,
Then limitless crimes will cease.
One will receive the incomparable bliss,
Finally and inevitably being born in Pure Land."

Then Kuan-yin rose from his [her] seat and recited the following verses:

"The two lords [Śākyamuni and Amitābha] who have come out like the sun
Can destroy the darkness of life and death,
Revealing the conditions for birth
Which cannot be lost throughout time.

I am mindful of the limitless eons
In which I have lived on the isolated island shore.
When I awoke to the thought of enlightenment
This caused my continual presence on Potalaka.

In the past when I was in the life-death cycle,
The two lords were my mother and father.
Now I am in the Pure Land
And together [with them] help change the world."

Then Mahāsthāmaprāpta recited the following verses:

"From the moment I awakened to the thought of enlightenment
I have followed the two lords, never parting.
Now I have heard of the past causes
And can know the causes do not end.

When I move one foot
The three evils are separated from the Bodhisattva.
When it is time for you to be born in the Pure Land
I will give my hand and we will meet in the west."

Then Dhāraṇīśvararāja recited the following verse:

"In the past I was a friend,
Today I am able to know this.

Those who are able to hear
Will definitely be born in Pure Land."

Then Amitābha Buddha was suddenly aware [of everything] and disappeared. The great assembly was joyous, revered him, and then left.

Notes

1. Ten of the heads represent the ten directions in Indian cosmology while the eleventh represents the Buddha Amitābha. For an excellent study of the textual and iconographic presentations of Avalokiteśvara in India and an analysis of various interpretations of the Sanskrit name, see Marie-Thérèse de Mallmann, *L'Introduction à l'étude d'Avalokiteçvara* (Paris: Presses Universitaires de France, 1967).
2. Edward Conze, *Thirty Years of Buddhist Studies: Selected Essays* (Columbia: University of South Carolina, 1968), p. 81.
3. Edward Conze, *Buddhism: Its Essence and Development* (New York: Harper Torchbook, 1959), p. 192.
4. Kenneth K. S. Ch'en, *The Chinese Transformation of Buddhism* (Princeton: Princeton University Press, 1973), p. 6.
5. See John J. Chamberlayne, "The Development of Kuan Yin, the Goddess of Mercy," *Numen*, 9 (January 1962), 45–52; Henri Doré, *Recherches sur les superstitions en Chine*, VI, 194–96; and Zenryū Tsukamoto, *Studies in Indology and Buddhology* (Kyoto: Hōzōkan, 1955). Whalen Lai, "Women and the Pure Land," unpublished paper, discusses the feminization of Buddhism in China.
6. C. N. Tay, "Kuan-yin: The Cult of Half Asia," *History of Religions*, November 1976, cites several instances of female portrayals of Kuan-yin before the T'ang dynasty (pp. 151–52).
7. Sanskrit: *Pāndaravāsinī;* Chinese *Pai-i.*
8. Edward Conze, tr., *The Perfection of Wisdom in Eight Thousand Lines and Its Verse Summary* (Bolinas, Ca.: Four Seasons, 1973), pp. 172–73.
9. *Kuan-p'u-hsien-hsing-fa ching,* T. v. 9, n. 277, p. 389. I have translated from the more popular Kumārajīva version.
10. Since this chapter of the *Lotus Sutra* became revered as a separate sutra by the Chinese who were devoted to the Bodhisattva Kuan-yin, sometimes called Kuan-shih-yin, the author has retained the Chinese name for the Bodhisattva to reflect the Chinese interpretation of the text rather than the Sanskrit name Avalokiteśvara and the Indian Buddhist interpretation.

11. "Kuan-yin" means "perceiving sounds," i.e., the sounds of those calling the Bodhisattva's name. "Kuan-shih-yin" (Sanskrit: *Avalokiteśvara*) means "perceiving the world's sounds."
12. The deity of the north.
13. The name of a Yakṣa of imposing and terrifying appearance; the epithet of Indra; the name of a Bodhisattva who is cited in the *Laṅkāvatāra-sūtra, Daśabhūmika-sūtra,* and in the *Śikṣasamuccaya,* among other texts; Franklin Edgerton, *Buddhist Hybrid Sanskrit Grammar and Dictionary* (Delhi: Motilal Banarsidass, 1970), p. 467 b.
14. According to the Sanskrit edition, the Buddha recites the verses. Cf. H. Kern, tr., *The Saddharma-puṇḍarīkā, or The Lotus of the True Law* (Oxford: Clarendon Press, 1884); reprinted in Delhi by Motilal Banarsidass, 1965, p. 413.
15. Verses 28–33 are excluded from Kumārajīva's translation. Verse 31 excludes women and sexual intercourse, Kern, p. 417: "There no women are to be found; there sexual intercourse is absolutely unknown; there the sons of Jina, on springing into existence by apparitional birth, are sitting in the undefiled cups of lotuses."
16. Arhats, Pratyeka-buddhas, and Bodhisattvas.
17. This is the only indication that the form of Bodhisattva Kuan-yin is probably appearing as a male in this story. However, son (nan tzu) is also applied to female Bodhisattvas.
18. The mother is trying to comfort her children by saying that she is not moaning because of the impending separation from her two young sons but because of the pains of sickness.
19. *Pien tso* literally means "changing into and becoming something." A literal translation would be making the claim that Kuan-yin would become the great land, water, fire, wind, etc., in order to help all beings. Since Bodhisattvas assume forms of sentient beings rather than of inanimate objects, the translator has interpreted this passage as a claim that Kuan-yin would vow to change useless or hostile inanimate objects into useful and harmonious ones. The "Kuan-yin Sutra" attributed to Kuan-yin the power to change the environment.

CHAPTER 8

A Female Buddha?

This chapter directly raises the question of the possibility of female Buddhas, a question which had continually vexed Buddhist scholars and commentators. They attempted to come to terms with the possibility of a relationship between a notion of ultimate spiritual perfection or Buddhahood and the feminine. Such a relationship was viewed ambivalently. This question was raised only by Mahāyāna Buddhists, particularly those who proclaimed one path to universal Buddhahood (Ekayāna). For these Buddhists, all men and women equally had the nature of the Buddha. But, what did Buddha nature then suggest for woman's physical and psychological nature? If women were truly capable of having a Buddha nature in this lifetime without undergoing any sexual transformation, this would implicitly indicate that women were not biologically determined as religiously, psychologically, and physically inferior to men.

In the early period of Buddhism, women were prohibited from realizing the "five stations" of being the god Brahmā, the god Indra, a great king, an emperor, or an irreversible Bodhisattva. The episode of the Nāga princess in the *Lotus Sutra*, described in Chapter 5, illustrated the adherence to that belief in a woman's limitations. The teaching of a sexual transformation from female to male, a popular theme in Mahāyāna Buddhist texts, provided a means by which women could become irreversible Bodhisattvas. We have seen several cases in Chapter 5 of female Bodhisattvas who changed their sex either before or immediately after receiving the prediction of future Buddhahood.

According to the *Lotus Sutra* commentary, *Miao-fa lien-hua ching wen-chü,* (*chüan* eight), which cites the *Bodhisattva in the Womb Sutra* as its authority, the females in the heavens of Māra, Brahmā, and Indra attained Buddhahood in their present bodies without sexual transformation.[1] The verses in the *Bodhisattva in the Womb Sutra* declare that:

> The nature of the Dharma is like the great sea. One cannot say it is true or false. The common man and the saint are equal, neither being superior or inferior. There is only the extinction of impurities of the mind. . . [2]

Other commentaries on the *Lotus Sutra* also claim that there is no necessity to undergo sexual changes prior to Buddhahood. For example, the *Fa-hua wen-chü chi* commentary claims that if an individual has attained the patience to understand the Emptiness (nonarising) of all phenomena, then there would be no necessity to relinquish one's present physical form for another.[3] According to the complete teaching of the T'ien-t'ai school of Chinese Buddhism, sudden Buddhahood within the present lifetime is possible. The Nāga princess episode from the *Lotus Sutra* is an example of the "complete teaching."[4]

The issue of the Nāga princess' awakening to the thought of enlightenment is discussed in another commentary on the *Lotus Sutra* entitled *Fa-hua i-shu.* Based upon a sutra known as the *Chia-yeh shan-ting ching* (*The Mt. Gāya Sutra*), the *Fa-hua i-shu* distinguishes four kinds of awakening to the thought of enlightenment: (1) the awakening experience immediately prior to entering the first stage of the Bodhisattva practice, (2) the practitioner who awakens to the thought of enlightenment during the second through seventh stages of the Bodhisattva practice, (3) the mind which is irreversible in its awakening experience at the eighth or ninth stage of Bodhisattva practice, and (4) the awakening experience of one who has only one more lifetime[5] as a Bodhisattva, that is, the tenth stage Bodhisattva.[6] According to the commentator, the Nāga princess had experienced the fourth kind of awakening and was therefore an imminent Buddha.

The *Fa-hua i-shu* maintains that there are four types of Buddhahood: (1) those who have skill-in-means of a slow nature; their enlightenment process will take ten eons to complete; (2) those who have skill-in-means of a sudden nature like the Nāga princess' instantaneous Buddhahood; (3) those who have skill-in-means which is both slow and sudden like Śākyamuni; and (4) those who have skill-in-means which is neither slow nor sudden like Buddhahood in Pure Land.[7] Instantaneous Buddhahood is attributed to the Nāga princess whose skill-in-means was sudden, reaffirming the fact that she is an imminent Buddha.

The commentator's discourse on the sex and age of the enlightened or imminently enlightened individual are critical to establishing whether feminine attributes were appropriate qualifications of the notion of Buddhahood. The *Fa-hua i-shu*, in delineating the sexual characteristics of a Buddha, implicitly interprets sexual transformation as a physiological process: (1) In a male body there is enlightenment like Śākyamuni. (2) In a female body there is enlightenment. There is a specific sutra[8] which states that a Buddha appeared in a land of women and in a female body became a Buddha. (3) In both a male and female [body] like the Nāga princess. Originally a female she changed into a male. And (4) in neither a male or female [body] nor in a divine or human [body] like Buddhahood in Pure Land.[9]

The Nāga princess is an imminent Buddha in which the maleness is not emphasized as in the first claim, nor is the femaleness emphasized as in the second. The implicit presupposition is that both males and females become enlightened. In the fourth claim an asexual enlightenment is the case. Asexuality implies the transcendence of physical characteristics and dualistic oppositions because of false discriminations.

With reference to age, the *Fa-hua i-shu* lists three possible qualifications of Buddhahood: (1) The very young become Buddhas; the Nāga girl is such a case. (2) Those who are not very young become Buddhas; Śākyamuni is such a case. And (3) those who are neither, like the Buddha in Pure Land.[10] The very young age of the Nāga princess, combined with her female sex, perhaps suggests the innocence of the female before puberty. Young females are not involved with the sensual realm. On the other hand, the commentator may only be asserting that there is ultimately no age or sex discrimination in Buddhist literature. All of the statements concerning sudden and gradual enlightenment, sexuality and enlightenment, and age with relationship to enlightenment are accepted as expedients for helping others receive and accept Buddhism. From the above commentaries, one may conclude that sudden enlightenment is possible within one's present lifetime, that a female body does not preclude enlightenment, and that regardless of age enlightenment is a viable option. Enlightenment is sexless and ageless.

Buddhahood is discussed in the *Fa-hua i-shu* as neither sudden nor gradual, neither male nor female, and neither young nor adult. Relieving both men and women from their existential suffering implies a transcendence of all distinctions which limit us in our everyday lives. This transcendence of limitations is the elimination of all distinctions, including those of sexuality.

Throughout the episodes of Bodhisattvas depicted in Chapter 5, the tension between the egalitarian view toward both sexes based upon the teaching of Emptiness and the discriminatory view toward women was readily apparent. Chapter 6 considered the notion of sexual transformation as a latent form of discrimination. With regard to the female as a Buddha, the Mahāyāna texts are silent in explicitly naming any. All of the Buddhas in their various Buddha lands are depicted in Mahāyāna sutra literature as either male or androgynous. The Buddha Amitābha, who was metaphorically represented as either the mother or father in Pure Land,[12] is an example of an androgynous notion of Buddhahood. The Bodhisattva Kuan-yin may also be androgynous or, more precisely, asexual because of the perpetual transformations attributed to this particular Bodhisattva.

Although the characterization of Buddhas is predominantly male, less commonly androgynous, the traditional attitudes toward sexuality and attachment to the secular world in general have been negative. "Neutralizing" or controlling sexual desires, ultimately aiming for total elimination of desire, was conceived as essential to the attainment of spiritual states of meditation and Bodhisattva practice. Therefore, when one views the ideal spiritual state as desireless, the notion of Buddhahood must be viewed as sexless, illustrating the emptiness of all distinctions which result from desire.

Deities generally had been accorded an asexual status in the *Agañña-suttanta.* Celestial Bodhisattvas such as Kuan-yin also are viewed as asexual, magically transforming to suit the needs of the devotee. The possibility of assigning feminine imagery to Buddhas was usually ignored although, in many ways, cults to female and male images of celestial Bodhisattvas preempted devotion to the various male images of Buddhas. The qualifications of any given cult Buddhas as female were never developed, nor was the relationship between a male divine principle with a female divine principle explored until the emergence of Tantric Buddhism. It is only in Tantricism that we find androgyny in its most precise sense, namely, the unity of the best attributes of both sexes conceived as a state of perfection. Mahāyāna Buddhists outside the Tantric tradition construed sexuality as the antithesis to a perfected or enlightened state. Consequently, the state of androgyny would not be desirable, if Buddhist texts were to be consistent with their traditional attitudes toward sexuality. Implicit androgynous overtones to Buddhas such as Amitābha focused on asexual characterizations, namely, mother and father, and were not strictly speaking androgynous in the sense defined above, namely, as the ultimate fulfillment of femininity and masculinity, usually associated with sexual union rather than parenthood.

Images of the feminine with respect to Buddhahood are implicit, nonetheless, in *The Sutra of Queen Śrīmālā Who Had the Lion's Roar* (*Śrīmālādevīsiṃhanāda-sūtram*), translated below, where we find the main character, Śrīmālā, is an astute teacher of the Tathāgatagarbha.

Unlike the queen by that name in earlier Buddhist literature who was the exemplar of the dutiful wife, Queen Śrīmālā, who had the lion's roar of a Buddha, is very much her own person. She first converts the women of her kingdom, then her husband, a non-Buddhist, and finally the men. Unlike Bodhisattvas discussed in Chapter 5, Śrīmālā is praised for her intelligence and compassion, not for her beauty or wealth, which are implicit. She is eloquent in expounding the Dharma and is charismatic, as are all Bodhisattvas.

The level of Bodhisattvahood which Śrīmālā represented was the subject of many commentaries. The difficulty in differentiating between the higher stages of the Bodhisattva path in the Queen Śrīmālā sutra is well illustrated by the commentaries on the text. According to the Chinese commentaries *Sheng-man i-su pen-i* and the *Sheng-man pao-k'u*,[13] Queen Śrīmālā is an eighth-stage Bodhisattva, an irreversible Bodhisattva. The *Sheng-man i-su pen-i* does not mention a sexual change while the *Sheng-man pao-k'u* claims that Śrīmālā is really a male appearing as a female. According to another commentary, the *Shōmangyō gisho*, Queen Śrīmālā is a seventh-stage Bodhisattva who is about to enter the stage of irreversibility.[14]. The *Sheng-man ching i-chi*, also a commentary on the Śrīmālā sutra, disagrees with all of the above commentaries, placing Śrīmālā at the first stage of the Bodhisattva path.[15]

The controversy which arose among scholars concerning Queen Śrīmālā's level of attainment may reflect continual controversy among Buddhists with regard to the Bodhisattva ideal and image of Buddhahood as female. If Bodhisattvahood and Buddhahood were states of asexual perfection, both feminine and masculine images would not pertain to those ideals. If Śrīmālā were a male Bodhisattva assuming the likeness of a female, as indicated in the *Sheng-man ching pao-k'u*, then sexuality was implicitly construed as a critical factor for Buddhahood. It is only when sexuality remains a criterion for enlightenment that feminine images of Buddhahood are untenable. The enduring association of the feminine with sexuality becomes a "double-edged sword" in images of Buddhahood. When sex is conceived as an important factor for attaining Buddhahood, the perfect sex is always masculine. The inconsistency in beliefs and values is readily apparent in maintaining the elimination of sexuality as essential to Buddhahood, but adhering to masculinity as the ideal state rather than to one of asexuality. By definition, feminine images of Buddhahood are a contradiction in terms if asexuality denotes the masculine state. To claim that Śrīmālā is an eighth-stage Bodhisattva and imminent Buddha, as claimed in the *Sheng-man i-su pen-i* and *Sheng man pao-k'u,* is to give the feminine a remarkable status, namely, an association with the highest ideals of Mahāyāna Buddhism. The portrait of Śrīmālā is an exception to the traditional association of the feminine with sexuality and the masculine with asexuality.

The sutra of *Queen Śrīmālā Who Had the Lion's Roar* is an

exceptional text in several distinctive ways. (1) The assembly of those who listen to Queen Śrīmālā consists entirely of laymen and laywomen who are the attendants and citizens in Queen Śrīmālā's court and kingdom. The religious community of monks and nuns are absent. (2) Queen Śrīmālā is the central figure, preempting even the Buddha, with regard to the length and content of the speeches. No other Bodhisattvas share the center stage with Śrīmālā, which was not the case in other texts depicting female Bodhisattvas. (3) The entire exposition is addressed to both the good sons and daughters who love and accept the true Dharma, teaching all other living beings to do likewise. These good sons and daughters are compared to a great rain cloud pouring forth countless benefits and rewards, reminiscent of the parable in the *Lotus Sutra*. They are also compared to the great earth which carries the weight of the sea, mountains, vegetation, and sentient life, bestowing compassion like a great Dharma mother of the world. At no time is there a hierarchical pattern of the division of labor in which good sons are the administrators and teachers while good daughters are the assistants. (4) After the discourse, the order of the conversion of the citizens in Queen Śrīmālā's kingdom is extraordinary. First, the women of the city seven years of age and older are converted; then, Queen Śrīmālā's husband, and finally the men of the city who were seven years of age and older. The preeminence of women over men in the order of conversion may either suggest a concession for the sake of the narration since Queen Śrīmālā is the central figure, or it may suggest that there was either a prominent woman in the ruling class at that time or that women could ideally have such a societal and religious position in a Buddhist community.

The entire tone of the text in which the Bodhisattva is the supporter, acceptor, and compassionate Dharma mother suggests female imagery. Whether or not women were ever recognized as potential or imminent Buddhas remains unanswered. The evidence which would plead Śrīmālā's case, namely, that she is an eighth-stage female Bodhisattva, depends upon whether or not she was ever considered an eighth-stage female Bodhisattva and not an eighth-stage male Bodhisattva in female appearance. The more conservative commentators certainly were not supportive of imminent female Buddhahood. Queen Śrīmālā awakens to the thought of enlightenment, receives the prediction of future Buddhahood, and then begins her long discourse on the ultimate and most difficult teaching in Buddhism. If any portrait of the feminine indicates the association of the feminine with Buddhahood, in a religious tradition which had an ideal of egalitarianism and nondiscrimination, on the one hand, but in practice at times represented a poor facsimile of that Mahāyāna Buddhist ideal, on the other, the portrait of Queen Śrīmālā closely approaches the image of a female Buddha. She epitomized the Mahāyāna ideal, that of a sentient being who, regardless of sex or status, strives to realize his or her spiritual potential or Buddhahood.

Introduction to Selections from *The Sutra of Queen Śrīmālā Who Had the Lion's Roar*

Of all the Buddhist texts which teach the principle known as the Tathāgatagarbha, none is as popular as this sutra. Queen Śrīmālā, the central figure in the text, represents a portrait of the ideal Buddhist laywoman as a teacher and philosopher who is committed to assisting all beings through the supreme teaching of the Tathāgatagarbha.

The text emphasizes total devotion to the Tathāgatagarbha or Buddha nature which is the means for universal salvation (Ekayāna). Each individual has this potential Buddha within his or her mind but must nurture and develop the awareness of this potentiality so that one may "give birth" or realize this nature of the Buddha. This theory of Buddha nature or Tathāgatagarbha became increasingly popular in China and Japan, particularly in Zen Buddhism where the notion of universal Buddha mind (Busshin) was identified with the mind that understands Emptiness (mushin).

The Sutra of Queen Srīmālā Who Had the Lion's Roar inspired first the Indian royal patronesses of Buddhism and then the court ladies in China and Japan. The popularity of this text undoubtedly was due not only to the portrayal of a woman as both a compassionate and helping human being, but also as an example of a human being in her struggle to exist and understand the world in freedom.

Although the text is no longer available in Sanskrit, fragments are cited in other Buddhist Sanskrit texts, attesting to the text's wide circulation throughout India at one time. In addition, both the Chinese and Tibetan collections of scripture have preserved redactions of the text. Commentaries on the *Śrīmālā Sutra* are extant only in Chinese and Japanese. According to the Chinese commentator Chi-tsang, monks at one time studied and composed commentaries in this sutra in great numbers from the time of the North-South dynastic periods through the Sui (that is, from approximately 440–618 of the common era).

Guṇabhadra, the central Indian *Tripiṭaka* master (ca. 394–468) who translated the older of the two Chinese redactions (one of which was the source of the following translations), was a Central Indian scholar who departed for Canton in 435 via Ceylon, bringing the first Buddhist idealist (Vijñānavādin) texts with him. His translations of these texts were virtually neglected until the late Wei dynasty, when Ratnamati, Bodhiruci, and others came to China to translate texts from the same school of thought. He translated, among others, the *Great Dharma Drum* (*Mahābherihārakaparivarta*), which is a Tathāgatagarbhan text, and the *Saṃdhinirmocana-sūtram* and *Laṇkāvatāra-sūtram*, both considered Vijñanavādin in doctrine.

Queen Śrīmālā and her historicity still remain obscure. In other Buddhist literature she is sometimes identified with King Prasenajit's wife, Mallikā, instead of with his daughter as described in the Śrīmālā sutra. According to the Sarvāstivādin books of discipline (*Vinaya*) which are preserved in the Chinese, Śrīmālā was the daughter of a village administrator who was raised by the king. Because she loved to pick flowers for her hair, she was known as Śrīmālā, which means "Beautiful Flower Garland." One day when King Prasenajit was visiting her guardian, Śrīmālā, through her foresight, ordered the palace gates closed during the period of his stay. Later, King Prasenajit discovered that his enemies had attempted to seize the palace and assassinate him but had failed in their plot because of Śrīmālā. He immediately asked her to be his queen, and she accepted. From that time on, Queen Śrīmālā compassionately ruled over the kingdom with her husband.

In the following sutra Queen Śrīmālā, with her eloquence or "lion's roar," receives the prediction that she will become a Buddha, and all of her kingdom subsequently practices according to the Buddha's teaching.

The Sutra of Queen Śrīmālā Who Had the Lion's Roar (Śrīmālādevīsiṃhanāda-sūtram).*[16] T. v. 12, n. 353, pp. 217–23.

[Chapter 1: The Merits of the Tathāgata's True Doctrine," T. v. 12, n. 353, p. 217 a 1–b 22:]

Thus I [Ānanda] have heard [from the Buddha who preached this sermon to me]:

At one time I, the Buddha, was residing in the Jeta garden in the city of Śrāvastī in the kingdom Kośala. At that time King Prasenajit and Queen Mallikā, who had only recently attained the faith in the Dharma, said these words together: "Śrīmālā, our daughter, is astute and extremely intelligent. If she has the opportunity to see the Buddha, she will certainly understand the Dharma without doubting [its truth]. Sometime we should send a message to her to awaken her religious state of mind."

His queen spoke: "Now is the right time." The king and queen then wrote a letter to Śrīmālā praising the Tathāgata's immeasurable merits, dispatching a messenger named Candirā to deliver the letter to the kingdom of Ayodhyā [where Śrīmālā was queen]. Entering the palace, the messenger respectfully conferred the letter to Śrīmālā, who rejoiced upon receiving it, raising the letter to her head [as a sign of reverence]. She read and understood it, arousing a religious mind of rare quality. Then she spoke to Candirā in verses:

"I hear the name 'Buddha,'
The one who is rarely in the world.
If my words are true [that the Buddha is now in the world]
Then I will honor him.

*This English translation is by Diana Paul.

Since I humbly acknowledge that the Buddha, the lord
Came for the sake of the world,
He should be compassionate with me
Allowing me to see him."

At that very moment of reflection,
I appeared in heaven,
Radiating pure light in all directions,
And revealing my incomparable body.

Śrīmālā and her attendants
Prostrated themselves reverently at my feet;
And with pure minds,
They praised my true merits.

"The body of the Tathāgata, excellent in form,
Is unequaled in the world,
Being incomparable and inconceivable.
Therefore, we now honor you.

The Tathāgata's form is inexhaustible
And likewise his wisdom.
All things eternally abide [in you].
Therefore, we take refuge in you.

Having already exorcised the mind's defilements
And the four kinds [of faults] in body [and speech][17]
You have already arrived at the undaunted stage.
Therefore, we worship you, the Dharma king.

By knowing all objects to be known,
And by the self-mastery of your body of wisdom,
You encompass all things.
Therefore, we now honor you.

We honor you, the one who transcends all measures [of space and time].
We honor you, the one who is incomparable.
We honor you, the one who has the limitless Dharma.
We honor you, the one beyond conceptualization."

[Śrīmālā:]

"Please be compassionate and protect me,
Causing the seeds of the Dharma to grow [within me].
In this life and in future lives,
Please, Buddha, always accept me."

[I respond:]

"I have been with you for a long time,
Guiding you in former lives.
I now again will accept you.
And will do likewise in the future."

[Śrīmālā professes:]

"I have produced merits
At present and in other lives.
Because of these virtuous deeds
I only wish to be accepted."

Then Śrīmālā and all of her attendants prostrated themselves before my feet. I then made this prediction among them: "You praise my true merits because of your virtuous deeds. After immeasurable periods of time, you will become sovereign among the gods. In all lives you will continually see me and praise me in my presence, in the same manner as you are doing now. You will also make offerings to the immeasurable numbers of Buddhas, for more than twenty thousand immeasurable periods of time. Then you [Śrīmālā], will become the Buddha named 'Universal Light' [Samanta-prabhā], the Tathāgata, Arhat, Perfectly Enlightened one.

"Your Buddha land will have no evil destinies and no suffering due to old age, sickness, deterioration, torments. . . . There will be no evil whatsoever. Those who are in your land will have the five desires [of the senses fulfilled], longevity, physical power, and beauty, and will be happier than even the gods who control enjoyments created by others[paranirmitavaśavartin].[18] They all will be exclusively Mahāyāna, having habitually practiced virtuous deeds, and assemblying in your land."

When Queen Śrīmālā had received this prediction, the countless gods, men, and other beings, vowed to be born in her land. I predicted to everyone that they all would be born there.

[After professing her vows to practice the path of the Bodhisattva through the six perfections, Śrīmālā, preaching eloquently with the "lion's roar" of a Buddha, begins to explain what is entailed in accepting the teaching of the Dharma. The focus of her discourse is the teaching of Tathāgatagarbha, the ultimate Dharma in this sutra.]

[T. v. 12, n. 353, p. 218 b 7–219 b 3:]

"Moreover, [the Acceptance of the true Dharma] is like the great earth which supports four weights. What are the four? The great seas, the mountains, vegetation, and living beings. Similarly, like that great earth, the good sons and daughters who accept the true Dharma build the great earth and carry four responsibilities. Who are the four? (1) Living beings who have parted from good friends either have not heard [the Dharma] or are without the Dharma. By advising them to cultivate the good deeds of men and the gods, they [the good sons and daughters] prepare them [for entering the path]. (2) For those who want to be disciples, they present the disciple vehicle. (3) For those who want to be Pratyeka-buddhas, they present the Pratyeka vehicle. And (4) for those who want to be Mahāyānists, they present Mahāyāna. These are the good sons and good daughters who accept the true Dharma, build the great earth, and carry the four responsibilities.

"Therefore, lord, good sons and daughters who accept the true Dharma, build the great earth, and carry the four responsibilities, become friends without being asked, for the sake of all living beings. In their great compassion, they comfort and sympathize with living beings, becoming the Dharma mother of the world.

"Again, the Acceptance of the true Dharma is like the great earth that has four kinds of jeweled storehouses. What are the four? (1) the priceless, (2) the supremely valuable, (3) the moderately valuable, and (4) the slightly valuable. These are the great earth's four kinds of jeweled storehouses.

"Similarly, the good sons and daughters who accept the true Dharma and build the great earth, obtain the four kinds of most precious jewels, namely, living beings. Who are the four? (1) Those who have not heard [the Dharma] or are without the Dharma to whom the good sons and daughters who have accepted the true Dharma present the [cultivation of] merits and virtuous deeds of men and the gods. (2) Those who want to be disciples are presented with the disciple vehicle. (3) Those who want to be Pratyeka-buddhas are presented with the Pratyeka vehicle. And (4) those who want to be Mahāyānists are presented with Mahāyāna.

"Therefore, all the good sons and daughters who obtain the great jewels, namely, living beings, realize extraordinarily rare merits because of the Acceptance of the truc Dharma. Lord, the great jeweled storehouse is the Acceptance of the true Dharma.

"Lord, 'the Acceptance of the true Dharma' means the true Dharma [itself] is not different from the Acceptance of the true Dharma. The true Dharma [itself] is identical with the Acceptance of the true Dharma.

"Lord, the perfections are not different from the one who accepts the true Dharma. The one who accepts the true Dharma is identical with the Perfections. Why?

"(1) The good sons and daughters who accept the true Dharma give even their body and limbs for those who respond to giving. By protecting these [living beings'] intentions, they teach them. When they are thus taught and caused to abide in the true Dharma, this is called the Perfection of Giving.

"(2) The good sons and daughters teach the protection of the six senses, the purification of action, speech, and thought, and the cultivation of the four correct postures [in walking, standing, sitting, and reclining], to those who respond to discipline. By protecting these [living beings'] intentions, they teach them. When they are thus taught and caused to abide in the true Dharma, this is called the Perfection of Discipline.

"(3) The good sons and daughters teach nonhatred, liberality, supreme patience, and neutrality in facial expression to those who respond to patience. By protecting these [living beings'] intentions, they teach them. When they are thus taught and caused to abide in the true Dharma, this is called the Perfection of Patience.

"(4) The good sons and daughters do not teach indolence, but the desire [to practice], supreme perseverance, and the cultivation of the four correct postures to those who respond to perseverance. By protecting these [living beings'] intentions, they teach them. When they are thus taught and caused to abide in the true Dharma, this is called the Perfection of Perseverance.

"(5) The good sons and daughters teach tranquillity, constant mindfulness not conditioned by external objects, and recollection of all actions and speech over long periods of time, to those who respond to meditation. By protecting these [living beings'] intentions, they teach them. When they are thus taught and caused to abide in the true Dharma, this is called the Perfection of Meditation.

"(6) The good sons and daughters, when questioned concerning the meaning of all things, extensively teach all treatises and all arts, without trepidation, causing those who respond to wisdom to reach the ultimate in science and art. By protecting these [living beings'] intentions, they teach them. When they are thus taught and caused to abide in the true Dharma, this is called the Perfection of Wisdom.

"Therefore, O lord, the perfections are not different from the one who accepts the true Dharma. The one who accepts the true Dharma is identical with the perfections.

"O lord, now receiving your power, I will further explain the greatness [of the true Dharma]."

I spoke: "Please do so."

Śrīmālā said to me: " 'The Acceptance of the true Dharma' means the Acceptance of the true Dharma is not different from the one who accepts the true Dharma. The good sons and daughters who accept the true Dharma are identical with the Acceptance of the true Dharma. Why? Because the good sons and daughters who accept the true Dharma, abandon three things for the sake of the Acceptance of the true Dharma. What are the three? They are body, life, and property.

"When the good sons and daughters abandon the body, they become equal to the last limit of the life-death cycle [saṃsāra]. Having parted from old age, sickness, and death, they realize the indestructible, eternal, unchanging, and inconceivable merits of the Tathāgata's Dharma body.

"When they abandon life, they become equal to the last limit of the life-death cycle. Ultimately, having parted from death, they realize limitless, eternal, and inconceivable merits, penetrating all the profound Buddha dharmas.

"When they abandon property, they become equal to the last limit of the life-death cycle. Having realized the inexhaustible, indestructible, ultimately eternal, inconceivable, and complete merits which are not common to all other living beings, they obtain the excellent offerings of all living beings.

"Lord, the good sons and daughters who have abandoned these three and have accepted the true Dharma, will always obtain the predictions of all the Buddhas [concerning their Buddhahood], and will be honored by all living beings.

"Furthermore, O lord, the good sons and daughters who accept the true Dharma without distortion and without deception or misrepresentation, will love the true Dharma and accept the true Dharma, entering the Dharma friendship when monks, nuns, laymen, and laywomen are forming rival factions, which cause the destruction and dispersion [of the Saṃgha]. Those who enter the Dharma friendship will certainly receive the prediction [of their future Buddhahood] by all the Buddhas.

"O lord, I see that the Acceptance of the true Dharma has such great powers. Because you are the eye of truth, the wisdom of truth, the source of the Dharma and penetrate all things, you are the basis for the true Dharma and know all things."

At that time, I was joyous over Śrīmālā's explanation concerning the great powers of the Acceptance of the true Dharma. [I spoke:] "Śrīmālā, what you have said is true. The great powers of the Acceptance of the true Dharma are like a very strong man who briefly touches a [vulnerable] part of one's body and causes great pain. Similarly, Śrīmālā, barely accepting the true Dharma causes suffering to Māra, the Evil One. I do not see even one remaining good act which can cause suffering to Māra in the manner that barely accepting the true Dharma does.

"Moreover, the bull king has a form without equal, surpassing all other bulls. Similarly, barely accepting the true Dharma in Mahāyāna is superior to all the virtuous deeds of the two vehicles because it is so extensive.

"The majestic bearing and uniqueness of great Mt. Sumeru surpasses all other mountains. Similarly, the [merit of] abandonment of body, life, and property in Mahāyāna, accepting the true Dharma with a benevolent heart, surpasses [the merit of] those who have just engaged in the virtuous deeds of Mahāyāna but do not abandon body, life, and property. Because of its extensiveness, of course it is superior to the two vehicles.

"Thus, Śrīmālā, through the Acceptance of the true Dharma, explain [this teaching] to living beings, teach and convert living beings, and make living beings confirmed [in the Dharma].

"Therefore, Śrīmālā, the Acceptance of the true Dharma has these great benefits, these great blessings, and these great fruits. Śrīmālā, even if I explain the merits and benefits of the Acceptance of the true Dharma for countless periods of time, I shall not reach the end [of explaining]. Therefore, the Acceptance of the true Dharma has immeasurable and unlimited merits."

[Chapter 15: "Śrīmālā," T. v. 12, n. 353, p. 222 c 27 to p. 223 a 12:]

[Śrīmālā spoke:] "All the remaining living beings who stubbornly cling to false teachings instead of to the most profound Dharma, turn their backs to the true Dharma, and habitually practice the corrupt ways of various heterodoxies. These corrupt ways must be subdued by the king's [that is, your] powers and by the powers of the divine Nāgas."

When Queen Śrīmālā and her attendants paid obeisance to me, I spoke: "Excellent, excellent, Queen Śrīmālā! In the most profound Dharma, protected by skill-in-means, subdue what is not the Dharma. Maintain well its correctness. You have already been very close to the one hundred billion Buddhas and can explain this [Dharma's] meaning."

At that time I emitted a most excellent light, radiating everywhere over the crowd. My body ascended into the sky, higher than seven Tāla trees. Walking in the sky, I returned to the kingdom of Śrāvastī. Then Queen Śrīmālā and her attendants together faced me and were transfixed by the sight of me, not moving for even a moment. Having passed by their field of vision, I caused them to be exalted. Each individual praised my merits and was mindful of me.

I then reentered the city. Turning toward King Mitrayaśas [Queen Śrīmālā's husband], I praised Mahāyāna. All the women of the city, seven years of age and older, were converted to Mahāyāna. King Mitrayaśas was also converted to Mahāyāna. All the men, seven years of age and older, were converted to Mahāyāna. Then all of the citizens of the state were introduced to Mahāyāna.

Notes

1. T. v. 34, n. 1718, p. 117 a 21—22.
2. T. v. 34, n. 1718, p. 117 a 22–24.
3. *Fa-hua wen-chü chi,* T. v. 34, n. 1719, p. 314 b 29–c 1.
4. See Chapter 5, section b.
5. Sanskrit: *Ekajātipratibaddha.*
6. T.v. 34, n. 1721, p. 592 b 16–19.
7. T. v. 34, n. 1721, p. 592 b 21–24.
8. The sutra is not identified.
9. T. v. 34, n. 1721, p. 592 b 24–28.
10. T. v. 34, n. 1721, p. 592 c 2–3.
11. See Chapter 7 for a brief discussion of the vow which purportedly excludes women from Pure Land.
12. See Chapter 7, section b, *The Bodhisattva Kuan-yin [who Explains] the Conditions to Be Born in Pure Land.*
13. Koizumi Enjun, "Shōmangyō gisho hongi," in *Shōtoku taishi kenkyū,* V, 1973 (Osaka: Shitennōji Joshi Daigaku), p. 15.
14. *Shōmangyō gisho,* T. v. 56, n. 2184, p. 2 b 11–12.
15. *Dai nihon zokuzōkyō,* part 1, 30.4 p. 283.
16. The subtitle: "A Comprehensive Text That Teaches the Skill-in-Means of the One Vehicle." The One Vehicle (Ekayāna) doctrine proclaims universal salvation for all living beings.
17. Actually, there are three faults of the body: killing, stealing, and sexual misconduct; and four faults of speech: false speech, slander, unkind speech, and idle talk.
18. This heaven is a place where others constantly provide all the pleasure the heart desires.

Conclusions

The present investigation of portraits of women and the feminine has demonstrated the extreme views of misogynist attitudes, on the one hand, and the religious ideals of nondiscriminative wisdom, emptiness, and universal salvation, on the other. These views were upheld in varying degrees throughout a wide range of Mahāyāna Buddhist literature. The most popular Mahāyāna texts did not support hostile arguments against women who endeavored to realize their spiritual goals. Negative attitudes toward women were insignificant in influence and popularity among the monks and laity of the time. The correlation between popular and widely influential texts with more liberal and egalitarian views is significant in order to understand to what extent misogynist texts were accepted by Buddhist followers. What we found in translating and analyzing textual materials was an increase in both popularity and influence among Buddhists as the texts became more egalitarian. As a result, the organization of our materials in three parts illustrated not only a gradual elevation in the attitudes toward women and the feminine as the reader proceeds from Part I to Part III, but a gradual increase in popularity and esteem, particularly noticeable in Chapters 4 through 8 as contrasted with Chapters 1 through 3.

Part I reflected the traditional attitudes toward women, relegating the feminine to the sensual realm as opposed to the Dharma realm. The prototype for the negative attitude toward the feminine was embodied in the daughters of Māra, personified as Lust, Aversion, and Craving. The imminent seductive powers of the feminine suggested that monks perceived women as potential threats to their spiritual welfare, as illustrated in Chapter 1. Monastic insecurity and resentment were made explicit; the bestial and evil powers of sexuality were associated with women and the household life. Possible notions of pollution or contamination through any interactions with women remained implicit. Women were viewed as the cause of mental anguish and pain, as competitors to the Buddhist monastic community, and as threats to familial stability because of women's adulterous behavior. There is no acknowledgment of the corresponding threat which monastic life posed on society by its retreat from both the maintenance of the family structure and from engagement in sexuality.

Woman as mother was also tied to the sensual realm, to a state of attachment to home and children. In contradistinction to the view of woman as the source and fountainhead of man's anguish and pain, the attitude toward the mother is one of intrinsic pain and attachment. Although woman as mother does not threaten the family structure, being almost synonymous with the household life, woman as mother cannot move out of that domestic sphere to the religious. She is respected as the paragon of womanhood through her procreative function as the bearer of sons, but she is also inextricably entwined with a world of suffering, namely, a world of children and attachment to them, which prevents active involvement with religious institutions.

Part II discussed practical statements concerning soteriological paths open to women. The paths to salvation represented the compromising efforts of reconciling the tensions between ingrained prejudice and religious goals of universal salvation. The paths open to Mahāyāna Buddhists, as described in sutra literature, were sex-typed to some degree. Limitations, which the authors of Buddhist texts imposed upon women, were primarily due to: (1) fear of losing their own spiritual position, particularly in the case of the monks; (2) recognition that women were constrained by society, particularly by their close association with familial responsibilities which were more demanding for women than for men; and (3) the association and imposition of inordinate sexual powers to the feminine, generalized to all women as inherently sensual and destructive beings.

Considerations of the differences in paths for men and women were interpreted with reference to the traditional stereotypes of the feminine as attached to sensuality and domesticity. Textual descriptions of the path of the nun, for example, reflected the Buddhist concern for the disintegration of the family structure, indicating that the establishment of the order of nuns could possibly threaten the societal structure of the family if women were to leave their homes. The account of the origin of the nuns' community indicated a closer association of women to domestic life. The text suggested that there was a potentially disruptive force to the stability of society if women became estranged from familial responsibilities. The fact that estrangement of the monks from household life is not discussed in the text as a parallel threat contributing to the destruction of social institutions reflects probable authorship by a monk. Moreover, unless nuns were subordinated to monks, the institution of the order of nuns implicitly would threaten the acknowledged hierarchical position of men in patriarchal society. The resulting compromise with social norms assumed deference by all nuns, regardless of seniority, to even the youngest monks. Nonetheless, nuns were teachers of the Dharma in their own right.

Textual accounts of the good daughter and the good friend also implied, in some instances, dependence and subordination. Like the nun, the good friend and good daughter were capable of teaching and respecting the Dharma. They were supporters of the Dharma through their daily activities, according a religious function to women in both the domestic sphere and in the small range of more "public" careers. The familial association, if any, with a husband, father, or child, was not mentioned, suggesting that a woman's familial responsibilities at home were obstacles to an independent pursuit of the Dharma.

The soteriological path of the Bodhisattva and its accessibility for women demonstrated a variety of interpretations of women's capabilities. Since the Bodhisattva path was much more significant than either the path of the nun or the good daughter or the good friend, many of the ambivalences toward women become more explicit in descriptions of the Bodhisattva path as contrasted with the less important paths of nun, good daughter, and good friend. The texts were divided on the issue of a woman's practice of the Bodhisattva path. Some sutras declared that women could not enter the path until their rebirth as men, demonstrating misogynist attitudes. Another alternative to denying women the discipline of Bodhisattva practice was suggested in a wide range of sutras. Through the notion of sexual change, women were believed to be capable of participating in even the advanced stages of Bodhisattva practice.

Sexual change or transformation was interpreted in Chapter 5 in two ways: (1) as a physiological process involving a mental sexual power which controlled physical changes pertaining to sexual characteristics; and (2) as a symbolic process involving a mental transition from a state of attachment to a sensual existence to a state of desirelessness and eventual enlightenment. In both instances the "male" state of mind was equated with the Bodhisattva state of mind, which was capable of understanding the teaching of Emptiness. In the first case, the interpretation of female birth as a limiting state of existence precluded the accessibility of the Bodhisattva path. The second interpretation permitted women full involvement with Bodhisattva practice.

Chapter 6 advanced another interpretation of sexuality and its relationship with the soteriology of the Bodhisattva.

Rather than attempting to identify "maleness" with Bodhisattvahood, the sutras in this chapter claimed that all notions of sexuality, either male or female, were mental attachments contradicting the Buddha's teaching that all phenomena are Empty. Instead of using the motif of sexual change, the sutras in Chapter 6 explained the asexual nature of the Bodhisattva. Illusions of innate sexual characteristics were refuted. In addition, symbolic representation of the masculine and feminine as spiritual perfection and sexuality, respectively, were considered implicitly discriminatory,[1] suggesting that the interpretation of the Bodhisattva path in asexual terms was the most egalitarian and compatible with expositions on Emptiness.

Part III provided a sharp contrast to Part I. Intensely misogynist attitudes toward women in Chapter 1 imposed negative attributes to the feminine as sensual, destructive, and sometimes bestial. Chapter 2, in its depiction of the mother, destined women to a life apart from religious activities, attributing to the feminine a sorrowful and suffering nature. In contrast, the feminine in Part III exalts the image of the feminine by the association of feminine qualities to certain deities, particularly to the celestial Bodhisattva Kuan-yin. However, Kuan-yin, assuming a wide variety of male and female forms, does not, strictly speaking, exemplify male and female perfection, but rather an asexual ideal in which notions of sexuality are removed. Kuan-yin is the "compassionate mother of sentient beings," an asexual figure in the sense that sexual desire is disassociated from her. Moreover, by devotion to Kuan-yin, the faithful relinquished all desires and passions.

The Buddha, even more so than the celestial Bodhisattva, exemplified a spiritual state of perfection, totally desireless, asexual, and omniscient. Although sutra literature tended to consider the Buddha a paternal figure, residing in a Buddha field, several Buddhas were a combination of both maternal and paternal images. Amitābha was frequently described as both the mother and father of all living beings, suggesting androgynous imagery to indicate the nature of Buddhahood. Perhaps the most applicable attribute attesting to the asexual rather than the androgynous quality of the Buddha is the distinguishing characteristic of concealment of the male sexual organ. Although the concealment suggested masculine disciplinary efforts to "neutralize" sexual desires and eventually remove them through meditation, the concealment also indicated that the masculine dimension of sexual energies had also been eradicated.

The suggestion that women were biologically determined to be more "defiled," more passionate than men, is never totally eliminated, however. Texts generalized that the female sex was weaker both physically and mentally, more vulnerable to ignorance, and perhaps even somewhat defective, both in terms of spiritual weaknesses and physical handicaps. *The Sutra on Changing the Female Sex* makes explicit the psychological and physical constitution of the female:

The Buddha:

> "The female's defects—greed, hate, and delusion and other defilements—are greater than the male's. . . . You [women] should have such an intention[1]. . . . Because I wish to be freed from the impurities of the woman's body, I will acquire the beautiful and fresh body of a man.' "[2]

The physiological theories of ancient India and China undoubtedly contributed to creating and maintaining certain biases which the Mahāyāna Buddhist literature described. If, on the one hand, women were viewed as biologically inferior by society, they would have little hope of being full participants in their communities. On the other hand, a religious tradition which did not advocate equality of the sexes would provide fuel to the fire of prejudice which biological theories of the day would foster. In general, physiological weaknesses and handicaps were not the main thrust of misogynist arguments. Rather, the authors of the texts developed psychological theories concerning traits of the feminine personality such as lustful, desirous, jealous, and destructive. These psychological traits imposed on women by a minority of monks actually mirrored the monks' insecurities and fears with regard to their own sexuality, as illustrated in Chapter 1.

The prevailing societal restrictions on women also undoubtedly influenced descriptions of women and the feminine. Portraits of women frequently focused on the woman's important functions within the household life as a limitation to Bodhisattva practice or the nun's discipline. While men could more freely leave their families to either enter a monastic community or teach the Dharma as lay Buddhists, women were expected to bear the majority of familial responsibilities. If women also left the domestic sphere of activities, social institutions would collapse with the expected breakdown of the family.

Nonetheless, many sympathetic portraits of women and the feminine have been preserved in Mahāyāna Buddhist literature of which a representative sample has been interpreted in the above selections. Texts such as *The Sutra of the Teaching of Vimalakīrti* and *The Sutra of Queen Śrīmālā Who Had the Lion's Roar* did not ignore the needs of women but attempted to explore the options available to both sexes in observing the Bodhisattva practice. As a result of the dissemination of these texts, the predominant tendency in Mahāyāna Buddhism was undoubtedly to promote the welfare of all living beings and to alleviate their suffering without prejudice or favor.

In short, the tension between sexual prejudice and religious ideals was reflected throughout Buddhist literature. More popular and appealing texts usually did not deny the spiritual potential of women as well as of men. The most significant and persuasive theme for acknowledging women's full and active participation in the various soteriological paths was the notion that all attachments to sexuality must be removed. The celestial Bodhisattvas and Buddhas illustrated the asexual nature of the deity, reminiscent of the *Agañña-suttanta* in which the Golden Age was an asexual one. Sexuality was eradicated in attributes ascribed to the divine, either by androgynous images or, more precisely, epicene images.

A prejudiced mind which, nonetheless, adhered to notions of sexuality was an unenlightened mind, a mind not "emptied" of discrimination. The following anecdote illustrates both the humor and inconsistency of maintaining misogynist attitudes, summarizing the untenability of the "monkish" attitude toward women and providing a fitting conclusion to this study:

> Tanzan, a Zen monk, was walking with another monk named Ekidō when they met a beautiful woman who was unable to cross the river. She asked Tanzan to lift her up and carry her across. Tanzan agreed to assist her and carried her in his arms to the other side. Ekidō and Tanzan then continued to walk along in silence. Ekidō could no longer contain himself and finally angrily retorted: "How could you carry a woman, especially a beautiful one, across the river! Monks are not supposed to have anything to do with women!" Tanzan quietly replied: "I carried the woman across a river and left her at the other side. Are you still carrying her in your mind?"[3]

Notes

1. According to a Tibetan myth, "those who wish to attain supreme enlightenment in a man's body are many, but those who wish to serve the aims of beings in a woman's body are few indeed." Cf. Stephan Beyer, *The Cult of Tārā* (Berkeley and Los Angeles: University of California Press, 1973), p. 65.
2. T. v. 14, n. 564, p. 919 a 26–27; p. 919 c 11–13. *Nan tzu,* literally "son," is translated as "male" in this passage. Celestial Bodhisattvas such as Kuan-yin are called good sons even when assuming female forms. *Nan tzu* may imply either a virtuous mental state or a physiological one. Cf. T. v. 11, n. 310, p. 563 c 2, for a female Bodhisattva named Vimalaprabhā who is called "good son."
3. A paraphrase from Conrad Hyers, *Zen and the Comic Spirit* (Phila.: Westminster Press, 1973), pp. 176–77.

Glossary

Agañña-suttanta.
The title of the twenty-seventh chapter in the *Dīgha Nikāya* in the Pāli canon. This text is the early Buddhist equivalent of the book of Genesis, including a myth on the origin of the universe in a golden age. This myth is also found in the *Mahāvastu,* a Mahāsaṃghikan text.

Amitābha.
The Buddha of Infinite Light. Each Buddha has a field of influence, a Buddha land, in which he teaches the Dharma and helps sentient beings become enlightened. The Buddha Amitābha presides over the Pure Land Sukhāvatī.

Ānanda.
The Buddha's favorite disciple. According to the Buddhist tradition, Ānanda recited all the sermons, or sutras, from memory after the Buddha's final Nirvana. He was rebuked for advocating the establishment of the nuns' order.

Apadāna.
The title of the thirteenth division of the *Khuddaka Nikāya* in the Pāli canon. Stories of the former lifetimes of Buddhist saints, of monks and nuns who were believed to have lived during the time of the Buddha.

Apsara.
A celestial female deity whose male counterpart is Gandharva and whose enticing ways captivate the hearts of men.

Arhat.
"Worthy of respect." The religious ideal, the saint, the highest stage of development in early Buddhism. One who seeks Nirvana for himself or herself alone. The extinction of the "outflows," that is, sensual desire, the desire for coming to be, and ignorance and false views: These are what distinguish the Arhat.

Āsuras.
Antigods; mythical beings of evil intent.

Avadāna.
See *Apadāna*. *Avadāna* is a form of literature similar to *Apadāna* but composed in Sanskrit by the Sarvāstivādins, rather than in Pāli, and of a more recent period.

Awakening to the Thought of Enlightenment.
The beginning of the Bodhisattva path; an experience through which one first decides to obtain the full enlightenment of a Buddha.

Āyatanas.
The six senses (sight, hearing, touch, taste, smell, and conceptualization) and their sense fields.

Bodhisattva.
"Enlightenment being." The religious ideal in Mahāyāna Buddhism. The Buddha-to-be who, through compassion, vows to assist all beings to enlightenment. The Bodhisattva abandons the world but not the beings in it.

Brahmā.
The reputed creator of this world in the Brahmanic tradition; the highest god in this religion.

Brahman.
The highest of the four classes in Indian society.

Buddha (583–463 B.C.).
"The enlightened one." The founder of Buddhism; the Buddha lived in northeast India (Kapilavastu). See also, Gautama and Śākyamuni.

Buddha dharmas.
The qualities of a Buddha.

Buddha nature.
The Mahāyānists identified the Buddha with every part of this world and, consequently, with each human being. Therefore, an innovation of the Mahāyāna school consisted of the idea that Buddha nature is present in all of us, that is, that we are all potential Buddhas.

Celestial Bodhisattvas.
The advanced Bodhisattvas of the seventh stage and above, who have nearly mastered the superpowers of a Buddha. The chief innovation of the Mahāyāna pantheon, the celestial Bodhisattvas, are nonhistorical, mythical figures. Al-

though objects of cult worship, they are often personifications of Mahāyāna ideals.

Dhāraṇī.
Incantations; similar to mantra.

Dharma.
Doctrine, scripture, truth, reality, the teaching of the Buddha.

Dharma body.
The collection of the Buddha's teachings or the absolute body of Buddhahood that on occasion projects into this world phantom bodies of Buddhas with definite qualities to do its work.

Dharma realm or Dharmadhātu.
The ideal world of the Dharma.

Dharma wheel.
The wheel set in motion by the Buddha when he first espoused his doctrine.

Divyāvadāna.
The title of a Buddhist Sanskrit text belonging to the *Avadāna*, composed by the Sarvāstivādin Buddhists.

Ekayāna.
Universal salvation.

Emptiness.
The fundamental teaching, central to all Mahāyāna schools, which denies the self-existence or substantiality of all phenomena. The teaching of nonduality and of the cessation of all cognitions, distinction-making, and discursive reasoning. The teaching of Emptiness is not a negation or an affirmation of the phenomenal world but an attempt to transcend all opposites.

Gandharva.
A celestial male deity associated with the secret knowledge of the heavens and with seductive powers over women.

Garuḍa.
A mythical birdlike spirit.

Gautama.
Siddhārtha Gautama or Gautama is the name for the historical Buddha.

Good daughter.
Refers to a woman who has entered the Bodhisattva path.

Good friend.
One who helps in conversion to or progress in the Dharma by example and teaching. A spiritual friend who supports and encourages the good daughter or good son.

Good son.
Designates a man who has entered the Bodhisattva path.

Indra.
A great Āryan god, also known as Śakra, of the Brahmanic tradition.

Irreversibility.
The irreversible stage of a Bodhisattva; the stage at which a Bodhisattva can no longer regress from the path to the full enlightenment of a Buddha.

Jātakas.
"Birth stories." The Jātaka tales relate how the Buddha Gautama, in his former lives, fulfilled the six perfections of a Bodhisattva: giving, morality, patience, energy, meditation, and wisdom.

Kuan-yin (Avalokiteśvara).
A famous celestial Bodhisattva. As the personification of compassion, Kuan-yin (Chinese) or Avalokiteśvara is usually represented iconographically by eleven heads, facing all directions, in order to save all living beings. In China, Avalokiteśvara became Kuan-yin and was metamorphosed into a female.

Lokadhātu.
The secular world.

Mādhyamika.
One of the two great traditions of Mahāyāna Buddhism, founded about A.D. 150 by Nāgārjuna, Mādhyamika means middle, and the Mādhyamikas are those who take the middle way between affirming and denying. Considering all phenomena as Empty but not mental, the

Mādhyamikas expected salvation from the perfection of wisdom, that is, the contemplation of Emptiness.

Mahāprajāpatī.

The Buddha's aunt. She became the first nun in the Buddhist Saṃgha.

Māhasthāmaprāpta.

A celestial Bodhisattva in the Mahāyānist pantheon, sometimes accorded more status than the Buddhas. A chief assistant to the Buddha Amitābha along with Avalokiteśvara. In Far Eastern art, he is frequently represented standing on the right of Amitābha while Avalokiteśvara stands on the left.

Mahāvastu.

The title of a Buddhist Sanskrit text, sometimes classified as an *Avadāna;* composed by the Mahāsaṃghikans and containing a legendary account of the Buddha's life as a Bodhisattva.

Mahāyāna.

"The Great Vehicle." The movement within Buddhism originating around the beginning of the Christian era. The Mahāyāna innovation was to prescribe a path for Bodhisattvas, leading to Buddhahood or Supreme, Perfect Enlightenment, to proclaim that all humans possess the spiritual potential of Buddhahood and to develop a metaphysical doctrine of the Emptiness of all phenomena.

Mantra.

Chants or magical formulae used in meditation and rituals.

Māra.

The Evil One, the Buddhist Satanic figure, the tempter. The personification of all evils and passions, Māra's entrapments consist of the sensory pleasures.

Mudrā.

Symbolic hand gestures used in meditation and rituals.

Nāgas.

Mythological water spirits in the form of serpents or dragons that inhabit rivers, lakes, and oceans; they are either protective or destructive.

Nāgārjuna.

The founder of the Mādhyamika school of Mahāyāna Buddhism, about A.D. 150. One of the most subtle dialecticians of all times, he hypothetically stated Emptiness as a worldview. His best-known work is the *Middle Stanzas* (*Mādhyamaka-kārikās*), a polemical treatise of about 450 verses in which he refutes a wide range of views.

Nirvana.
"Extinction." The enlightenment of an Arhat or Buddha. The incomprehensible peace of complete spiritual release. The real truth, the supreme reality, the ultimate good.

Pāli canon.
The three collections of Theravāda scripture usually referred to as the *Tripiṭaka*.

Perfection of Wisdom.
The highest of the six perfections of the Bodhisattva. The Perfection of Wisdom consists of the direct realization that all phenomena in their true nature are Empty. It is often personified as a goddess, and in the *Perfection of Wisdom* sutras she is described as the mother of the Buddhas. Just as the mother gives birth to the child, so the Perfection of Wisdom produces the supreme enlightenment of a Buddha.

Pratyeka-buddha.
A self-enlightened Buddha who does not teach others.

Purāṇas.
A collection of sacred Hindu texts containing cosmology and genealogies of gods, sages, and rulers.

Pure Land.
The Buddha land of Amitābha. A world devoid of women, animals, ghosts, and the damned and inhabited only by Bodhisattvas of high spiritual development.

Śakra.
The name of Indra, the chief of the gods. He is devout, reveres the Buddha, and protects the Dharma.

Śākyamuni.
A name for Buddha.

Saṃgha.
The Buddhist community consisting of four assemblies: monks, nuns, laymen, and laywomen.

Samādhi.
Concentration; a meditative trance of intense absorption.

Saṃsāra.
The existentially confining condition of perpetual rebirth. The birth-death cycle caused by desire.

Śāriputra.
The name of one of the Buddha's principal disciples renowned for wisdom and philosophical skill in Abhidharma. The Theravādins regarded Śāriputra almost as a second founder of Buddhism. But as the representative of conceptual reasoning, an inferior wisdom to the Mahāyānists, he is one of the favorite antagonists in Mahāyāna Buddhist literature.

(Mūla)sarvāstivādin.
A branch of the Sarvāstivādins who were one of the two branches of the Old Wisdom School (Hīnayāna) of Buddhism. The Theravādins, the other branch, predominated in East India while the Sarvāstivādins flourished in West India for 1,500 years. The Sarvāstivādins professed a doctrine that became the cornerstone of the Mahāyāna, the six perfections fulfilled by the Bodhisattva.

Skandhas.
The five psychophysical elements or aggregates which comprise an individual person, forming the basis for attachment to existence. The five elements are form (rūpa), sensations and feelings (vedanā), conceptions (samjñā), predispositions or experiences conditioned by past events (saṃskāra), and consciousness (vijñāna).

Streamwinner.
The first stage of the eight-stage path of development that leads to Nirvana. One who has entered the path by understanding the four noble truths.

Stūpa.
A reliquary for the historical Buddha's remains. Later, the object of worship in popularized forms of Buddhist practice.

Subhūti.
A chief disciple of the Buddha, noted for friendliness and compassion. The foremost disciple in the Mahāyāna, he is the principal interlocutor of the *Perfection of Wisdom* sutras.

Sugata.
"Well-gone"; an epithet for the Buddha.

Sutra.
A collection of discourses believed to be the words of the Buddha. One of the three collections in the Pāli canon.

Tathāgata.
A title of the Buddha meaning either "Thus-gone" or "Thus-come," that is, as the other Tathāgatas have come or gone. This epithet refers to the Buddhas as a spiritual principle or as one who has obtained the Supreme, Perfect Enlightenment. It emphasizes the fact that the historical Buddha is just one of an endless series of Tathāgatas, who appear throughout history and proclaim the same doctrine.

Tathāgatagarbha.
A concept of great soteriological importance. Tathāgata refers to the one who has obtained the Supreme, Perfect Enlightenment. Garbha has a twofold meaning: first, the womb and, by extension, the calix of a lotus, a storehouse; and, second, the womb's contents, that is, an embryo. The womb may be interpreted either as Buddhahood with the accompanying virtue and merit or as a defiled consciousness, that is, womb of darkness, depending on the context. The embryo represents the potentiality in all sentient beings for Buddhahood.

Theravāda.
The major sect of early Buddhism and the composer of the Pāli canon. The Mahāyānists usually denote the Theravāda pejoratively as "The Subordinate (or Lesser) Vehicle." The Theravādins now practice principally in Burma and Ceylon, but also in other parts of Southeast Asia.

Therīgāthā.
A collection of hymns believed to have been written by nuns.

Therīs.
Nun Arhats.

T'ien-t'ai.
A school of Chinese Buddhism that believes in sudden enlightenment and the attainment of Buddhahood in this lifetime.

Transference of Merit.
Spiritual progress is contingent upon the accumulation of merit. But to desire merit implies a considerable degree of self-seeking that must be abandoned at higher spiritual stages. The Mahāyāna drew this conclusion and embodied in the Bodhisattva vows the transference of one's own merit to help those less spiritually endowed.

Trayastriṃśas.
In Indian cosmology, a class of thirty-three gods.

Vijñānavāda.
One of the two great traditions of Mahāyāna Buddhism. As the idealist school of Mahāyāna Buddhism, the Vijñānavādins maintained that all phenomena are both Empty and mentally constructed.

Vimokṣa.
Special attainment; salvation or final liberation.

Vinaya Piṭaka.
The discipline and training rules that regulate the Saṃgha. One of the three collections in the Pāli canon.

Yakṣa.
A spirit or ghost of semidivine status.

Yama.
The guardian of the underworld.

Bibliography

A. *English and French Sources*

Bapat, P. V. "Change of Sex in Buddhist Literature," in *Sripad Krishna Belvalkar Felicitation Volume* (Benares: Motilal Banarsidass, 1957).

Beal, Samuel, tr. *Si-yu-ki: Buddhist Records of the Western World* (Delhi: Oriental Books Reprinting, 1969).

Beyer, Stephan. *The Buddhist Experience: Sources and Interpretations* (Belmont, Ca.: Dickenson Publishing Co., 1974).

———. *The Cult of Tāra: Magic and Ritual in Tibet* (Berkeley and Los Angeles: University of California Press, 1973).

Bollée, W. B., tr. *Kuṇālajātaka* (London: Luzac & Co., 1970).

Brown, Norman W. "The Metaphysics of Truth Act (Satyakriyā)," *Mélanges d'indienisme á la mémoire de Louis Renou* (Paris: 1968).

Bruns, J. Edgar. *God as Woman, Woman as God* (New York: Paulist Press, 1973).

Bühler, George, tr. *The Laws of Mānu* (Oxford University Press: 1886; reprinted in Delhi by Motilal Banarsidass, 1964).

Burlingame, E. W. "The Act of Truth (Saccakiriyā): A Hindu Spell and Its Employment as a Psychic Motif in Hindu Fiction," *Journal of the Royal Asiatic Society* (*JRAS*), July 1917, pp. 429–67.

Chamberlayne, John J. "The Development of Kuan Yin, the Goddess of Mercy," *Numen*, 9 (January 1962), 45–52.

Ch'en, Kenneth K. S. *Buddhism in China: A Historical Survey* (Princeton: Princeton University Press, 1964).

———. *The Chinese Transformation of Buddhism* (Princeton: Princeton University Press, 1973).

Conze, Edward. *Buddhism: Its Essence and Development* (New York: Harper Torchbook, 1959).

———, tr. *Buddhist Wisdom Books* (New York: Harper & Row, 1958).

———, tr. *The Large Sutra on Perfect Wisdom* (Berkeley and Los Angeles: University of California Press, 1975).

———, tr. *The Perfection of Wisdom in Eight Thousand Lines and Its Verse Summary* (Bolinas, Ca.: Four Seasons Foundation, 1973).

———.*The Prajnāpāramitā Literature* (The Hague: Mouton & Co., 1960), Indo-Iranian Monograph Series, vol. 6.

———. *Thirty Years of Buddhist Studies: Selected Essays* (Columbia: University of South Carolina, 1968).

Cowell, E. B., ed. *The Jātaka or Stories of the Buddha's Former Births* (London: Cambridge University Press, 1897), 6 vols.

Dayal, Har. *The Bodhisattva Doctrine in Buddhist Sanskrit Literature* (London: Routledge & Kegan Paul, 1932; reprinted in Delhi by Motilal Benarsidass, 1970).

De la Vallée Poussin, Louis, tr. *L'Abhidharmakośa de Vasubandhu* (Paris: Paul Guethner, 1925), 3 vols.

Doré, Henri. *Recherches sur les superstitions en Chine* (Shanghai: 1914), vol. 6.

Edgerton, Franklin. *Buddhist Hybrid Sanskrit Grammar and Dictionary* (Delhi: Motilal Banarsidass, 1970; reprinted by arrangement with Yale University Press).

Eliade, Mircea. *Patterns in Comparative Religion* (New York: Sheed & Ward, 1958).

Emmerick, R. E., tr. *The Sutra of Golden Light* (London: Luzac & Co., 1970).

Falk, Nancy. "An Image of Woman in Old Buddhist Literature—The Daughters of Māra," in *Women and Religion*, eds. Judith Plaskow and Joan Arnold Romero (Missoula, Montana: Scholars' Press for the American Academy of Religion, 1974).

Francis, H. T., and E. J. Thomas, trs. *Jātaka Tales* (London: Cambridge University Press, 1916).

Guenther, Herbert V. *Philosophy and Psychology in the Abhidharma* (Berkeley: Shambala, 1974).

Hare, E. M., tr. *The Book of the Gradual Sayings (Anguttara Nikāya)* (London: Luzac & Co., 1952), 3 vols.

Horner, I. B., tr. *The Book of the Discipline (Vinaya Piṭaka)* IV (*Mahāvagga*), Sacred Books of the Buddhists, XIV (London: Luzac & Co., 1962).

———, tr. *Minor Anthologies III* (London: Routledge & Kegan Paul, 1975).

———. *Women Under Primitive Buddhism* (London: George Routledge, 1930).

Hyers, Conrad. *Zen and the Comic Spirit* (Phila.: Westminster Press, 1973).

Jones, J. J., tr. *Mahāvastu* (London: Luzac & Co., 1949), 3 vols.

Jung, Carl Gustav. *Psychology and Religion* (New Haven: Yale University Press, 1938; 16th printing, 1966).

Kajiyama Yuichi. "Bhāvaviveka, Sthiramati, and Dharmapāla," *Beiträge zur Geistesgeschichte Indiens: Festschrift für Erich Frauwallner*, vols. 12–13, 1968–1969.

Kern, H., tr. *The Saddharma-puṇḍarīkā, or The Lotus of the True Law* (Oxford: Clarendon Press, 1884), Sacred Books of the East XXI; reprinted in Delhi by Motilal Benarsidass, 1965.

Kinsley, David R. *The Sword and the Flute: Kāli and Kṛṣṇa, Dark Visions of the Terrible and the Sublime in Hindu Mythology* (Berkeley and Los Angeles: University of California Press, 1975).

Lai, Whalen. "Women and the Pure Land," unpublished paper.

Lal, Kanwar. *The Cult of Desire* (New York: University Books, 1967).

Lamotte, Etienne, tr. *L'Enseignement de Vimalakīrti* (Louvain: Université de Louvain Institut Orientaliste, 1962).

Lancaster, Lewis R. "An Analysis of the Aṣṭasāhasrikā-prajñāpāramitā-sūtra from the Chinese Translations," unpublished dissertation, University of Wisconsin, 1968.

———. "The Story of a Buddhist Hero," *Tsing Hua Journal of Chinese Studies*, 10:2 (July 1974), 83–89.

Leach, Edmund. *Genesis as Myth and Other Essays* (London: Cape Editions, 1969).

Majumdar, R. C., ed. *The Classical Age* (Bombay: Bharatiya Vidya Bhavan, 1954).

Malalasekera, G. P. *Dictionary of Pāli Proper Names* (London: Pāli Text Society, Luzac & Co., 1960), 2 vols.

Mallmann, Marie-Thérèse de. *L'Introduction á l'étude d'Avalokiteçvara* (Paris: Presses Universitaires de France, 1967).

Matics, Marion L., tr. *Entering the Path of Enlightenment: The Bodhicaryāvatāra of the Buddhist Poet Śāntideva* (London: Macmillan, 1970).

Müller, F. Max, ed. and tr. *The Larger Sukhāvativyūha* (Sacred Books of the East, XLIX) (Oxford: Clarendon Press, 1894).

Neumann, Erich. *The Great Mother: An Analysis of the Archetype* (New York: Bollinger Foundation, 1955).

O'Flaherty, Wendy Doniger. *Asceticism and Eroticism in the Mythology of Śiva* (New York: Oxford University Press, 1973).

———. *The Origins of Evil in Hindu Mythology* (Berkeley and Los Angeles: University of California Press, 1976).

Pulleyblank, E. G. "Chinese and Indo-Europeans," *Journal of the Royal Asiatic Society*, April 1969, 9–39.

Rhys Davids, C. A. F., tr. *The Book of Kindred Sayings (Saṃyutta Nikāya)* (London: Luzac & Co., 1950), 3 vols.

Rhys Davids, T. W., and C. A. F. Rhys Davids, trs. *Dialogues of the Buddha (Dīgha Nikāya)*, 5th ed. (London: Luzac & Co., 1966), 3 vols.

Rhys Davids, T. W., and Hermann Oldenberg, trs. *The Vinaya*

Texts (Delhi: Motilal Banarsidass, 1968; first published by Oxford University Press, 1881).
Ricoeur, Paul. *The Symbolism of Evil* (Boston: Beacon Press, 1967).
Ridding, C. M., and Louis de la Vallée Poussin, "Fragment of the Sanskrit *Vinaya*: 'Bhikṣuṇīkarmavācanā,'" *Bulletin of the School of Oriental and African Studies* (London), vol. 1, part 3, pp. 123–43; India Office, Stein Tibetan Manuscripts, no. 30.
Robinson, Richard H. *The Buddhist Religion: A Historical Introduction* (Belmont, Ca.: Dickenson Publishing Co., 1970).
Saddhatissa, H. *Buddhist Ethics: Essence of Buddhism* (New York: George Braziller, 1970).
Spiro, Melford. *Buddhism and Society* (New York: Harper & Row, 1970).
Tay, C. N. "Kuan-yin: The Cult of Half Asia," *History of Religions*, November 1976.
Thomas, Edward J. *The Life of Buddha as Legend and History* (London: Routledge & Kegan Paul, 1927; reprinted 1969).
Vogel, J. Ph. *Indian Serpent-Lore, or The Nāgas in Hindu Legend and Art* (London: Arthur Probsthain, 1926).
Warren, H. C., tr. *Buddhism in Translation* (Cambridge: Harvard University Press, 1896; reprinted in New York by Atheneum, 1968).
Wayman, Alex. "The Hindu-Buddhist Rite of Truth: An Interpretation," *Studies in Indian Linguistics* (Poona: 1968), 365–69.
Wayman, Alex, and Hideko Wayman, trs. *The Lion's Roar of Queen Śrīmālā* (New York: Columbia University Press, 1974).
Zimmer, Heinrich. *Myths and Symbols in Indian Art and Civilization* (Princeton: Princeton University Press, 1946), Bollingen Series VI; reprinted 1962.
Zürcher, Erich. *The Buddhist Conquest of China: The Spread and Adaptation of Buddhism in Early Medieval China* (Leiden: E. J. Brill, 1959).

B. *Chinese, Japanese, and Sanskrit Sources*

Akanuma Chizen. *Indo bukkyō koyū meishi jiten* (Kyoto: Hōzōkan, 1967).
Aṣṭasāhasrikāprajñāpāramitā-sūtram (*The Sutra of the Perfection of Wisdom in Eight Thousand Verses*), ed. P. L. Vaidya (Darbhanga: Mithila Institute, 1960), Buddhist Sanskrit Texts, no. 4.
"Bhikṣuṇīkarmavācanā" ("Nuns: The Stating of the Matter"), from the *Vinaya Piṭaka* (*The Book of the Discipline*), in C. M.

Ridding and Louis de la Vallēe Poussin, "Fragment of the Sanskrit *Vinaya*: 'Bhikṣuṇīkarmavācanā,' " *Bulletin of the School of Oriental and African Studies* (London), vol. 1, part 3, pp. 123–43; India Office, Stein Tibetan Manuscripts, no. 30.

Bodhisattva-bhūmi: A Statement of Whole Course of the Bodhisattva, ed. Unrai Wogihara (Tokyo: Sankibō Buddhist Bookstore, 1971).

Dai nihon zokuzōkyō (*Hsü tsang ching*), (Kyoto: 1905–1912; reprinted in Hong Kong, 1967), 150 vols.

Fa-hua i-shu, composed by Chi-tsang of Sui; T. v. 34, n. 1721, pp. 451–633.

Fa-hua wen-chü chi, composed by the T'ien t'ai monk Chan-jan of T'ang; T. v. 34, n. 1719, pp. 151–361.

Fo shuo ch'i nü ching (*The Sutra of the Buddha Teaching the Seven Daughters*), tr. Chih Ch'ien, third century; T. v. 14, n. 556, pp. 907–09.

Fo shuo chuan nü shen ching (*The Sutra on Changing the Female Sex*), tr. Dharmagupta of Liu Sung; T. v. 14, n. 564, pp. 915–21.

Fo shuo yüeh-shang nü ching (*The Sutra of the Dialogue of the Girl Candrottarā*), tr. Jñānagupta and Chih-te of Sui in 591; T. v. 14, n. 480, pp. 615–23.

Gaṇḍavyūha-sūtram (*The Harmony of the Young Sapling Sutra*), ed. P. L. Vaidya (Darbhanga: Mithila Institute, 1960), Buddhist Sanskrit Texts, no. 5.

Hai-lung-wang ching (*The Sutra of Sāgara, the Nāga King*), tr. Dharmarakṣa in 285; T. v. 15, n. 598, pp. 131–57.

Koizumi Enjun, "Shōmangyō gisho hongi," in *Shōtoku taishi kenkyū*, V, 1973 (Osaka: Shitennōji Joshi Daigaku).

Kuan-shih-yin p'u-sa wang-sheng ching-t'u pen-yüan ching (*The Sutra of the Bodhisattva Kuan-yin [Who Explains] the Conditions to Be Born in Pure Land*), translator unknown; in *Dai nihon zokuzōkyō, part 1, 87.4.*

Mahāratnakūṭa (*The Collection of Jewels*), see *Ta-pao chi ching.*

Mānavadharmaśāstra (*Law Books of Māṇu*), ed. V. N. Mandlik (Bombay: 1886).

Miao-fa lien-hua ching (*Lotus Sutra*), tr. Kumārajīva in 406; T. v. 9, n. 262, pp. 1–63.

Miao-fa lien-hua ching wen-chü, composed by Chih-i of Sui; T. v. 34, n. 1718, pp. 1–151.

"Miao-hui t'ung-nü hui" ("Questions Concerning the Daughter Sumati"), assembly 30 of *Mahāratnakūṭa* (*Ta-pao chi ching*), tr. Bodhiruci of T'ang; T. v. 11, n. 310, pp. 547–49.

Mochizuki Shinkō, ed. *Bukkyō daijiten* (Tokyo: Sekai shōten, 1955–1960), 10 vols.

Nakamura Hajime. *Shin Bukkyō jiten* (Tokyo: Seishin shobō, 1972).

Ono Masao, ed. *Busshō kaisetsu daijiten* (Tokyo: Daitō shuppansha, 1966), 11 vols.

Saddharmapuṇḍarīka-sūtram (*Lotus Sutra*), eds. Unrai Wogihara and C. Tsuchida (Tokyo: Sankibō Buddhist Bookstore, 1958).

Sheng-man ching i-chi, composed by Hui-yüan of Sui, *Dai nihon zokuzōkyō*, part 1, 30.4, pp. 275–94; also T. v. 85, n. 2761, pp. 253–61.

Sheng-man ching pao-k'u, composed by Chi-tsang of Sui; T. v. 37, n. 1744, pp. 1–90.

Sheng-man shih-tzu-hou i-sheng ta-fang-pien fang-kuang ching (*The Sutra of Queen Śrīmālā Who Had the Lion's Roar*), tr. Guṇabhadra of Liu Sung; T. v. 12, n. 353, pp. 217–23.

Shōmangyō gisho, attributed to Prince Shōtoku; T. v. 56, n. 2185, pp. 1–20.

Taishō shinshū daizōkyō, compiled by Takakusu Junjiro and Watanabe Kaigyoku (Tokyo: Taisho shinshu daizokyo kanko kai, 1924–1929; reprinted 1970), 85 vols.

Tao-hsing pan-jo ching (*The Sutra of the Perfection of Wisdom in Eight Thousand Verses*), tr. Lokakṣema, between 179–180; T. v. 8, n. 224, pp. 425–77.

Ta-pao chi ching (*The Collection of Jewels*), tr. Bodhiruci of T'ang; T. v. 11, n. 310, pp. 1–686.

Ui Hakujiu. *Bukkyō jiten* (Tokyo: Daitō shuppansha, 1971).

Wei-mo-chieh so shuo ching (*The Sutra of the Teaching of Vimalakīrti*), tr. Kumārajīva in 406; T. v. 14, n. 475, pp. 537–57.

Wu mu tzu ching (*The Sutra of the Child and His Five Mothers*), tr. Chih Ch'ien, third century; T. v. 14, n. 555, p. 907.

"Yu-t'o-yen yang hui ("The Tale of King Udayana of Vatsa"), assembly 29 of *Mahāratnakūṭa* (*Ta-pao chi ching*), tr. Bodhiruci of T'ang; T. v. 11, no. 310, pp. 543–47.

C. *Texts with English Translations*

The Book of the Discipline (Vinaya Piṭaka)

Horner, I.B., tr. *The Book of the Discipline (Vinaya Piṭaka)*, Sacred Books of the Buddhists X, XI, XIII, XIV, XX, and XXV (London: Luzac & Co., 1938–1962).

Prebish, Charles. *Buddhist Monastic Discipline* (University Park: Pennsylvania State University Press, 1975).

Rhys Davids, T. W., and Hermann Oldenberg, trs. *The Vinaya Texts*, Sacred Books of the East, XIII, XVII, and XX (Oxford: Oxford University Press, 1881).

Ridding, C. M., and Louis de la Vallée Poussin. "Fragment of the Sanskrit *Vinaya*: 'Bhikṣuṇīkarmavācanā,' " *Bulletin of the School of Oriental and African Studies* (London), vol. 1, part 3, 123–143; India Office, Stein Tibetan Manuscripts, no. 30.

Lotus Sutra (Saddharmapuṇḍarīka-sūtram)

Fa-hua i-shu, composed by Chi-tsang of Sui; T. v. 34, n. 1721, pp. 451–633.

Fa-hua wen-chü chi, composed by the T'ien-t'ai monk Chan-jan of T'ang; T. v. 34, n. 1719, pp. 151–361.

Hurvitz, Leon, tr. *Scripture of the Lotus Blossom of the Fine Dharma*, (New York: Columbia University Press, 1976).

Kern, H., tr. *The Saddharma-puṇḍarīka, or The Lotus of the True Law*, (Oxford: Clarendon Press, 1884; reprinted in Delhi by Motilal Banarsidass, 1965).

Miao-fa lien-hua ching, tr. Kumārajīva in 406; T. v. 9, n. 262, pp. 1–63.

Miao-fa lien-hua ching wen-chü, composed by Chih-i of Sui; T. v. 34, n. 1718, pp. 1–151.

Wogihara, Unrai, and C. Tsuchida, eds. *Saddharmapuṇḍarīka-sūtram* (Tokyo: Sankibō Buddhist Bookstore, 1958).

The Sutra of the Perfection of Wisdom in Eight Thousand Verses (Aṣṭasāhasrikāprajñāpāramitā-sūtram)

Conze, Edward, tr. *The Perfection of Wisdom in Eight Thousand Lines and Its Verse Summary* (Bolinas, Ca.: Four Seasons Foundation, 1973).

———. *The Prajñāpāramitā Literature* (The Hague: Mouton & Co., 1960), Indo-Iranian Monograph Series, vol. 6.

Tao-hsing pan-jo ching, tr. Lokakṣema, between 179–180; T. v. 8, n. 224, pp. 425–77.

Vaidya, P. L., ed. *Aṣṭasāhasrikāprajñāpāramitā-sūtram* (Dharbhanga: Mithila Institute, 1960), Buddhist Sanskrit Texts, no. 4.

The Sutra of the Teaching of Vimalakīrti (Vimalakīrtinirdeśa-sūtram)

Lamotte, Etienne, tr. *L'Enseignement de Vimalakīrti* (Louvain: Université de Louvain, Institut Orientaliste, 1962).

Thurman, Robert A. F., tr. *The Holy Teaching of Vimalakīrti* (University Park: Pennsylvania State University Press, 1976).

Wei-mo-chieh so shuo ching, tr. Kumārajīva in 406; T. v. 14, n. 475, pp. 537–57.

The Sutra of Queen Śrīmālā Who Had the Lion's Roar (Śrīmālādevīsiṃhanāda-sūtram)

Koizumi Enjun. "Shōmangyō gisho hongi," in *Shōtoku taishi kenkyū*, vol. 5, 1973 (Osaka: Shitennōji Joshi Daigaku).

Sheng-man ching i-chi, composed by Hui-yüan of Sui, *Dai nihon zokuzōkyō*, part 1, 30.4, pp. 275–94; also T. v. 85, n. 2761, pp. 253–61.

Sheng-man ching pao-k'u, composed by Chi-tsang of Sui; T. v. 37, n. 1744, pp. 1–90.

Sheng-man shih-tzu-hou i-sheng ta-fang-pien fang-kuang ching, tr. Guṇabhadra of Lui Sung; T. v. 12, n. 353, pp. 217–23.

Shōmangyō gisho, attributed to Prince Shōtoku; T. v. 56, n. 2185, pp. 1–20.

Wayman, Alex, and Hideko Wayman, trs. *The Lion's Roar of Queen Śrīmālā* (New York: Columbia University Press, 1974).

INDEX